D0850311

German Voices

German Voices

*Memories of Life during
Hitler's Third Reich*

Frederic C. Tubach

with Sally Patterson Tubach

UNIVERSITY OF CALIFORNIA PRESS

Berkeley   Los Angeles   London

University of California Press, one of the most distinguished university presses in the United States, enriches lives around the world by advancing scholarship in the humanities, social sciences, and natural sciences. Its activities are supported by the UC Press Foundation and by philanthropic contributions from individuals and institutions. For more information, visit www.ucpress.edu.

University of California Press
Berkeley and Los Angeles, California

University of California Press, Ltd.
London, England

Library of Congress Cataloging-in-Publication Data

Tubach, Frederic C.
  German voices : memories of life during Hitler's Third Reich / Frederic C. Tubach with Sally Patterson Tubach.
    p.   cm.
  Includes bibliographical references.
  ISBN 978-0-520-26964-4 (cloth : alk. paper)
    1. National socialism—Social aspects.   2. Germany—History—1933–1945. 3. Germany—Social conditions—1933–1945.   4. Germany—Social life and customs— 20th century.   5. Germany—History—1933–1945—Biography.   6. World War, 1939–1945—Social aspects—Germany.   7. World War, 1939–1945—Personal narratives, German.   I. Tubach, Sally P. (Sally Patterson), 1946–   II. Title.
  DD256.6.T83   2011
  943.086—dc22   2010051218

Manufactured in the United States of America

19 18 17 16 15 14 13 12 11
10 9 8 7 6 5 4 3 2 1

This book is printed on Cascades Enviro 100, a 100% postconsumer waste, recycled, de-inked fiber. FSC recycled certified and processed chlorine free. It is acid free, Ecologo certified, and manufactured by BioGas energy.

For Maria Tubach, née Zink

CONTENTS

List of Figures ix

Preface xi

Acknowledgments xv

Introduction
1

1. Jobs and the Olympic Games
20

2. *Jungvolk* and Hitler Youth
42

3. War and the Holocaust
60

4. In Search of Individuals
100

5. German Soldiers Write Home
198

Notes 263

LIST OF FIGURES

1. Eberhard Weinbrenner, Karls-Gymnasium, Heilbronn, 1943 *107*

2. Volker Schätzel at eighteen as a reserve officer candidate, 1943 *114*

3. Lore Ziermann, 2006 *138*

4. Hannelore Mehnert as a nurse in training, 1946 *143*

5. Klaus Conrad as a pilot in the German air force, 1940 *146*

6. Johannes Kuhn on a JU87 Stuka wing, 1944 *149*

7. Pastor Johannes Kuhn preaching to pilgrims on Mt. Tabor, Israel, 1989 *151*

8. Manfred Fischer on his mother's lap and his brother Hans, near the entrance to their garage, 1936 *154*

9. Private Gerhard Neizert in East Prussia, before the invasion of the Soviet Union, 1941 *157*

10. Helga Stursberg, 1939 *161*

11. Princess Ruth-Erika and Prince Alfred-Ernst zu Löwenstein-Wertheim-Freudenberg, 2007 *172*

12. Werner Bertsch, 2007 *174*

13. Dola Ben-Yehuda Wittmann and Matthias Bertsch, in Israel, 1995 *178*

14. Klaus Tiedje, standing apart from companions in the mountains, 1943 *187*

15. Hans-Bernhard Bolza-Schünemann, 2005 *196*

PREFACE

I was born in San Francisco on November 9, 1930. In 1933, when I was three, my father and mother, Germans by birth, returned with me to Nazi Germany and the village of Kleinheubach on the Main River, southeast of Frankfurt. Shortly before I turned four, my mother died suddenly at the age of twenty-seven. I was raised first by my paternal grandparents and then by a stepmother, to whom this book is dedicated. Thus, I spent my childhood and teenage years in Germany during Hitler's ascent to power, World War II, and the immediate postwar years. An American by birth, I reclaimed my citizenship in 1949 and returned to California at the age of eighteen.

I belong to the *young* generation of Germans born between 1925 and 1935 who grew up during the most tumultuous period in twentieth-century German history, and I share many experiences, thoughts, and emotions with my German compatriots. After I returned to the United States, my life diverged drastically from those of relatives and friends I left behind. I came of age personally and intellectually while an undergraduate in foreign language studies and then as a graduate student in the German Department of the University of California at Berkeley. In addition to the professors in the French and German departments who guided my academic development, I became closely associated with many fellow students who had fled Nazi Germany because they were Jewish. Like me, they felt like cultural and social outsiders in California, even if our histories were not the same.

The personal bonds to my Jewish friends were strong and abiding. We spent lively hours discussing existentialism in Old Europe, a coffee shop on Telegraph Avenue, and socialized regularly together. Above all, we studied with an intense commitment not only to traditional German literature and culture, but also to the works and worlds of Shakespeare, Dante, Dostoevsky, and, of course, Franz Kafka. Anxious to make our way in a strange country, we were very much alike in harboring strong ambitions mixed with deep insecurities. Whatever our priorities and personal preferences, we shunned politics and were loath to dwell on our pasts in Germany. Protected within academia from the uncertainties we perceived in the world outside, we created our own world of the mind.

Then came the 1960s. That era, with its war protests and passionate championing of civil rights, woke me up politically, and I became active on the Berkeley campus in progressive causes—my way of giving shape to my antifascist views. In teaching German culture to undergraduates, I felt compelled to study the Holocaust as a personal and moral commitment. Yet the more I learned about this defining moment of twentieth-century German (and European) history, the more dissatisfied I became with the comprehensive explanations provided by an ever-growing body of academic research. There seemed to be a disconnect between academic explanations, on the one hand, and the horrors experienced by the victims of Nazism, on the other.

In the 1980s I became friends with Bernat Rosner, a Hungarian Jew and Auschwitz survivor. In the mid-1990s, at the age of sixty-two, Bernie decided he wanted to tell his story, one he had kept to himself ever since he was deported from his Hungarian village to Auschwitz, where his parents and brother were exterminated in the gas chambers. He wanted me to narrate his story—a challenging undertaking for someone who had marched in a *Jungvolk* (Pre–Hitler Youth) uniform at the same time Bernat was forced to wear concentration camp garb. The result of our joint efforts became *An Uncommon Friendship: From Opposite Sides of the Holocaust* (University of California Press, 2001; a revised edition with an epilogue was published in early 2010). Bernie and I appeared at many public events to read and discuss our double biography—what we had experienced and who we had become.

Our common efforts at reconciliation and mutual understanding found a receptive audience, both in the United States and in Germany. At the core of our collaboration was the belief in the importance of the individual, and how the grand brushstrokes that serve to explain history tend to cover up precisely what we wanted to preserve—namely, the value of individual lives and the texture of human experience in all its rich variety and complexity.

During the years of our public presentations, I was surprised to find a great interest in my experiences in Nazi Germany. I also became aware how little most Americans knew about life in Hitler's Third Reich beyond established clichés. Hitler attempted to destroy the individual identities of Jews through extermination en masse, but he also wanted to eliminate the individual identities of Germans, the better to use them as a monolithic instrument in fashioning his Nazi utopia.

Several years ago I began collecting letters and interviewing Germans who lived during the Third Reich, my intention being to counteract generalizations about "all Germans" that Hitler wanted the world to believe and to rebut the common belief that Germans who lived during that time are best understood by broad, condemnatory assertions. In order to make these differentiated German voices intelligible, I try to explain how Hitler manipulated the younger generation within his revolutionary system and how he was able to succeed so quickly. I believe that the German voices in this work illuminate the variety and complexity of circumstances that in fact existed during that terrible time, and that they open another window on Hitler's Third Reich. It is not my intention to present a polemic but merely to add—for the record—German voices that have not been sufficiently heard in the United States.

Frederic Tubach
Orinda, 2010

ACKNOWLEDGMENTS

I would above all like to express my deep respect and love for my stepmother, Maria Tubach, née Zink. She was an outspoken anti-Nazi at a time when it was dangerous to admit it. She taught me that civil courage is a virtue and that swimming against the stream is sometimes a moral necessity.

Without the help of many active participants, this project would never have seen completion. First and foremost, about sixty members of the Evangelische Wirtschaftsgilde (Protestant Business Association) entrusted me with memories they wrested from the most traumatic period of their lives. Through many hours of taping, we dug deep into our shared past. I was impressed with how open they were about details of their years in Hitler's *Reich*, without making exculpatory excuses or attempting to whitewash. Although I didn't include every story in this book, they all contributed to my understanding of the period. A former president of the *Wirtschaftsgilde*, Hansjörg Weitbrecht, was an indispensable help in organizing venues and interviews in Germany and, more important, in offering his moral support through the years that I worked on this book.

The staff at the Institut für Zeitgeschichte (Institute of Contemporary History) in Munich was most helpful in guiding me to relevant source material. The letters written home by German soldiers during World War II made available to me at the *Feldpostsammlung* (collection of war letters) at the Museum für Kommunikation in Berlin, under the direction of Dr. Veit Didczuneit, were invaluable for rounding out the project. I owe a special debt of gratitude to Thomas Jander at the *Feldpostsammlung,* who generously provided me with a thematic overview of a representative sampling of the letters. During my second visit, in April 2009, he made particularly telling letters available to me. Without his help it would have been much more difficult to sift through the largely uncatalogued, raw material housed in this archive.

Colleagues, family, and friends, particularly Horst Rademacher, Gerd Hillen, Herlinde Spahr, and my children, Karen and Michael Tubach, aided me in presenting a more differentiated view of the Nazi years. Our neighbor, Steven Strange, generously came to my rescue at crucial moments with expert computer help. I am also grateful for the encouragement I received from a larger circle of acquaintances, including the Jewish book discussion group of Orinda, California, organized by Ron Gross, who urged me to complete this project. I am deeply indebted as well to my cousin Manfred Zink, who assisted me in the archives in both Munich and Berlin. His devotion to the project and superb organizational talent were of immeasurable help.

Critical and insightful evaluations of the manuscript by Professors Joyce Appleby, UCLA, and Gunter Hertling, University of Washington, were essential in helping me to shape the final version of the manuscript. I am very grateful for the excellent attention University of California Press editors Suzanne Knott and Anne Canright devoted to the manuscript. Their work made it a better book. Finally, the trust, patience, and support of Stan Holwitz and Reed Malcolm at the Press gave me what I needed to finish this project.

Introduction

In the summer of 1933, the situation in which non-
Nazi Germans found themselves was certainly one
of the most difficult imaginable; it reflected our sense
of having been completely overwhelmed without the
possibility of escape, along with the aftereffects of
the shock of having been brutally shoved aside. The
Nazis had a merciless grip on us. All fortresses had
fallen; any collective resistance had become impossible; individual resistance was merely another form
of suicide.

  Sebastian Haffner, 1939, while living in Germany

It was a youth full of intense experiences and dramatic events. The party recognized early on that the
most efficient way to bind youngsters to the Nazi state
was to provide them with the kind of experiences
that would guarantee loyalty. For that reason they
arranged celebrations, marches, sporting events, and,
in general, a life that seemed free and full of exciting
diversions. . . . The party was . . . able to shape a generation into conformists and, in the end, to people who
followed orders willingly when things turned serious.
We may have experienced that world on the whole
as free and lacking in coercion, simply because of the
penchant of the young for the excitement provided us.

But on a deeper level, we were taken in by the creeping and subtle manipulation that coerced us into the world of Nazi ideology.

Eberhard Weinbrenner, reflecting on the 1930s

For days, Ivan [the Russian army] was stationed to the right and left of us. He attacked us, and when we had fifty or sixty [soldiers] lying [dead or wounded] in front of our foxholes, he turned on his heels. Then the shooting of human beings began, as if it were a hunting expedition. Afterward, we gathered up the weapons he left behind and hammered away at him with his own weapons. You cannot really stop to think about all of that. We were no longer capable of it. You just became too numbed. What it means to aim, shoot, and a person falls, and then you walk up to him and you take everything you can use from him and leave the remaining piece of a human being drowning in a lake of melting ice—all of this can be done and written about in such a cold way, as if I were missing a piece of clothing. I am beginning to become horrified of myself.

Emil B., February 7, 1945, from the Russian front

The initial impulse for this project arose during a conference of Germans, many of them elderly, who grew up during the Third Reich. My wife and I became members of the *Evangelische Wirtschaftsgilde* by chance. The organization, founded after World War II, was made up originally of business leaders and company owners located primarily in southern Germany who had grown up in Hitler's *Reich* and then played an important role in the economic reconstruction of postwar Germany. Their meetings have been devoted primarily to the study of ethics in business and society within the emergent market economy. At present the membership includes a variety of professionals— academics, artists, journalists, public servants, bankers, and doctors. It is a cosmopolitan group; most members have personal and professional contacts all over the world. We are the only American members.

Some years ago during an annual conference, I was surprised when a number of the older members decided to meet informally, outside the official program, to share with each other their experiences during World War II. I sat in the back of the room listening while memories of a vastly different world were evoked. For decades no public arena had been available where these people could tell the stories of their personal lives between 1933 and 1945, and it was obviously difficult for them to dig these memory fragments up from their pasts. The images emerged fresh and raw, with an intensity that was palpable. It struck me that for these old friends and acquaintances, no narrative context existed to facilitate the relating of their histories to the larger issues of their country's past and present. In spite of the group's solidarity, each speaker was on his own. For most of them, indeed, it was the first time they had dared talk about the most traumatic period of their lives, about experiences they had held inside in lonely isolation for decades. I was impressed by the utter seriousness with which these individuals told their own truth as conscientiously and in as much detail as possible, whether they had been convinced of the Nazi cause or opposed to it. Listening to them, I became convinced that their voices needed to be heard for the record, even at this late date and in spite of the inevitable lapses and distortions to which memory is subject.

It wasn't until some years later, after I had interviewed most of those who participated in this gathering as well as others, that I decided to supplement their recollections with letters written during the period of totalitarian control, which would not be subject in the same way to the influences of time. Beginning in 2000, the German Post Office began to collect unpublished letters written by German soldiers from the various European theaters of World War II, particularly from the Russian front; currently it has about 80,000 archived in the Museum für Kommunikation in Berlin.[1] As eyewitness testimonials, these letters provided me with a great variety of voices, from all social classes and many different educational and cultural backgrounds. Central to both the postwar recollections of elderly Germans and the written thoughts of these young soldiers was the traumatic experience of war, as well as a strong sense of these individuals' unique identities.

Research in the Nazi records concerning surveillance of private German citizens archived at the Institut für Zeitgeschichte in Munich expanded my knowledge of the period.[2] My own childhood (from ages three to eighteen) in Nazi Germany and my research and teaching as a professor of German at the University of California, Berkeley, have shaped my insights as well, particularly concerning the pre–World War II years. As I heard people's stories and read letters and other documents, it became increasingly clear to me that a crucial aspect in the study of the Nazi years is generally neglected, namely, the role of the everyday in shaping individual Germans' experiences and beliefs—their *Lebenswelt*. A closer look at this neglected aspect of history brings out German voices not yet heard, or when heard, often misunderstood because of preconceived notions, influenced in large part by Hitler's propaganda image of "the Germans," upon which historians have expanded after the fact.

In what follows, I concentrate on aspects of the Nazis' rise to power and the influence they held over Germany that throw light on individuals, their values and experiences. The German voices that emerge from this period are varied and often contradictory and do not allow for facile generalizations and judgments. Rather—and this is the central point of this book— to understand ordinary Germans, we must examine the complexities of that place and time, and of the lives lived there, this despite Hitler's malevolent propaganda on the one hand, and the moral compass the Shoah gives us, on the other. History is lived and suffered by individuals, each of whom brings a complicated personality and varied experience onto the stage. Attributions of collective guilt cannot hold in the face of all this complexity.

We know that the Nazis did not create the death camps only to exterminate millions of individuals; they were also determined to wipe out their victims' history from our collective memory. It is to Germany's credit that, since World War II, and particularly in recent decades, great efforts have been made to keep the memory of Holocaust victims alive and, when possible, to recapture the rich tapestry of their everyday lives before the Nazis took over. In this way, a cautionary tale is spun that can, perhaps, shine a light on new forms of abstract totalitarianism, with their leveling, dehumanizing effects.

One group of Germans that has been studied in depth consists of the perpetrators of Nazi crimes. Their deeds have been analyzed and now stand as part of the historical record. Nazi bureaucrats aided historians in acquiring this knowledge through their own detailed documentation of their genocidal work.

There was more to Nazi record keeping, of course, than the documentation of their own crimes—which they were eager to preserve for history on behalf of the "Aryan race." Nazi leaders were equally thorough in another area, namely, in their exploitation of every available propaganda tool to project onto Germans a thoroughly distorted image of a unified, collective society, a monolithic, totalitarian whole in which all members were in total agreement. To this end, the Nazis employed all modern means of communication exhaustively—newspapers, films, pamphlets, monumental spectacles, and above all, radio. The transformation and reduction of a complex society into *ein Volk, ein Reich, ein Führer* was projected by the Nazis to the world at large as an established fact virtually overnight.

The grand rallies, the enthusiastic crowds, the triumphant marches are amply recorded. Carefully orchestrated by the Nazis, they have become part of our collective memory. Without the advent of radio and film the Nazis could not have constructed their "new world." Hitler, the architect, created a virtual reality, a brilliantly designed set on which, as with any successful show, only vigilantly managed events were allowed to take place. At opportune moments, selected by Chancellor Hitler himself, a freshly minted, quasi-sacred community— a *Volksgemeinschaft*—appeared onstage, with Germans serving either as willing actors or as fascinated and stunned onlookers. Often drawn by what one of my interviewees called *freiwilliger Zwang* (voluntary coercion), however, most Germans lacked the historical points of reference by which to measure what it all meant—both on the face of it and in the long run.

From the Nuremberg rallies in 1934 when Hitler evoked a "new Germany," to Joseph Goebbels's call for "total war" in the Berlin Sports Arena in 1942, masses of people were always present and highly visible. But who were these masses that Hitler's propagandists captured on film? In the main, they were members of the party—not just average card-carrying members, but rather, *committed* members. And what of the rest of Germany, the vast majority of Germans, who were not members of the Nazi Party? Most onlookers simply hoped these thrilling spectacles would lead to a better day, one with jobs, peace in the streets, and freedom from the oppressive Treaty of Versailles of 1918. Certainly, in 1934 the average German watched with fascination and reacted in varied ways to these unprecedented public displays, trying to get used to the "new" Germany of the radio and movies. We can be sure that by the time of Goebbels's total war proclamation, however, despite the wild applause and acclaim of Nazi fanatics, the same average German wanted the war to end soon—with victory, if possible, but if not, then at least with peace terms less vengeful than those of Versailles. Aside from the extremists, who believed in a final victory up until the very end, Germans weren't interested in glory or honor anymore, and certainly not in Aryans or Jews; they just wanted not to starve or be killed, their horizons having narrowed to a basic interest in personal survival.

This unrepresented majority, however, remained silent after the war. In recent years, efforts have been made to allow some of these voices to come forth in all their variety, to the degree that the passage of time and the tricks of memory still permit; nevertheless, a reconstruction of German lives and views during this period is fraught with serious obstacles, for obvious reasons. For one, Germans have never been a monolithic tribal society explainable by simple generalizations. Social and economic class, education, religion, geographical location, rural versus urban lifestyle, and regional history all contribute to individuals' uniqueness. Add to this the considerable variety of German loyalties to the Nazi regime, and it is clear that Germany remained a complex and heterogeneous society even under the Nazis.

Another problematic aspect of my endeavor is this: in my narrative reconstruction of individual German lives, the Holocaust is not a main point of reference, for the simple reason that it did not play a major role in the lives of the majority of Germans. For some readers, this may seem a scandalous assertion. Even for me the assertion is unsettling, because it implies that some key aspects of the Holocaust remain unexplained—above all, the quantum leap from traditional anti-Semitism to the systematic slaughter of millions. Rather than smoothing over the enormous crime of genocide under the Third Reich, my assertion points if anything to the need for continued vigilance against prejudices of all sorts. Anti-Semitism in Germany was no worse than in other European countries until Hitler used all the modern means of control and organization at his disposal to actualize its deadliest potential. To carry it through to genocide, however, he needed World War II, and in particular, the ferocious assault he unleashed upon the Soviet Union, proclaiming it to be a war of survival between civilizations.

We judge past historical traumas through the inescapable filter of our own contemporary values and societal norms. Perhaps the American trauma of 9/11 helps us better understand how the burning of the German parliament building *(Reichstagsbrand)* in early 1933 could serve as a catalyst propelling the Nazis into absolute power. Our sensitivity to financial catastrophes, such as the one that currently affects the United States, may also sharpen our hindsight in relation to Germany's economic collapse before 1933 and Hitler's massive and generally successful attempts to bolster its economy through reconstruction efforts that dwarfed even Roosevelt's New Deal. Playing into this near-total collapse of Germany by 1933 were the Versailles Treaty and the effects of defeat on Germany after World War I; an exaggerated belief in the state ever since Bismarck; authoritarian family structures; and last but not least the fear of communism within the frightened middle and upper classes. Nonetheless, all these causes, even when taken together, do not create enough critical mass to explain Hitler's swift ascent to power in 1933.

. . .

How was it possible for Hitler to gain total control over Germany in such a short time? The many answers given to this question have played out in the public sphere long after the events, filling libraries, making and breaking professional reputations, and continuing to shape values and attitudes. My objective is not to provide comprehensive answers, but to raise still-unanswered questions while introducing an American audience to the lives of some individual Germans. Above all, I hope to avoid the ideological traps that all too often shape the debate on Nazism and its causes.

Backed by the conservative parties in parliament, Hitler became chancellor on January 30, 1933. But the real takeover did not occur until several weeks later, spurred by the *Reichstagsbrand* event of February 27. Germans were already gripped by a fear of chaos and anarchy, and when the parliament building, a symbol of their tenuous democracy, went up in flames in Berlin, their extraordinary desire for security increased dramatically.

A Dutchman by the name of Marinus van der Lubbe was taken to be the arsonist. Apprehended near the parliament building, he exhibited behavior at the time that was considered odd. He was a massive man, with shoulders hunched forward, an over-large head, and slightly grotesque features, as well as a person of low intelligence. He was furthermore a card-carrying member of the Communist Party of Holland. Foreigner, communist, and "subhuman," he was a scapegoat ideally suited to shock Germans about horrible things to come if such people were allowed to gain power in Germany.

A Nazi image of this man appeared in the schoolbooks read by the younger generation; in early 1933, it explained history in the making. Historical analysis through the spoken and written word became secondary to the impact of this visual image; with this symbol, propagandists could make a disturbing point directly to a confused population.

Yet there was also considerable disagreement and skepticism among Germans as to the real culprit or culprits. While the Nazis inflamed fear through propaganda, claiming that a war of civilizations was coming true and that only Hitler could defend Europe against the "Asiatic pestilence and Bolshevism,"[3] the political Left, particularly the communists and socialists, blamed the Nazis for the *Reichstagsbrand*. And in the weeks following the conflagration, as the Nazis consolidated their power both in the streets and in the government, any statement blaming them would quite likely land the accuser in jail or, worse, in Dachau, one of the first major concentration camps, opened on March 22, 1933, to imprison German political dissidents.

Hitler was ready. As early as February 3 he had outlined to military generals his plan to undo the Treaty of Versailles and to pursue an expansionist policy in Europe—by means of war, if necessary. Some generals were incredulous; others worried about the implications of their new chancellor's rhetoric.

On February 20, even before the Nazis' victory in the elections of March 5, Hermann Göring, then president of the parliament, expanded the range of control over the population in a proclamation "für den Schutz von Volk und Vaterland" (for the protection of the people and the fatherland) and assigned complete authority over all aspects of law enforcement to the Gestapa (*Geheimes Staatspolizeiamt*, Secret State Police Office), a predecessor of the Gestapo (*Geheime Staatspolizei*, Secret State Police, created in April 1934 under the administration of the SS—the *Schutzstaffel*, or Protection Squadron). The Gestapa defined what constituted treason in the broadest terms, including issues of conscience and hidden motives attributed to the accused. They not only handled the fact-finding part of investigations, but they also functioned as judges and executed verdicts.[4]

The swiftness of the Nazis' ascent to power immediately after January 1933 was stunning. While most of the other parties talked, the Nazis acted. The only others to act were the communists, and Göring moved against them without hesitation. On February 28, 1933, an Oldenburg newspaper in northern

Germany (typical for the headlines nationwide) reported two events on page one: "Kommunistischer Brandstifter verhaftet" (Communist arsonist arrested) and, further down, "Schutzhaft für die gesammte Kommunistische Reichstagsfraktion" (Protective custody for the entire Communist parliamentary faction).[5]

This move against the political opposition was not only rapid, but comprehensive as well, right down to the village level. In my childhood village of Kleinheubach, eight Communist Party members were arrested and taken to Dachau between March 14 and April 8, 1933. Eventually all were released, but one of them, Fritz Breitenbach, was so undone by the experience that he committed suicide soon thereafter, throwing himself in front of a train. The Socialist and Communist members of the German parliament who managed to avoid "protective custody" and fled Germany found their way to Prague, Moscow, or Paris. One such refugee, a Herr Ludwig, a former representative of the German parliament, published a pamphlet in Paris soon after the disastrous election of March 5. His comments still impart a sense of immediacy: "The elections on March 5 took place in an all-pervasive atmosphere of terror, fear, and heated nationalism. For the enemies of National Socialism, free elections were no longer feasible. Their newspapers, publications, pamphlets, and posters were confiscated, their meetings forbidden, their members incarcerated. [German] auditoriums, theaters, movie houses, and radio stations were placed in the service of a propaganda that knew no limits."[6]

Resistance was not only dangerous but also increasingly futile. The brilliant timing of the Nazi takeover in the spring of 1933, which combined the use of fear, a cataclysmic event (the burning of the parliament), and the evocation of a stable order to come, proved persuasive for the disoriented population. Once the Nazis gained power, their ability to remove violence from the stage, to a degree at least and for a time, and to promote their glittering new world left people fascinated but with little opportunity to make informed moral choices. The gradual, largely covert concentration of power in the hands of an ever-smaller circle of executors (the SS and Gestapo) preserved a sense of social peace for a risk-averse population that craved stability.

While the Nazis' anti-Semitism and their response to the economic depression are generally understood, less known is their brilliant use of staged reality in conjunction with violence. Ultimately, this strategic application, nationwide, of persuasion and coercion enabled them to consolidate total control.

In this regard, events in the nearby cities of Göttingen and Moringen provide a telling example. On March 6, 1933, the day after the overwhelming Nazi victory and a week after the *Reichstagsbrand*, the *Göttinger Tageblatt* reported that the venerable university town was festooned in full Nazi regalia,

> symbols of freedom and hope strictly watched over by ramrod-straight members of SA [*Sturmabteilung*, Storm Troopers, a.k.a. "Brown Shirts"] and SS units carrying flaming torches. Chancellor Hitler's call to action rang forth from loudspeakers as he addressed a wildly enthusiastic crowd in Königsberg that had hurriedly assembled there from all parts of East Prussia to join him in celebration. At the end of the speech, when a Dutch prayer of thanks mingled with the deep metallic voices of the bells of the Königsberg cathedral, thousands of rapt listeners stood bare-headed in the rain and spontaneously began to sing the German national anthem ["Deutschland, Deutschland, über alles"]. Greeted enthusiastically

by onlookers, they marched in orderly columns to the southern part
of town, an area that had overwhelmingly voted for the movement.
Here many houses were festively illuminated ... and their windows
displayed flags with the swastika. A brief and condensed address by
the SA leader Soest concluded the greatest patriotic demonstration
that Göttingen had ever experienced.[7]

This town, where Einstein lectured on relativity in 1915, where
Grotefend deciphered Mesopotamian cuneiform, and where
the Brothers Grimm fought for democratic freedoms, was now
transformed into a stage for the Nazi revolution.

Only one month later and about thirty kilometers northwest
of Göttingen, a makeshift concentration camp was opened in
Moringen, a small town in Lower Saxony. With this move, organized violence trumped staged persuasion. In March 1933, two
men in "protective custody," August Baumgarten from Hannover and Karl Ebveling from Lauenstein, were transported to
Moringen and incarcerated. At the so-called workers' housing,
two large halls housed 280 Communists, twenty Social Democrats, and twenty members of other parties. According to a
report by Baumgarten and Ebveling, the prisoners attempted a
hunger strike to protest shabby treatment associated with the
forced labor demanded of them. Under the assumption that they
were still governed by the civil laws of the Weimar Republic,
the prisoners registered their complaints. For a while their conditions improved. The report continues: "In the meantime, the
fascists had assumed power in Germany. After four weeks, the
camp guards were replaced. Now came the SS! What now happened was indescribable."[8] The report goes on to detail beatings and concludes with a description of the *Prügelhaus* (house of
flogging) that many prisoners were forced to enter, individually.

None of the Jews among them escaped brutal beatings in this building. Communist Party functionaries and Communist candidates for local or national elections were the first to find themselves in these camps, pursuant to the Order for the Protection of the People and the State.[9]

In Moringen, as in many other towns all over Germany, the Nazis exercised their power removed from the public eye as much as possible. The seeds of this preferred modus operandi (the *hidden* application of violence), sown at the very beginning of their revolution, came to full deadly fruition a decade later in the Holocaust.

. . .

Not enough has been made of the fact that Germany's fate was all but sealed during the first crucial months of 1933 with the Nazis' ascent to power. These months constituted the third of three radical collective events that had occurred in Europe since the late eighteenth century—the third of three revolutions, as they might be more appropriately called: the French Revolution of 1789, the Bolshevik Revolution of 1917, and in 1933, the Nazi revolution. The first two revolutions were revolts of the masses, though after they rose up against their rulers, the king in France and the czar in Russia, the initial violence did not abate, even after the old regimes were gone. The third revolution, designed and carried out by the Nazis, was not a revolution of the masses against oppressors; rather, it was organized from above and arrived in increments. The subtle interplay of show—a kind of Nazi virtual reality—on the one hand, and violent oppression, on the other, proved very effective. The vast majority of Germans were caught in the tight vise of persuasion counterposed against coercion. Options and alternatives disappeared in very short order.

To be sure, Germans had directed widespread resentment against real or imagined enemies in the past, but no hatred for any oppressors was pervasive or strong enough to have fueled a violent overthrow of the status quo. Yet in the early months of 1933, revolutionary change took place by virtue of the very speed with which the Nazis removed opposition groups from positions of power—Communists and Socialists, above all—and installed trusted Nazis in key positions throughout German society. For a time, the Socialists held on to the hope that established laws would prevail. On January 31, 1933, the executive committee of the Social Democratic Party (SPD, *Sozialdemokratische Partei Deutschlands*) declared: "We will fight on the basis of the constitution, and we will defend civil liberties against attacks with all the legal means at our disposal."[10] But a year and a half later, in August 1934, the Socialists had become discouraged. "There is nothing that can be done; we cannot do battle, the sacrifices are too great."[11]

Unlike the French and Russian revolutions, in which open displays of violence enforced the new systems, the Nazi revolution frequently used stealth and concealed violence, especially in the early stages. Executions of Germans considered inimical were not carried out in public but rather hidden away, their nature and location receiving a low profile. Execution by guillotine took place in only a few towns. At first, the press reported on Nazi executions of dissenting Germans, but as time went on, the regime asked and then ordered that newspapers stop publishing details of executions. Decree #211, for example, stated that "executions shall be centralized and take place in only a few locations in Germany. So that the reputation of these locales will not be damaged due to frequent reference to them as places of execution, no reference to the precise location will be provided to the public."[12] Inconsistent compliance by the press apparently led to Decree #256, which repeats and reinforces the earlier directive: "We recommend once more that the locations where the executions are to take place should not be mentioned and no information be provided in advance of the impending executions."[13] By contrast, during the French Revolution, led by the masses, executions were public celebrations around the guillotine in the center of the Place de la Concorde. Anyone could witness them, and once the blade fell, executioners raised high the severed heads for the crowds to behold.

Into the mid-thirties the Nazis were very much aware that their revolution had not yet achieved its goal of fully persuading the German masses of the righteousness of their cause. Consequently, they moved incrementally and as quietly as possible. Secretiveness was maintained to the degree feasible, even when mass transports into death camps were in full swing.

· · ·

What was life like for the youths of this "new" country that called itself *Großdeutschland* under the Nazi banner? Compelling for this younger generation were the Olympic Games of 1936, because sports constituted an important Nazi vehicle for binding young people to their system. At the same time, their parents enjoyed a measure of economic security heretofore unknown, and they appreciated the international legitimacy that these games brought to their country. Hitler and his movement spent an extraordinary amount of time and energy not only integrating young people into the Nazi system, but also preparing them for the agenda to come.

With the collapse of Nazism in 1945, Germany's devastation was both physical and moral. In the aftermath of the war, Germans collectively engaged in a serious soul-searching in relation to this disastrous period of their history. And attempts to come to grips with the past have not let up to this day. The sober German voices of my interviewees, which I reproduce here as accurately as possible, lie at the heart of this book. The intense, confessional character of these elders' recollections of their lives in Nazi Germany before and during the war vouchsafes their authenticity, devoid of whitewashing or self-serving rationalization.

The sampling of soldiers' letters from the Museum für Kommunikation I include in chapter 5 also brings individuals into view; as they make very clear, these men, too, suffered the consequences of the disaster that Hitler brought upon all Europeans, Germans included. The letters held many surprises for me—unexpected points of view, insights gained in the heat of battle or during endless night watches. The greatest surprise, however, was the sheer variety of perspectives I found. Some letter writers were convinced fanatics and racists, while others criticized the regime they had to serve; some were appalled by the violence of the war, or withdrew into reflections on their private lives, now put on hold; still others were distressed by the suffering of the local populations in their battle zones. Most of them would have preferred to be home, Hitler's ambitions notwithstanding.

Finally, although the Holocaust is not at the center of this project, it remains a dreadful and powerful reminder that in a democracy, *ordinary citizens* should be wary of political leaders who provide simplistic answers to complex social, political, and economic problems. I hope this work is a similar reminder that what government does in the people's name should be recognized and understood—before it's too late.

CHAPTER ONE

Jobs and the Olympic Games

Following the swift Nazi takeover in 1933, the interplay of persuasion and coercion alone was not enough to consolidate the party's authority. Other factors, including the Olympic Games of 1936, which legitimized the Nazi movement before the world,[1] and the completion in 1937 of Hitler's first, successful Four-Year Economic Plan—profound displays of harmony and accomplishment, requiring three years of careful preparation on all levels of society—brought Hitler to the apex of power.

JOBS

The generation growing up in the early 1930s saw hunger and unemployment all around them. If they lived in nice houses and their parents patronized the neighborhood butcher, baker, and grocer, these individuals nevertheless remember the beggars who knocked on their doors and asked for work, food, or handouts. "Meister, hast du keine Arbeit?" (Boss, don't you have any work?) still echoes in the memory of a man from Cologne, whose father owned a sizable carpentry shop. For the parents, who had no knowledge of rough-and-tumble, open-ended capitalism, such need was hard to take. Since Bismarck, the older generation had come to believe in social and economic stability, and whenever that broke down, they expected the state to step in and help.

After January 30, 1933, when Hitler was handed control in the German parliament, he lost no time in making his first move. On February 2, he presented his first Four-Year Plan to the public. Relief from economic hardship was exactly what Germans wanted to hear, and he addressed this concern directly:

> We see in the terrible fate that has been haunting us since 1918 only an expression of our decay. However, the entire world is in the grips of a deep crisis. The historical balance of forces has been removed. The insane idea of victors and vanquished prevents any confidence from developing between nation and nation, and with that a chance for an economic recovery.
>
> But the misery of our people is horrible. The proletariat of the hungry and unemployed millions in industry is now joined by the progressive deterioration of the entire middle class. If this general decay engulfs the German peasantry as well, then we will face a catastrophe of unimaginable proportions.[2]

Hitler, of course, was interested not only in providing his views of economic conditions, but also in evoking an apocalyptic vision of total collapse that only the Nazi movement could prevent.

During the three years leading up to the Olympic Games, most Germans—even those not fond of the Nazi regime—thought that the Nazis had made good on their promise to lift the German economy out of the depression. Those who, with the help of hindsight, now stress that Hitler was already mobilizing the German economy for war miss the point. The vast majority of Germans did not and could not know that mobilization for war was foremost in Hitler's mind.[3] What they did know was that work materialized, living standards rose, and unemployment largely disappeared. On March 26, 1937, a few days before the general election of March 29, a student wrote a composition for a class assignment with the title "Wahlzeit" (Election time): "Now the German people have the chance to show their gratitude toward the Führer. . . . Things are moving, chimneys are smoking again, farmers are filled with hope, workers' brigades till the land and soil, the army marches, youth sings and has faith, and the Saarland has returned home."[4] He received an A–/B+ for his efforts.

This young student welcomed the advent of an astonishing new age of work, hope, and flag-waving; for the millions of older Germans who had been unemployed, however, the changes came largely as a great relief. Looking back at the Nazi era after World War II, the child of a father who had been unemployed remarked:

> After all, the party called itself, oddly enough, the National Socialist German Workers Party [*National Sozialistische Deutsche Arbeiterpartei*, or NSDAP]. Work was promised and work was created. Now we know the reasons why work was created. But you have to see it from the point of view of the father of a family, who had been unemployed for three, four, five, seven years and had to make do with a few pennies from social welfare. The Nazis gave him a uniform and boots. Hunger is what churned around in my stomach and intestines. Mother cried because she was unable to give us

anything to eat, and we were four children. I can really understand that a father who looks at his children and finds a job will say, "Well, that is to the credit of Hitler." And then there was this immense propaganda effort that influenced the masses. I can really understand all of that.[5]

One of my interviewees recalled a remark of an anti-Nazi whom his father had known. Although this opponent of Hitler had fought against the Nazis in the 1920s, he still praised their economic accomplishments when he mused, "Is Hitler a genius or what?" The economic success attributed to the Nazis only added to Hitler's nimbus as savior—an aura carefully constructed since 1933. Hitler's magic lasted among the true believers throughout the war, in some cases to the very end. And Hitler himself believed in his own invincibility; had he not, after all, survived a whole string of assassination attempts?

By the late 1930s, propaganda had convinced the Germans not only that their economy was strong and growing stronger, but also that there was no war agenda hidden behind the economic data. Eventually, many critics began to waver in their negative views of the Nazis and to fall in line. One such individual, a good Catholic born in 1913, remarked, "In 1936–37—I still remember it well—pronouncements of the church were read from the pulpit that were considered to be propaganda against the Nazis. . . . I still remember my mother saying, 'Good God, how can they proclaim such stuff in church? After all, everything is turning out just fine.'"[6]

The Nazis implemented programs to improve workers' lives and enhance their leisure time. The leadership was well aware that German labor had been a strong supporter of the Socialists and Communists, and they wanted to destroy the last vestiges of leftist loyalties among the working class. Robert Ley, for example, was in charge of the *Deutsche Arbeiterfront* (DAF, German Labor Front) and developed vacation philosophy and policy for workers:

> When someone arrives at a beach resort, he must be able to forget his past right away. I would like to arrange things in such a way that he is swept off his feet immediately by a general mood filled with excitement, so much so that it will take his breath away and he will not come to his senses with all that music, dancing, theater visits, and so on. Up until now you needed seven days just to get adjusted to vacation time and to get in touch with other people. And during the last seven days you already had to get used again to the worries of everyday life. That must be stopped. Starting with the first hour, the vacationer must be submerged in an intoxicating environment [and it must last] up to the very last second, when he climbs back onto his train to go home. This is also the wish of *der Führer*, and so we want to construct this beach resort with these leisure principles in mind: a theater, a movie, evening shows, music, dance locales and so on.[7]

Kraft durch Freude (KdF, Strength through Joy) was the Nazi organization charged with implementing vacation policy. It administered a wide range of activities, including propaganda rallies, theater performances, operas, symphony concerts, cabarets, nightclub acts, and group travel. Except for the meetings designed specifically for ideological advertising, many of these vacation programs had little explicit political content. During the 1930s Germans began to experience and enjoy mass entertainment and the glitzy, modern world of escapist illusion. The Nazi utopia of a *Reich* to last a thousand years and this world of entertainment mutually reinforced each other.

The Nazis never flagged in their efforts to control all aspects of leisure time. They developed, for instance, special cultural programs for the handicapped, such as the blind, the deaf, and those who had become invalids as a result of workplace injuries. Their efforts paid off. In 1934, only 9,111,663 participated in the KdF programs; by 1937, the number of participants had grown to 38,435,663—as the KdF authorities pointed out with utmost precision.[8]

In the early years, the economic mobilization and upswing also included efforts to feed the hungry—not unlike in the United States in the 1930s, but with an important addition. In a major campaign to collect money and food for the neediest citizens, the Nazis, thanks to their centralized command structure, were able to mobilize everyone down to the village and even city block level. Anyone who was employed, even for minimum wages, had to sacrifice 10 percent in additional taxes to benefit their poorest fellow citizens. The Nazis drove such efforts to collect money so hard, however, that in many communities complaints arose about the pressure to contribute. Grumblings were closely monitored by the party and, in more prolonged and severe cases, reported to the Gestapo.

By collecting money from every German household, the Nazis nurtured a sense of solidarity among all members of society, rich and poor, well fed and hungry. Nothing symbolized the Nazis' aid to the elderly, sick, and poor better than the ubiquitous *Sammelbüchsen* (collection boxes) for small change. Painted bright red, the cone-shaped metal boxes had small slots on top surrounded by metal cuffs, meant for coins, as well as holes for depositing rolled-up bills. A metal grate covered the slot on the inside, preventing deposited coins from escaping even if the box were turned upside down and shaken. These boxes had a dual function: to collect money and to make it apparent to every

German that the Nazi state cared for everyone, even its weakest citizens. The younger generation could not fail to notice this display of altruism, which for the Nazis, of course, was also a way of inculcating a sense of loyalty to the regime. Virtually every German with spare change deposited money into these boxes. Such actions constituted one of the *social* elements of the National *Socialist* German Workers Party.

I had a great-aunt, a member of the older generation. She was the spinster sister of my step-grandfather and beloved by all the villagers for her volunteer work at the local kindergarten and at the home for the poor and sick. She was also known for her poetry, which mourned the dead and celebrated weddings and anniversaries. She wrote her poems in a neat notebook. This gentle old woman wrote "Heil Hitler" at the bottom of the page of each of her poems. Her world was simple. She liked Hitler because he fed the poor.

Young Germans may have been just as impressed by the anti-poverty efforts of the Nazis, but for them these were plainly heady times. By 1936 earlier fears about unemployment had vanished. The young believed in better days to come, a secure future with fulfilling work, to be created in the new Germany they would inherit. For them it was all sunshine as the Zeppelin flew over the various regions of Germany, the swastika ablaze on its tailfins.

.   .   .

By 1936 the Nazis had succeeded in splitting the public sphere into two distinct but mutually supportive elements: the "big show," with its projection of a new utopia, on the one hand, and the ever-more-secretive application of violence against all those who opposed them or whom they considered undesirable, on the other. To create a vision of themselves as they wanted to be seen by others, however, they organized two grand events in addition: for Germans, the 1934 Nuremberg party rally; and for the rest of the world, the 1936 summer Olympic Games.[9]

THE NUREMBERG PARTY RALLY

More than any other medium, Leni Riefenstahl's 1934 documentary film about the annual Nuremberg party rally, *Triumph des Willens* (Triumph of the Will), introduced the Nazi Party to the astonished audience of the German population at large, and to this day it stands as a masterpiece of propaganda. There was no television, after all, and news consisted of after-the-fact reports in newspapers and visual summaries at the beginning of entertainment films. Only the radio projected the immediacy of the events the Nazis staged for public consumption, but the radio was a poor substitute for Nazi happenings that were arranged primarily for the eye. A stage was needed for Hitler's words, and a stage had to be seen to be appreciated. Riefenstahl's film had an enormous impact, particularly on the younger generation. It also set the tone for Nazi propaganda films in general, and eventually led to her internationally acclaimed documentary on the Berlin Olympics of 1936.

What made *Triumph of the Will* so effective as a visual introduction to the Nazi movement? The movie opens with a view out the window of an airplane. The spectator (eye of the camera) sees clouds move by swiftly as the plane descends for a landing—a new visual experience for most Germans, who had never flown in an airplane. The anonymous spectator, a German

Everyman who takes in this novel scene—clouds, sky, and the city slowly unfolding below—though not identified until after the landing, is Hitler, who debarks to a tumultuous reception at the Nazi Party Rally in Nuremberg, the *Reichsparteitag* of 1934. In this opening scene, the identification between Hitler and the passive moviegoer takes place on a preconscious level: the eye of the camera and the eyes of the viewers watching the film in theaters all over Germany turn out to share Hitler's own field of vision as his JU-52 prepares to set down in Nuremberg.

The documentary then switches to individual Germans pursuing various private tasks as they prepare to participate in the mass rally. Their activities are familiar to all: the old woman peering out the window from behind geranium boxes; young men polishing their shoes, washing themselves, or playing catch in a springtime meadow. The backdrop to all this is a sun-drenched Nuremberg, the ancient and familiar city of the trade guilds and the *Meistersinger*, though now it is festooned with swastikas and striking streamers.

As the film continues, individual Germans slowly transform into a mass. In one scene, uniformed members of an *Arbeitsdienst* (work brigade) are lined up in formation, with each member shouting out in turn: "Comrade, where are you from?" and another member of the group answering, "From the Alps," or another, "From the seashore." The subliminal message is clear: only in this tightly knit formation is it possible for them to hear and contact each other, to ask questions and give answers as to their origins. The scene concludes with a ritual chant by the entire group that gives voice to their solidarity as one body.

Similar transformations of the individual are repeated throughout the documentary, up to the climax, when approximately 100,000 Nazi Party members, all assembled on the Nuremberg rally grounds, are organized into two huge blocks of black (the brown color of the Nazi uniforms in a black-and-white film) separated by a broad white concrete pathway, on which Hitler walks, slowly and silently, up to the tribune and the speaker's platform. The masses now become an aesthetic foil; all individual differences are obliterated in a metamorphosis that presents only *one individual,* Adolf Hitler, in splendid isolation. This central scene of the Nazi celebration brings us back to the beginning of the documentary, where the eye that sees is initially our own; the propaganda equation is solved as we have become him, and he us.

Depicted in this way, the masses are a centerpiece of Nazi aesthetics, signifying power. The film creates a realm of its own, one in isolation from anything around it, and Hitler emerges in the middle as a self-contained symbol devoid of any contingencies. This quasi-religious Hitler persona, created over time, first appeared full-blown in this film. The cinematic images were replete with self-referential significance, while nothing was said about any moral sensibilities the passive participants might have brought, whether to the stadium in Nuremberg or to the movie theaters all over Germany. The Germans and the world had never seen anything like it.

What about German moviegoers curious about their new leader? In a series of visual tableaux, they are coaxed to identify with the enthusiastic masses. But the masses in this right-wing revolution have little in common with the masses of the French Revolution, who were the subjects of their history, storming the barricades and bringing down the old order. They also share nothing with the more recent revolution, that of the Communists in 1917, who took over streets and towns and murdered the czar. The Germans who participated at Nuremberg were portrayed as representing the entire *Volk,* but in reality they were a prop for Hitler in his big show. To create such a grand impression, members of the various Nazi organizations from the entire country came together, arriving by train, bus, and bicycle and filling the parade grounds with the brown uniform of the Nazi Party. For anonymous moviegoers sitting in darkened theaters, it was all a novel experience, disconnected from their daily lives.

For most Germans, that broad band of white concrete on which Hitler slowly marched up to the speaker's platform in Nuremberg created an extraordinary, defining image and moment. A few years later, a different broad band of concrete appeared as an expansion of the utopia: the *Autobahn,* flowing through forests and fields, over hills and mountains. While most Germans did not yet own a Volkswagen, some started to buy coupons that eventually would qualify determined savers to drive the new roads in these cars built for the *Volk.* In taverns all over Germany, old and young gathered around the radio to listen to coverage of the car races now being held on the marvelous new highways of speed. Shock and mourning swept the country when a popular race-car driver exceeded safe limits and a side wind thrust his car off the road, hurling him to his death in a forest clearing between Heidelberg and Frankfurt. A spectacular event typical of the new Germany, it embodied daredevilry, heroism, and violent death.

Most documentary films about Hitler, the weekly movie theater newsreels *(die Wochenschau),* and many newspaper photos from the time included masses of people as a charismatic backdrop to the *Führer's* appearances. The presence of large crowds projected solidarity and implied the Nazi movement's great power from the beginning. But large numbers did not necessarily appear automatically or spontaneously; rather, Nazi organizers closed schools, offices, and often factories in advance and ordered the local population to appear at these events. Hannelore Schmidt, wife of the former chancellor of the Federal Republic, Helmut Schmidt, notes that attendance at the rallies was more or less mandatory. On one occasion, she recalls, "Hitler was visiting Hamburg.... Schools remained closed for that day, because all pupils were to line up on the road between the airport and the city center. Our school had been assigned to stand at the Alsterkrugchaussee, where we lined up in three rows. I had firmly decided neither to raise my hand nor to shout."[10]

By contrast, the Germans who had joined the Nazi movement felt elated to participate in this new Germany. They also felt a special sense of entitlement, one denied the rest of the population. They returned all aglow from Nuremberg, basking in what Germans called the *innerer Reichsparteitag* (inner party rally)—an ironic term that described the heightened emotion a participant enjoyed at one of these glorious events. As time went on, the term was applied to any personal experience that made you happy.

THE OLYMPIC GAMES OF 1936

On the occasion of the Olympic Games in Berlin, Propaganda Minister Joseph Goebbels addressed a gathering of the international press with the following words: "We did not intend to place Potemkin villages before your eyes. You may freely move around in Germany among our people. Thus you can observe the Germans at work and as they celebrate the games; you will see how the people have become better and happier.... I ask you to consider in what a [terrible] condition we had to take over this country and to keep in mind the incredible crisis that we had to overcome during the past three and a half years."[11]

This statement was perfectly crafted for the festive occasion. Only a discerning architect with political savvy might have noticed that the monumental façade of the Olympia Stadium in Berlin was indeed a Potemkin village, despite Goebbels's claim to the contrary. Indeed, the virtual reality that he proclaimed to the international press hid more than it revealed. Any German reporters who sat in that press conference were no longer free to express their own views or those of their newspapers. Goebbels had seen to that several years earlier. Already on April 13, 1933, a report on a meeting of the local press association in Berlin summarized its plight succinctly: "The way things are now, it seems that the only question that remains for the press is to express its readiness to pay homage voluntarily to the rise of Nazi nationalism or to stand aside and watch as events take their course beyond everyone's control.... The principle of journalistic neutrality no longer has a right to exist. There is no self-evident validity for the press, except inasmuch as it participates in the greater and much more important Nazi transformation of the nation."[12]

The Nazis left nothing to chance, and control of the means of communication allowed them to invent or evoke any social condition they needed as a way of furthering their goals. To this end they passed laws that specified in great detail the new role of the press. Editors and publishers needed one simple qualification: loyalty to the Nazi party. The authorities paid close attention to permissible topics of publication, as well as the notion of deviance. Essentially, any point of view that did not adhere to the party line was considered deviant—though if any such reporters or publications still existed in 1936, they had long lost their accreditation and their ability to publish, let alone to be admitted to this international gathering. The Nazis' justifications were clear: "We [the Nazis] have never hidden our opinion—even during the times we were in the opposition—that we considered it political insanity to grant the individual free rein over self-expression to further an absolute freedom of thought and opinion, since granting this absolute freedom does damage to the body politic of the entire nation."[13]

With the Berlin Olympics the Nazis were catapulted onto the international stage. It was a great coup to present the new Germany to the world without major disruptions. Although the American Olympic Committee (AOC) considered a boycott partially because of the anti-Semitic Nuremberg Laws of 1935, the Nazis made every effort to prevent such an act. They even contemplated asking the president of the International Olympic Committee (IOC), the Belgian Henri de Baillet-Latour, to go to the United States to intercede on their behalf. This became unnecessary, however, when rumors spread that AOC president Avery Brundage had claimed that Jews were not suppressed in Nazi Germany and, further, that African Americans had not been treated any too well during the 1932 games in Los Angeles either.[14]

A few Jewish Germans participated in the 1936 games. One athlete, Helene Mayer, an instructor at San Francisco City College in the late 1940s, was a tall, lanky, blond Jewish-German immigrant—a gold medalist in fencing in the 1928 Olympic

Games in Amsterdam—who heeded the Nazis' call to participate in the 1936 games on behalf of Germany. According to both
Jewish and Nazi laws, she fell between the cracks. Her father
was Jewish, but her mother was not, which made her a non-Jew
by Jewish law. By Nazi law, however, she certainly was Jewish; they accepted her for the duration of the games, however,
because she might earn a medal for the *Reich*. And she did: a
silver medal in fencing.

Olympic events in Berlin were carefully planned to present
an image of a modern, united, forward-looking nation. The great
majority of people who attended the games were impressed. A
German visitor from one of the provinces put it this way: "Truly,
this city has adorned itself in a festive garb. Clean, scrubbed-
down, freshly painted house fronts, clean streets on which you
could not find even the smallest piece of paper. This cleanliness
really gets the attention of the visitors. The main street, Unter
den Linden, is no longer recognizable. The endless row of flags
and the ocean of lights at nightfall when the new lanterns are lit
leave a profound impression on us visitors, and it even impresses
the Berliners, who are not easily fooled."[15]

Foreigners were impressed as well. For one, the American
author Thomas Wolfe was so taken by the spectacle that he
wrote a story about it. One of his friends reported that Wolfe
also fell in love with a pretty German woman, which made his
trip to Berlin a completely intoxicating experience. Almost as
an afterthought, Wolfe mentioned police hauling a person off a
train, but he was too captivated by the brilliance of the Olympic spectacle to pay much attention. As he rhapsodized, "Such
a beautiful green cannot be found anywhere else in the entire
world."[16] By contrast, a Jewish German woman, who surely

disliked the fascistic flavor and fanfare surrounding the games, commented after the fact on foreigners' reactions to the event: "Well, they all came to the Olympic Games of 1936! The athletes and politicians! In their sweat suits, in uniforms or formal attire. They were all filled with enthusiasm. They did their business with the German government. Whereas we thought that the believers in democracy now had the opportunity to put pressure on the Nazis—break diplomatic relations, close German businesses and trade offices and the offices of major firms abroad. That would have led to some results."[17]

Of course, such minority voices were drowned out by the grandeur of the games, which outdid even the elaborate party rally at Nuremberg staged primarily for Germans two years previously. Now, in Berlin, the entire world was the audience, and on the whole, it liked what it saw. Most Americans who remember the Berlin games point to Hitler's refusal to shake the hand of Jesse Owens, winner of three gold medals and star of the event. But the evidence seems to indicate that Hitler was not even in the stadium at the time. Originally, to be sure, Hitler wanted to shake the hands only of German medal winners. When the IOC deemed that unacceptable, he stopped shaking hands altogether. The Nazis resented the prowess of "non-Aryan" athletes and convinced themselves that "Aryan" people did best in middle-distance races, in spear throwing, and in non-Olympic contests such as stone throwing. It is reported that the Nazi racist par excellence, the notorious Julius Streicher, the NSDAP regional head of Franconia and editor of the virulently anti-Semitic paper *Der Stürmer,* sat in the VIP loges, a riding whip across his knees, and demonstratively refrained from applauding any medal winners with dark skin. As one anti-Nazi visitor to the games noted, however, the general public filling the stadium did not share these views. "I was there," he said. "The American Owens, a black, won. His victorious efforts were accompanied by the jubilant applause of the public, while at the same time I could see that no one in the loges reserved for prominent Nazis joined in the applause."[18] The radio broadcasts of Jesse Owens's races confirm that he was, indeed, loudly cheered on by the general spectators.

The racist undertone of the games, and of German sports in general, was not obvious; after all, the Nazis wanted to impress people, not hit them over the head with their hidden agenda. Slogans such as "The poisoning of sports by the Jews,"[19] for example—a cant with no other purpose than to radicalize Nazi activists and exploit traditional anti-Semitism—were suppressed during the 1936 games. Indeed, Nazi timing about how, when, and to what degree to state their views was carefully calibrated when it came to the Olympics, because gaining international acceptance was at that point more pressing than the need to push their racist agenda. "Our National Socialist educational objectives in the broadest sense can accept the type of Olympic games as presently constituted only to a limited degree, because these games are shaped by an ethos emanating from a world that has been made obsolete by the revolutionary uprising of National Socialism."[20] One Nazi sports functionary commented, "Every means is fine as long as it makes the task of *der Führer* easier, and nothing is more timely at this point than improving our international relations through sports."[21]

In retrospect, it is now obvious that behind the public display of harmony and enthusiasm over the games, the Nazis were pursuing hidden agendas. Despite the splendid rhetoric that celebrated the prowess of the individual athletes—as seen, for example, in the aura of heroics portrayed by Leni Riefenstahl in her documentary of the games—the Nazis were busy developing a strident, racist ideology of sports.

Already in the nineteenth century, the *Turnvater* (founding father of gymnastics) Friedrich Jahn (1778–1852) had linked sports with nationalism. During the Third Reich, the Nazis gave their own peculiar twist to this tradition, calling it *Wehrertüchtigung* (training for defense)—a term sufficiently vague for the unsuspecting participants, but clear enough to those who could see that it implied physical fitness for military purposes. The year 1935 was declared the Year of Defense Training, with the focus on a national sports competition that attracted 4.3 million young Germans. By 1937, shooting and paramilitary games were included in these competitive games, and 30,700 shooting ranges were built expressly for this purpose.[22]

Although the Nazis stressed the virtues and enjoyment of physical competition, the ultimate goal of these games was military preparedness. As Nazi propagandist Heinz Wetzel explained, "The army should no longer have to teach the young man the basics of military training, as has been the custom . . . but the army will take the recruit who has already been trained to physical perfection, leaving only the task of making a soldier out of him."[23] During this era, as young Germans were becoming inextricably linked with the Nazi movement, they did not realize that these keen and enjoyable competitions had an ulterior purpose. Any racist ideology that was promulgated was secondary for the participants, since these young athletes simply wanted to compete well. I was proud to come in second out of forty-five competitors in a shooting competition, for example. It didn't dawn on me that this target practice against a bull's-eye affixed to a bale of hay was designed to make me adept at shooting human beings.

Yet in actuality, failure in any sport marked one as a second-rate member of Nazi youth society; soon, by extension, a serious physical handicap marked individuals as having *ein unwertes Leben* (a life of no value). In time, most young people began to sense the deadly serious underpinnings at work in the sporting events. All performances were recorded in participants' dossiers. I, for one, knew I would fail in short-distance running, so in one of the important regional sports competitions I deliberately tripped and pretended to stumble a few steps after the start; in that way, no record of a poor result in the 100-meter dash could be held against me.

In all this the young were never told that they were being trained for military fitness. Yet the ultimate goal *was* war preparation. As time went on, war preparation included as one of its key elements propaganda against the Jews. The Nazi ideology of sports carried racism to the extreme, and the idea of a battle for supremacy of the races gradually took on an apocalyptic tone, somewhat akin to today's apocalyptic talk of a war between civilizations. Between contending civilizations—as the Nazi cried then and the ideological call to arms now—there can be no compromise and no end until one is victorious over the other. Wetzel wrote:

> Jews plan to soften and feminize the male and turn him into an internationalist. And to achieve their goals, they employ—clever as they are—sports, that is, competitive battle. They leave all *politics* out of this, and with internationalism as their goal, they propagate the idea that peaceful competition should replace battle-hardened,

competitive fighting, claiming that sports should unite the peoples of the world and prepare them for noble, peaceful deeds. But they are silent about the fact that this pacification of sports should be under the control of the Jews.[24]

For young non-Jewish Germans, every winning performance in competitive sports meant a move up the rungs of a ladder. At the top of the ladder were the German Olympic medal winners. In the description of an Olympic shot-put athlete, the Nazis constructed a glorious and exaggerated vision of the "perfect man" that almost defies communication outside their peculiar world:

> The iron shot put enraptures us in a mysterious joy. It releases forces in us that normally only the earth, untrammeled nature, and the sun itself are able to bestow. Firmly rooted in the earth's foundation, his head held high up to the heavens, reaching toward the sun, man [the athlete] tests his coiled strength playfully. . . . He takes the shot put, bends his knee and his sun-drenched, naked body, and then thrusts the shot put forcefully into the air. In one mighty gesture, the body leaves its bent posture, a powerful stream leaves the gravitational center of the body, fills thighs, knees, powerful leg muscles up to mighty shoulders and all the way up to the fingertips, and for a moment the body is motionless, immobile as if cast in bronze.[25]

The sexual undertone is unmistakable. In this context, physical strength and sensual stamina have nothing to do with individual self-expression. Rather, the athlete represents collective power, a power that is open to all kinds of projections. This flight of metaphoric fancy also inspired many of the songs young Germans were taught, such as "Wildgänse rauschen durch die Nacht" (Wild geese flutter through the night), which tells of the birds' "shrill screams northward, unsteady flight—watch out, watch out, the world is full of murder." Other songs assured us that "the frightful night is now behind us, we move in silence, we move without words, we move on to perdition," or "as long as the flame of freedom burns, the world is not small." Many such songs contained an undertone that blended dreams of glory with readiness for death. Death and sacrifice were very often presented in a context that combined everyday events of nature with the charisma of Germany under Hitler: "'Germany must live, even if we have to die.' Profound experiences and sacred rituals shape the Hitler Youth as the rain and storm rages against their tents."[26] New laws prevailed in this virtual reality, which turned things upside down. Heroic perdition was good, and Nazi orders spelled freedom in a seamless, persuasive continuum that eliminated all rational discourse or personal reflection.

If young Germans did not think of actual war at the time, neither did most of their elders. Of course, it was the Nazi leadership that was planning the "dark night" for which they were told to prepare, but that was beyond the comprehension of the general population. *Gymnasium* (college preparatory school) history lessons about classical antiquity taught that it was heroic to accept one's fate. At the time of the 1936 Olympics, the dark night had not yet arrived for most non-Jewish Germans. Knowledge of the growing number of Nazi victims was not widespread. For the rest of Germany and, indeed, for the rest of the world who came to watch, the 1936 games evoked only sunshine, flag-waving, and celebration of the winners by enthusiastic throngs of spectators.

While the Nazis managed to foreground the aesthetic aspects of the Olympic Games in 1936, by 1938 the power games behind sports became explicit, and Nazi ideology now openly promoted the ultimate goal behind *Wehrertüchtigung*. Wetzel again: "The grand historical deeds of our nation are not merely the result of the historical decisions made by our leaders, but . . . these deeds are also the result of the physical efforts of all of us."[27] Tragically, the ultimate winners of the 1936 Olympic Games in Berlin were not the athletes, but Adolf Hitler and the Nazis.

CHAPTER TWO

Jungvolk and Hitler Youth

Once you were drawn into the regime, you somehow
lost your legitimacy as an individual.
 Gerhard Neizert

In Grimm's fairy tale "The Frog King," a girl tries to retrieve a
ball, loses her balance, and falls into a deep well. At the bottom
of the well she finds herself in an unfamiliar world governed by
unfamiliar laws. Strange rituals surround her, and tasks must be
completed for rich rewards or dire punishments. Laws of cause
and effect operate differently in this world, suspended as it is
between make-believe and a reality unlike our own. Motivations
for actions determine rewards and punishments: you may perform the same task, but if your motivation is wrong, you will be
punished. Hitler's *Reich* provided a similar fairy-tale landscape
for young Germans, conjuring up an illusory sense of freedom
while keeping its horrors well hidden. Young minds were initiated into a ritualized order and promised great rewards for
enthusiastic participation.

 Membership in the Nazi youth organizations—*Jungvolk*
(Young People), *Hitlerjugend* (Hitler Youth), *Jungmädel* (Young

Girls), and *Bund Deutscher Mädel* (Union of German Girls)—was accompanied by ideological indoctrination, the focus of which was Hitler as the ideal mentor and role model. The older generation, in contrast, had been influenced by what Hitler had accomplished since 1933, by either persuasion or coercion. Having experienced the trauma of the *Reichstagsbrand,* they craved order at all costs, and the more conservative members of that generation had been reassured by the blessing bestowed on Hitler by the venerable Field Marshal von Hindenburg and by the economic recovery they had experienced. For the young, however, it was Hitler himself that counted, not any specific Nazi ideology or accomplishments. The *Führer* was the center of the public stage show, and at the Nuremberg Party Rally of 1934 he took on an aura of greatness. His presentations to the young were performance oriented rather than content driven, effectively neutralizing any critical reflections that might have arisen.

The indoctrination of the young started when girls and boys joined a Nazi organization at ten years of age. As Franz Josef Heyen observes, "The swearing of the first oath to *der Führer* was supposed to represent the holiest hour of their lives," and strenuous effort was put into quasi-religious rituals to "make this hour of commitment also an hour imbued with profound personal emotions." Initiates were told that "millions of young Germans were swearing that oath at the same time, presenting a proud picture of solidarity of German youth to the entire world."[1] The hyperbole was meant to create a seamless and, therefore, insoluble Nazi social fabric.

Der Führer was represented as unique and yet at the same time intimately linked with each and every German. The Hitler mantra I remember as a ten-year-old member of the *Jungvolk* went something like this: His stature reaches the very stars, but deep down he is just like you and me ("und doch ist er geblieben, so wie du und ich"). Not only did the ritualized rhythm in which we repeated such mantras during our meetings give Hitler a special aura, but their magic also seemed to empower us personally, at least during those few hours. Their effect was much like when one attends church on Sunday and feels temporarily devout; when Monday comes, however, it's just another day and the mood is largely forgotten.

Hitler made sure that anything about his personal life that entered the public sphere could be integrated into this magic aura. During the Third Reich his everyday existence was presented in terms of carefully staged activities: picking flowers, stroking his German shepherd, patting the cheeks of small, blond, pigtailed girls. Whenever children handed him bouquets of flowers, it was always in bright sunshine and he always bent down to receive them. The smile of *der Führer* remained the same—not too much, not too little—so as to impart a sense of permanence in these programmed, fleeting gestures of affection. The snow-covered Alps, timeless and immutable, often provided the perfect background.

What about his earlier life in Munich and Vienna? He wanted all specifics expunged from his biography. In its stead we in the *Jungvolk* and Hitler Youth had to memorize a mythologized version of his past and recite it word for word, a secular liturgy that allowed for no deviation. It recounted his life from the day of his birth in 1889 in Braunau, Austria, to his assumption of power in 1933 in Berlin. I still remember fragments of it:

> Unser geliebter Führer, Adolf Hitler, wurde am 20. April 1889, zu Braunau am Inn geboren. . . . Im ersten Weltkrieg wurde er

in Frankreich durch Gas vergiftet und verbrachte sechs Monate im Lazarett in Pasewalk. Im Kampf gegen den Bolschevismus in München gründete er die Nationalsozialistische Deutsche Arbeiterpartei. . . . Am 30. Januar 1933, der Tag der Machtübernahme, nahm er das Schicksal Deutschlands in seine Hand und brachte Deutschland in eine bessere Zukunft.

(Our beloved *Führer*, Adolf Hitler, was born on April 20, 1889, in Braunau on the Inn River. . . . During World War I he was injured in France by poison gas and spent six months in a hospital in Pasewalk. In the struggle against Bolshevism in Munich he founded the National Socialist Workers Party. . . . On January 30, 1933, the day of the assumption of power, he took the fate of Germany into his own hands and brought Germany into a better future.)

This recitation of Hitler's life dovetails with many other ritualized recitations and songs that most members of my generation remember in fragmentary form. One such song, memorable because of its quasi-religious tone, began: "Deutschland, heiliges Wort. Du, voll Unendlichkeit über die Zeiten fort, seist Du gebenedeit" (Germany, hallowed word. You, filled with eternity all through the ages, may you be blessed).

Hitler wanted to be considered a man without a past *(ein Mann ohne Vergangenheit)*, a symbolic figure who emerged ex nihilo— a phoenix rising out of a world of his own making. Already in 1930, before he had realized his dream of self-invention, he pronounced: "People should not know who I am. They should not know where I come from and from which family."[2] When Hitler learned that an overeager high Nazi official had affixed a plaque on a house stating that Hitler had lived there, he flew into one of his infamous rages and ordered it removed.[3]

This self-invention relied heavily on visual media, a new technology at the time, and it was coupled with Hitler's unusual rhetoric, with its reliance on clichés, repetitions, crescendos, and sudden shifts of tempo. Content was sparse and secondary to the method of delivery, which was impressive—a kind of chant replete with emotion, inaccessible to logic, and unsuited for reflection. As many of those who had been at the Nuremberg Party Rally of 1934 attested, "He does not speak, but it speaks through him."[4]

The charismatic aura surrounding Hitler persisted almost until the end of the war. Considering him to be invincible, many believed that Hitler must have had his own, very personal reasons for allowing the Soviets to advance all the way to Berlin. All too often between 1933 and 1938, when the Nazis committed violent acts people complained that if Hitler only knew ("Wenn das nur der Führer wüßte") about the violence, he would not tolerate it. During the early part of his rule, his air of moral righteousness had an influence even on his political opponents. A Social Democrat from Bavaria who fled to Prague to escape persecution in Germany reported in a message back to the central office of the Social Democrats, "Many who criticize and complain still believe in the strength and honest goodwill of Adolf Hitler, who is not able to stand up against such wrongdoing."[5]

Aside from the *Führer*, a few submarine captains and fighter pilots were the objects of German hero worship during World War II, but it was not extended to other members of the Nazi elite. One did not make jokes about Hitler (or about the ominous, inaccessible SS head, Heinrich Himmler), but my generation heard many jokes about Göring and Goebbels, both of whom were turned into caricatures with relative ease, even in public. Derogatory remarks about Goebbels's clubfoot, physical scrawniness, and heated, hyperbolic rhetoric abounded.

My step-grandfather, a brave blacksmith, was the only person I knew who could tell anti-Hitler jokes in public with impunity. I assume that as the only blacksmith in our village, he was necessary to the village economy, and as a consequence no one turned him in.[6]

. . .

The great attention paid to the young reveals a central aspect of Nazi ideology, that of a utopia based on ethnic solidarity.[7] A new Germany would be built by brushing away the old, weak, and decrepit, in short, all those who no longer had the drive necessary to radically transform society. In embracing the young generation, the regime also challenged most traditional vehicles of inculcation, including the churches as moral guides, the schools and their cultural norms, and even the family, with its stabilizing, moderating effect on an individual's behavior.

Some of us remember this frontal attack on traditional values much more than the anti-Semitic propaganda to which we were exposed. It hit closer to home because it undermined authority as we knew it. The Nazis replaced traditions with a new legitimacy that granted the "freedom" (in actuality, the license) to give one's instincts free rein, as long as they were released in the name of the Nazi cause. Of course, this was the Nazis' intention: to redefine the superego in their terms, then to wed the new superego to the instincts and to eliminate the self as the battleground of desires and restraints. For example, many of my generation came from Christian homes and associated prayer with the beginning of the evening meal. In *Jungvolk* and Hitler Youth camps, before meals were served we were encouraged to raise a ruckus with our cutlery while screaming as loudly as possible, "We are hungry, hungry, hungry, give us some grub or else!" This replaced the saying of grace, perverting prayer to Nazi ends. The net result of this mix of superego with the instincts was, of course, the destruction of moral sensibilities and civilized behavior.

I experienced a similar incident, which I described in *An Uncommon Friendship: From Opposite Sides of the Holocaust:*

> During the *Bannausleselager* [preparatory camp], one of the twelve boys in my dormitory had brought along a condom. We blew it up like a balloon and floated it out of the window into the courtyard. Camp leaders seemed enraged by this prank. Their investigation traced the infraction to our quarters, and we were grilled for hours, pressured to reveal the culprit, and threatened with severe punishments. At the same time, however, I detected a certain ambiguity in these interrogations, which obviously implied an underlying compliment: "Ihr seid Kerle" (You're real men). We stuck together, refused to betray the instigator, and escaped punishment. The double message of our superiors linked a number of factors—sexuality, transgression, regulations, and male solidarity—that served both to maintain order and to inculcate in us a sense of rebellion and team spirit. They wanted to make us capable of doing anything in service of the grand Nazi design. They encouraged us to develop into a controlled horde, a gang, really, legitimized and led by the greatest tribal chief of all time, who sat in Berlin.[8]

Hitler had provided a blueprint for this dangerous mix of instincts and superego already in *Mein Kampf* (first published in 1925). He later wrote in *An seine Jugend* (To his youth, 1937), "It is unbelievable that it is prophesied that many a young person will end up on the gallows for personal characteristics that would be of priceless value if they became the common heritage of the entire *Volk*."[9] Hitler's early plans to integrate the asocial impulses of the young to serve his system were later elaborated on in leadership handbooks written for those in charge of training the young: "With their friends they [the young] form adventurous hordes, which at times develop a frightening fantasy for dangerous undertakings and 'uncivilized' ideas. A strange world of values, tightly knit and closed, appears before our eyes, quite independent of the views of the parental home or the school. The protection of the home and bourgeois behavior are despised. Industriousness in school is discarded for the sake of courage and physical prowess."[10]

Abstract as this may sound now, at the time conflicts between the younger generation and their elders brought tears, uncertainty in terms of roles, confusing disruptions in family life, and divided loyalties. In other words, these battles were very real for my generation. Occasionally teenagers turned against their parents, but most of these struggles were carried out behind closed doors, some of the more dramatic fights taking place between parents skeptical of the Nazi movement and their sons and daughters who were enthusiastic members of the *Jungvolk, Jungmädel, Bund Deutscher Mädel,* or *Hitlerjugend.* Such divided loyalties occurred in almost all spheres of private life.

·   ·   ·

The organized activities of the *Jungvolk* (boys ages ten to fourteen) and the Hitler Youth (fourteen- to eighteen-year-old boys) were inextricably linked to sports. While membership was not mandatory between 1933 and 1935, by the middle of the decade membership had become compulsory. All of the members of my generation of both sexes that I interviewed had belonged. The attractions of these Nazi organizations for the young were found in the "big show" and in "games," catchwords that describe constellations of events and programs. Violence played virtually no role. Several German Jews my age told me after the war that early on they had wanted to join the *Hitlerjugend*, with all its attractive singing, marching, and athletic activities. They begged their parents to let them, only to be told that Jews were not allowed.

While the Nazi party provided the general ideology for the youth organizations, no clearly defined national agenda guided weekly meetings. Consequently, these meetings varied greatly, depending on local leaders' fanaticism or personal preferences. Occasionally, higher-ups in the movement would visit and lecture on the virtues of being part of a new Germany. By singing or reading heroic tales of the Germanic past while gathered around campfires, the Hitler Youth often adopted traditions of pre-Nazi youth movements.

Probably the most popular of the Hitler Youth activities—for boys, anyway—were the maneuvers in the countryside, or *Geländespiele* (they were not called "war games," even though that's what they were). The aim was to conquer a particular point in the landscape—a tower, village main square, bridge, or similar object. Each participant had a band tied around his arm, either red or blue. Once an opponent had caught you and torn off your band, you were "dead" and could no longer participate. One of the exciting aspects of the *Geländespiele* was that the normal geography within which one lived was transformed for a day into territory to be defended or attacked by the young, beyond the control of our elders.

In preparation for these games, we were taught to focus on what we heard and saw, and we learned how to describe our physical surroundings so as to help our superiors plan an attack or defense. Strategy sessions were coupled with discussions of tactics. In this way the childhood game of hide-and-seek was translated into quasi-military activities. Variations abounded, as in this description from a 1934 book: "A boy hides in the forest and utters a few loud shrieks. The other boys look for the screamer, but they have to move cautiously because anyone struck by the beam of his flashlight is considered eliminated. The goal is to catch the boy who had screamed."[11] This was difficult, and it could only be done if certain boys sacrificed themselves in a frontal attack, while one sneaked up from behind to catch the screamer. The victory went to the team as a whole, however, and never to an individual—early training in "group-think" or, more accurately, in the value of sacrificing oneself for the common good. Occasionally, these games became violent, as when one village was pitted against another and old animosities characteristic of rural life broke out.

An important aspect of the Hitler Youth and *Jungvolk* was their hierarchical structure. As one ascended in rank, one gained control over an ever-increasing number of youngsters in the quasi-military exercises and marches. Leadership talents were recognized and promoted at an accelerated pace. Prowess in sports was particularly rewarded.

Next to weekly meetings, the authorities showed films created specifically for the young. None was more effective than *Hitlerjunge Quex,* depicting the life of a teenager who wants to join the Hitler Youth but whose father has signed him up for the *Jugendinternationale* of the Communist Party.[12] A deep political split in his family drove Quex's mother to suicide. Deeply moved by his mother's death, the young Quex becomes an activist for the Nazi cause and is murdered by the Communists as a traitor. The movie focuses on the natural preoccupations of young Germans: family conflicts, tragic consequences, divided political loyalties, and the need for personal guidance. Most of us saw the film. For many of my generation it became the defining moment of their anticommunism in the thirties. Later on, Soviet communism came to embody the evil that many of us had seen in *Hitlerjunge Quex*.

But the meetings and indoctrination, of course, did not constitute everyday life in all its variety. The youth organizations of the Hitler era (with the exception of the *Ordensburgen*, special schools for training the future Nazi elite) cannot be compared to present-day Islamic fundamentalist *madrassas*, in which youths live at the schools and are immersed in extremist religious propaganda twenty-four hours a day. In Nazi Germany, members of the Hitler Youth and *Jungvolk* had functioning family lives and commitments and loyalties outside of the youth meetings, in communities that operated on many levels and according to old habits.

. . .

The Nazis did not have a large contingent of trained ideologues to shape the canons of German history to their ends. The fact that Nazi concepts were so vague and unsupported by historical facts gave license to the fanatics to say whatever moved them, as long as it stimulated hatred and prejudice.

Occasionally, one of the higher-up Hitler Youth leaders from the district office would appear at one of our weekly meetings in Kleinheubach. All *Hitlerjugend* and *Jungvolk* members had to assemble on the soccer field to listen to his strident speech, in which he became increasingly animated. One day, he claimed, when the Nazi utopia had arrived, we would all throw away our watches (as a sign of a decadent civilization) and allow ourselves to be guided by the sun, moon, and stars. This surely did not reflect any official Nazi doctrine; rather, it was a spontaneous, creative (not to mention ludicrous) idea of his own making. None of the boys in attendance discussed this prospect afterward, because most of us would have loved to receive a wristwatch for Christmas, if only our parents had been able to afford it. In fact, most of us sensed the distance between such hyperbolic propaganda and our natural, youthful resistance to authority, Nazi or otherwise.

The Nazi call for an "ideal youth" (that is, ideally suited to their ends), of course, never fit the young generation as a whole, and Hitler decided early on, very much in keeping with his revolution from above, to select from the young German population those he considered good prospects for membership in his future elite. "My pedagogy is hard," he wrote. "Whatever is weak must be hammered away. In my *Ordensburgen* . . . a youth will grow up that will horrify the world. I want to have a violent, lordly, fearless, cruel youth. They must be full of youthful vitality. They have to suffer and conquer pain. Nothing gentle and weak in them must be left. The free, magnificent wild animal must flash forth in their eyes."[13]

The wilderness played a part in the dreams of German youth, but not as part of the military groups they were supposed to join or organize. Rather, the American Wild West with its Indians, as evoked in the novels of Karl May, was loved by young Germans. May's numerous stories came in conflict, however, with the stories that Nazis deemed ideal for young Germans. So the leadership developed a counterstrategy of emphasizing Germanic heroes; as one Nazi authority pointed out, "Winnetou and Old Shatterhand were the heroes of our youth, so all we had was the courage and bravery of a foreign people. But what are all the requisites of Indian life worth now—the peace pipe and feathered headdress—compared to the Germanic sword, the ornaments and tools of our Germanic ancestors, as we make them accessible to our youth? The courage of Siegfried, the loyalty of Hagen, and the love of Kriemhilde tell us more than the most beautiful stories of other peoples."[14]

Despite such Nazi efforts, their pedagogy couldn't compete effectively with the fantasies that Karl May evoked. After all, the Germanic epics were part of the canon taught in school and thus were associated with study and exams, not attractive flights of fancy to a distant, foreign land. Nazi pedagogy was instead more persuasive when it attacked modern art and abstract painting as another decadent symptom of "Weimar chaos." The widely discussed 1937 Nazi Degenerate Art exhibition convinced most Germans that expressionist paintings were a sign of moral decay. What Nazis wanted in art was the redundant reproduction of their reality.

In the indoctrination meetings of the Hitler Youth, and to some degree in geography and history classes taught by teachers who believed in the Nazi cause, much was made of the concept of *Lebensraum*. At first, this "living space" necessary for the German people to thrive was defined as lands cultivated by Germanic tribes, within which "the cultural treasures and the racial quality of the Nordic peoples were able to flourish throughout Europe."[15] A traditional linguistic sleight of hand—defining Indo-European as Indo-Germanic—allowed the Nazis to use their racist, expansionist notions to include lands to the east. As the Allies closed in on Germany, the definition of *Lebensraum* was increasingly redefined as the battlefield for the survival of the "Germanic race."

My generation listened to that propaganda and had difficulty believing the survival of the *race* was threatened. Nor was survival of the Nazi Party on our minds. But we *were* concerned with the survival of our fatherland, of Germany as our nation. Our elders had passed down to us the idea that World War I had been a war between nations, not between races. But after the fatal handshake between Hindenburg and Hitler that legitimized the Nazi movement in the eyes of cultural traditionalists, patriotism became conflated and therefore confused with Nazism. While Nazi teachers often attempted to weave propaganda into classroom lessons, such efforts were not necessarily effective. One interviewee told me that a common strategy used in his school to avoid a feared examination was to ask a fanatic teacher a question about the Nazi movement. In his enthusiasm to respond, the teacher would forget to administer the exam, instead praising the students for their astute political interests.

Whatever effect the Hitler Youth had in shaping the minds of young Germans, I believe it was not as great as one might think by watching all the *Jungvolk* and Hitler Youth marchers, fifers, and drummers in films about the Third Reich—and despite the fact that youth naturally enjoyed these activities immensely. The leaders of these organizations were, of course, convinced Nazis, but they came from the same social and familial environments as the rest of us, where their rank mattered less than the social status of their family. Hitler Youth leaders sat next to us in our classes, they sweated through the exams with the rest of us, and we were all aware of their fathers' professions. In short, the Nazi simplifications and slogans could not destroy the diversity of educational experiences the young received during the twelve years of the Third Reich. It mattered a great deal, for example, whether you attended a *Gymnasium* that emphasized classical languages (Greek or Latin) or a *Realgymnasium* that stressed modern languages and the sciences.

To be sure, the Nazis disseminated educational guidelines throughout Germany, but they were full of vague concepts that lacked any cultural canon to support them. Terms such as "the sphere of the people's soul" or "the biology of the innermost essence and laws that determine the fate of a *Volk*" were of no use in schools accustomed to a defined curriculum.[16] The Nazis were never able to develop an official curriculum to supplant the highly structured, traditional curricula of German *Gymnasien,* and pro-Nazi teachers usually stuck to their subjects, though they might try to give them an ideological twist.

The Nazis did develop a kind of variant school system in the form of the *Ordensburgen,* which were dedicated to training and indoctrinating a future Nazi elite. But these schools were reserved for a very small percentage of the student population. Forty or so students might be selected from a *Gymnasium* class and sent to a *Bannausleselager* (preparatory camp), from which four or five boys with the greatest potential for becoming devout Nazis were promoted to an *Ordensburg.*

Limits in the Nazis' control of German society became evident when they stepped outside their organizational framework. For instance, they offered a Nazi wedding ritual as an alternative to the traditional Christian wedding ceremonies, but these new ceremonies never gained much popularity. Nevertheless, anyone who married during the years of Hitler's regime, whether in a traditional religious ceremony or its Nazi variant, received a copy of *Mein Kampf* with the *Führer's* best wishes and printed signature. People generally shelved this book unread.

In 1938, the year before World War II was proclaimed, the Nazis declared *ein Jahr der Verständigung* (year of communication/understanding); they also made an effort to contact youth movements in other countries and bring them to one of their big shows—a tactic that had served them well just two years before when they invited the world to the Olympic Games. The Nazis believed that if young people from abroad were to experience one of their Hitler Youth meetings, they would, as historian Michael Buddrus puts it, "be freed from the belief that hatred of other nations and thoughts of revenge were being propagated in Germany."[17]

The sense of a dawning utopia in Germany faded in November of that same year with the Night of the Broken Glass *(Reichspogromnacht* or *Kristallnacht).* Ten months later, with the beginning of the war on September 1, 1939, it disappeared altogether. War spelled the end of false dreams. Hitler's earlier slogans about youth being the nation's hope and future and young people acting as the subjects of their own fate changed radically. We now realized that what he really intended was for our generation to be "hart wie Kruppstahl, zäh wie Leder, flink wie Windhunde" (hard as the steel of Krupp, tough as leather, and swift as greyhounds)—notions first propagated in Riefenstahl's *Triumph of the Will.* Most of us felt uncertain whether we could rise to this challenge. *Tough as leather* might be all right for some, *swift as greyhounds* for others, but to ask all three utopian virtues of most young Germans was too much. Hitler remained uncompromising when he proclaimed his educational goals in a speech of 1938:

> This younger generation will learn nothing less than to think and act German. And when this boy and this girl enter our organization at the age of ten and for the first time breathe the fresh air and begin to feel things, they will then be moved from the *Jungvolk* to the Hitler Youth, and there we will keep them for another four years, and after that we will most definitely not return them back into the hands of those who have created social classes and prestige, but we will take them immediately into the party, or the Worker's Division of the party, or into the SA or SS and so on. And if by then they have not yet become complete National Socialists, we will assign them to workers' brigades, and there they will be subjected to severe training for six or seven months. And if then there is anything left in them about social class or personal privilege, the army will take them over for further treatment. And they will never be free again, for their entire life.[18]

His ultimate goal was to turn an entire generation into robots, or as Dr. Robert Ley, one of his lieutenants, put it succinctly, "The pulse of the blood must blend in with the rhythm of the machine."[19]

· · ·

It is my belief that the majority of German youths neither could nor wanted to live up to the most extreme, utopian fantasies of the Nazis. School, church, and family continued to form a powerful counterbalance, and most of our teachers, priests, and parents had a different educational agenda. The Nazis themselves must have been aware of the limits of their propagandistic reach. In an opinion poll in 1937 that queried female members of a Nazi labor organization, political education ranked tenth on their scale of interests, well behind a preference for singing (which ranked first), sports and dancing, hiking and trips, festivals and celebrations, and basic job training.[20] Not only this poll, but my childhood memories, my interviews of older Germans, and archival material support my belief that in the everyday life of the German people, personal interests and preferences were more important to most individuals than the political hyperventilation of the Nazis as they attempted to shape the public sphere. Catholic children continued to take communion and their Protestant compatriots continued to be confirmed; fathers went to work, women scrubbed floors and cared for children, and young people attended school. All of this continued during the Nazi years, even though it did not make it into the history books.

Yet ultimately, the traditional influences of families, schools, and churches failed to stop the war machine from revving up to its full, catastrophic force. Whatever remained of individualism and dissenting opinions lost all public relevance after Hitler attacked the Soviet Union. Young men were ordered to fight in the war, and off they went. As draftees, they had no choice. Many were convinced they were fighting a patriotic battle for Germany's survival. Tragically, a sufficient minority performed the Nazis' bidding, escalating battles into a total war and unleashing the genocide.

CHAPTER THREE

War and the Holocaust

Before 1938, the Nazis hoped to remove Jews from the social fabric of the nation with a minimal use of force. A Gestapo report of September 1935, while noting with satisfaction that "Jews are being forced socially and economically into isolation," cautioned that public acts of violence, such as breaking windows and drawing graffiti on house fronts, should be avoided. Indeed, the Gestapo demanded that the *Kreisleiter* (district leaders) stop individual attacks against Jews and discouraged any posters and signs directed against the Jews.[1] Economic boycotts were encouraged, but the Nazis decided that German society in 1935 was not yet ready for widespread, open acts of violence, even though some, of course, took place. The amount and severity of violence depended on individual Nazi leaders and the degree of anti-Semitism they harbored. The *Lösung der Judenfrage* (solution of the Jewish question), which became a euphemism for removal and finally for extermination, was, even in the mid-thirties, still a carefully circumscribed concept, as the 1935 Gestapo report showed: "The solution of the Jewish question, which has made progress with the passage of the Nuremberg laws, is not helped when local authorities make decisions, apparently for propagandistic reasons, that prevent Jews from buying property, opening businesses, or, for those receiving governmental aid, from shopping at Jewish shops. Quite aside from the fact that such decisions at this point in time lack a legal basis, they encroach upon future plans of the government."[2]

The *Reichspogromnacht* of November 9, 1938, overturned the incremental employment of violence against German Jews in one fell swoop. If the future was not predictable before, events now began to take on an inevitable course as the ultimate agenda of the Nazis slowly came to the fore. Violence in the streets reminiscent of pre-1933 times returned on a national scale with the Jews as victims. Many Germans now began to fear that this organized violence constituted the first shot of World War II. Indeed, Hitler's war preparations accelerated behind the scenes and the Germans' intuition of worse things to come turned out to be correct.

This Night of the Broken Glass marked the beginning of political awareness for most of the Germans I interviewed. The summers of innocence were over; worry and uncertainty had arrived. The Nazis now made an adjustment in the modus operandi that had worked so well for them in the thirties after their takeover, and the split between their big show and the use of violence took a tragic turn. The war was to become the all-consuming reality for all Germans, Jew and non-Jew alike, with the genocide that came later being carried out largely hidden from view. November 9, 1938, brought the "Jewish question" to everyone's attention for a short time, but it quickly faded from overall German awareness. One contemporary assessment of

German reactions addressed the question of property: "One segment of the population is of the opinion that the actions [against the Jews] in question and . . . the destruction of property were much too mild. But the other segment of the population— and they represent the majority by far—believe that this kind of destruction was inappropriate. In this connection it might be worth noting that the population frequently raised the question of whether the people who had actively participated [in the vandalism] would be subject to prosecution."[3]

Much documentary evidence suggests that most Germans were appalled by the attacks against the Jews. In reaction to the Nuremberg race laws of 1935, for example, one German wrote: "Today a German might well consider suicide and leave the following note behind: 'Since I have realized that the German people have taken leave of their senses and succumbed to savagery because of people like Streicher [Julius Streicher, publisher of *Der Stürmer*], and have dishonored Germany and consequently are disdained by other nations, I prefer to end my life, because I am ashamed to be a German.'"[4] This, to be sure, was an extreme position, one not shared by most Germans. More typical was an attitude that justified a mild form of anti-Semitism but condemned physical violence against the Jews. "Anti-Semitism— that's fine, but not like *that*," was a frequently expressed point of view.

On the everyday level, of course, non-Jewish Germans and their Jewish compatriots enjoyed a variety of professional and personal relationships, including friendship and marriage. Since the war, more and more stories have emerged that tell of childhood friendships and their heartrending breakups, and of help provided to threatened Jews by gentile Germans. In his infamous 1942 speech to concentration camp guards in Poznan, Himmler granted cynically that "every German has his favorite Jew" whom he wanted to exempt from the genocide. The story (as related by the daughter) of one man, a non-Jewish employee in a Jewish-owned store in the city of Göttingen, is perhaps more common than we know:

> The Jewish shop Blumenkrohn was shut down, and my father lost his job after having been employed there for some thirty years. A tall, imposing man, my father lost all self-confidence within four to six weeks. My brother then got him a job as a night watchman. . . . This was not an easy thing for him to do after he had worked himself up to head clerk in the firm. But even this job did not last very long. The Gestapo ordered him removed from that position when they found out that he had worked in the Blumenkrohn firm until very recently. That put my father out on the street again, but a Göttingen businessman and friend, a contractor by profession, hired him. Now, though, he was forced to work underground [on building sites]. This heavy work finally destroyed all of his self-esteem. I still see him coming home in dirty tall boots, and my mother taking him to the kitchen and helping him out of that misery. . . . There were many tears. The fact that he once had been active as a Social Democratic Workers' Party representative also weighed against him.[5]

NOVEMBER 9, 1938:
A DAY FROZEN IN TIME

While the Jews were being physically separated from the German public sphere, no one—neither victims nor onlookers (nor most of the perpetrators themselves, the foot soldiers of Nazism, for that matter)—knew it was the first step on the way to the gas chambers. In December 1945, Johann Stab, a simple policeman in Kleinheubach, recorded with great care the events that transpired seven years earlier on the Night of the Broken Glass. Stab's report captures the slow transition from innocence to guilt and then to shame of those present, from the Nazi thugs to the confused bystanders. It was a historical moment repeated in thousands of German streets. Despite variations in the details, underlying all of these acts was the shift to war and the Holocaust.

My anti-Nazi stepmother was proud to possess a copy of Stab's typed, single-spaced, five-page report, which she guarded like a treasure. I read the account on one of my visits to her in the 1960s. She died in 1980, and her nephew, Manfred Zink, gave me a copy when I began work on *An Uncommon Friendship* in the mid-nineties. Now yellowed with age, the pages capture the policeman's sense of unease as he tries in painstaking detail to report on events he was by profession charged to prevent but in fact was only able to observe:

Around 17.30 in the evening, someone arrived—I no longer remember who it was—at our police station and reported that in the village all Jewish property was being laid waste and that unknown Brown Shirts were on their way to the synagogue. I immediately telephoned my superior officer [in the nearby town of Miltenberg] about what I had heard, and he informed me that the matter had already been settled in his town and that it was none of our business. Out of curiosity, I went into the village to see for myself what was happening and to prevent the perpetrators from committing illegal acts. When I arrived at the Hirsch-Platz [the main square of the village], I saw the gang; six or seven Brown Shirts among them were just entering, and some were already standing inside, the house of Samuel Wetzler [a Jew]. I immediately entered the property, since I was in charge of preserving public order on that night. These men, some civilians among them, were already standing in Herr

Wetzler's living room; others were still in the corridor. I gained entrance and made clear to them that the property had already been sold to a known non-Jewish firm. I succeeded in persuading this gang to refrain from committing acts of vandalism and to leave the property. I surveyed the damage and then discovered that this gang had already caused destruction to the properties of Jsak *[sic]* Sichel, Mina Freudenstein, the Sichel sisters, the Sichel shoe shop, and the synagogue. The scene that confronted me was terrible. All the windows of all the properties had been broken, furniture had been smashed, clothing and other objects had been thrown out into the streets, and even the items offered for sale in the shops had been ripped off their shelves and thrown onto the street. . . .

Herr Stab then received a message from police headquarters in Miltenberg:

"Do not take any measures against these actions." Who had telegraphed this order, Himmler or someone from the Gestapo? I could not tell. The same night, toward 23.00 or later, we received an order by telephone from the police headquarters to take all Jews into protective custody. My wife received that message and brought it to me. Before we followed that order, I locked up all damaged houses as far as it was possible, and with the assent of a leading Brown Shirt I had one SA man placed in front of each property with the order to protect it and prevent any further plundering. When we had gathered up all the Jews ready for the transport, two Nazi thugs pointed out that Sarah Sichel was still unaccounted for and that she also had to join the others. I explained to these thugs that Sarah Sichel was home in bed sick and therefore could not be taken into protective custody. The two thugs insisted that she also had to be taken. I refused them firmly by pointing out to them that she was sick. Since the above mentioned did not accept my justified objections, I demanded from them to provide a car so that she could be taken to the hospital, because it was impossible to transport her to a prison. These men refused that request also. I then requested that these two thugs accompany me to the apartment of Frau Sichel to inform themselves about her physical condition. They agreed. We then went to her apartment. As we entered the apartment, Frau Sichel was standing in her nightgown in front of her bed because she was very frightened. She was a truly pitiful sight. Now the thugs agreed that she would be allowed to stay behind.[6]

In precise bureaucratic language, Officer Stab goes on to chronicle in great detail the last days of the Jews in my childhood village, who had lived there peacefully, participating in everyday rural life, for centuries. With a synagogue, ritual bath *(mikva),* and school, the Jewish inhabitants of Kleinheubach constituted a Jewish community according to Jewish law. This simple police report removes the layers of abstract generalization that are so difficult to avoid when considering the genocide of millions in camps far away and now long ago.

. . .

The interval between the Night of the Broken Glass and the beginning of World War II in September 1939 was less than a year. Once the war broke out, many Germans believed that the Jews were simply being relocated and that it would be over by Christmas. Both notions proved illusory, and soon the sense of foreboding, the unease about an uncertain and dangerous future, took hold of the populace. Now, even those Germans who approved of the Nazis' excesses against the Jews realized that more violence lay in store for all of them, however it might be justified—whether as an annulment of the Treaty of Versailles or as necessary to defend Germany from "enemies," both foreign and domestic.

With the German attack on Poland, the nation's mood was one of dismay. There was none of the jubilant enthusiasm that had marked the entrance into World War I a generation earlier. "You were drafted and you went" is a phrase that echoed through the stories of the German men I interviewed. Families often grieved hearing again the stories of their elders who had lived through World War I and who understood the consequences of war beyond the triumphant trumpets of nationalist propaganda. One elderly woman, whose father had been seriously wounded in the trenches in France, told me that when her family heard the news of the war's outbreak, "They all sat down and cried. And then my father prophesied that terrible things would happen." She stopped, leaned back in her chair, and continued in a low voice: "My father's prophecy came true. Three of my brothers died in Russia; one came back. My husband died in Russia in December 1944; my son was born in December 1944. The Nazis fired my father in 1933 because he had been a representative of one of the liberal parties in parliament during the days of Weimar." This new world war was something entirely different.

"THE REICH UNDER THE PROTECTION OF THE ARMY"

The war against Poland was officially declared on September 1, 1939, with a telling headline: "The Reich under the Protection of the Army"—telling not just because of what it said, but also because of what it left out. It represented a purported shift of legitimacy away from the Nazi Party to the German army, that is, a shift from the swastika to military insignia, from propagation of Nazi ideology to the defense of the fatherland. The legitimacy that venerable Field Marshal von Hindenburg had bestowed upon the upstart Hitler finally bore fruit when, on

September 1, 1939, the High Command of the Armed Forces announced in its first report that "by order of the *Führer*, the Highest Commander of the Army, the army has taken over the active protection of the Reich. In fulfilling their task to stop Polish violence, German army units have started their counterattacks along the entire German-Polish border. At the same time, the *Luftwaffe* armada has taken off to destroy military objectives in Poland. The navy has taken over the protection of the Baltic Sea."[7]

Hitler's lie was that the Poles had launched raids on German territory, forcing the German army to retaliate with an invasion of Poland and a declaration of war. The "violence" cited in the report—an assault on the German radio station of Gleiwitz, near the border with Poland—was in reality carried out by the SD (*Sicherheitsdienst*, Security Service), the intelligence unit of the SS. Nevertheless, in strident tones Hitler proclaimed that the Poles had committed violence, even murder, against the German population, thus leaving the German government no choice but to act in its own defense. The lies worked, particularly because they were stated at a moment of high tension. One German reacted to the terrible news thus: "The Germans had to and still have to suffer unbearably. And the number of these poor and tormented people fleeing across the border is still increasing. . . . This Polish terror is so widespread because England has given Poland license to do anything by promising that if Germany were to defend itself against these Polish provocations, England would assist Poland militarily."[8]

This is exactly what Hitler wanted the Germans to believe. After England and France declared war in defense of Poland, Hitler once again employed the strategy that had worked so well throughout the 1930s: the incremental expansion of power. In a dissembling speech broadcast in Germany but meant for foreign ears as well, he declared: "The statesmen who face us desire peace—and we have to believe that they mean what they say. Unfortunately, their countries are governed internally in such a way that they can be removed from office at any time to be replaced by others who are not as devoted to peace. And these others are there. Just having Chamberlain replaced by . . . Churchill would make it clear that their goal is to start another world war."[9]

At this point, Hitler was still relying on an interplay between ostensibly peaceful intentions and hidden motives, a technique he had honed to perfection since 1933. Just a few months earlier, he gave quite a different kind of speech behind closed doors, meant for those who would conduct the war. On May 23, 1939, in remarks to the top echelon of his military staff, he made his war plans perfectly clear: "The war with England and France will be a life-and-death war."[10]

The German military high command did not spearhead the preparation for war. Instead, the SS took the lead. The elite guard unit had been partially reorganized and the membership increased in order to serve as a more effective force in the war to come. The Nazi leadership wanted to avoid repeating certain mistakes made earlier during the partial mobilization of the German army before Czechoslovakia was invaded.[11]

The first phase of the war (1939–41) was triumphant, the swift defeat of France being the high point. Every town and village in Germany celebrated the German troops' march down the Champs Élysées. A colleague of mine in the German Department at the University of California in Berkeley, whose Jewish father had fled Nazi Germany, told me that on the day Paris fell she was astonished to hear her father proclaim proudly, "We have conquered Paris." He, like many German Jews, had fought in the army during World War I; some received commendations from Hitler as late as 1935. Now she had to remind her father that this kind of German patriotism was no longer appropriate.

The second phase of the war (1941–44) was about the fight for survival and brought with it the proclamation of total war. With the attack on the Soviet Union in June 1941, the hostilities became a *Zweifrontenkrieg* (war on two fronts), recalling World War I in the minds of many Germans. And in December 1941, the entry of the United States again reminded Germans of their changing fortunes in that earlier conflict, when the sleeping giant across the Atlantic came to rescue the Allies in 1917. The giant arrived again, this time with its armada of bombers.

·   ·   ·

To prepare young men to march all over Europe, it was necessary to destroy their individualism. Inspirational, martial songs with such catchphrases as "the mighty storm" were meant to carry them into battle with youthful enthusiasm. As the war got under way, battlefield and sea victories were announced on the radio accompanied by the rousing music of Franz Liszt.

But the attitude of most Germans did not reflect the triumphalism that the Nazi authorities broadcast over the airwaves day and night. Less than three months into the war, on November 26, 1939, the police of one southern German town reported another tune: "The mood of the population at large about the war is with few exceptions not very good. There is, above all, much criticism that the members of the older generation have been drafted; those over forty years old have been called to arms, while on the other hand, quite a few younger people are still at home. This bad mood is particularly evident among peasant wives, who do not like to accept the fact that younger men are still at home pursuing their professions, while their husbands have been drafted."[12] One month later, on December 26, a police report from the small town of Aufseß in northern Bavaria likewise stated that "among a large part of the population of our local district, no enthusiasm for the war is to be found."[13] Although the official Nazi drumbeat about the Germans' universal eagerness to take on enemies at home and abroad and to give every male a chance to prove his manhood on the field of battle ("im Felde, da ist der Mann noch 'was wert"—on the battlefield a man is still worth his mettle) worked for some, most Germans would have preferred to stay home to improve the quality of their lives, as Hitler had promised them since 1933.

A prized possession of the German male at the time was an official slip of paper that made him *UK,* or *unabkömmlich*—exempt from military service because he was needed at home. The peasantry was accused of going to extremes to avoid the draft. "With all kinds of means at their disposal, every attempt is made [by peasants] to gain the *UK* status. If the application for draft exemption is refused in a specific case, then rather than a battle-ready soldier lining up behind the flag, you have an angry peasant not interested in defending blood and soil."[14]

"Blood and soil" was one of the pervasive Nazi slogans connected in a quasi-mythical way to the land owned or controlled by the "Aryans," that is, so-called pure-blooded Germans. For peasants, such slogans had little meaning. To them, soil was related to the sweat of their labors and not the blood of those mythical Aryans they started hearing so much about in 1933.

Not only the peasants, but most Germans grumbled about the rumors that prominent Nazis and their sons somehow managed to escape the draft: "The various decisions made by the authorities to grant exceptions to the draft cause a pervasive mood of poisonous resentment in the population. Especially the financial support for families, next to the applications for draft dispensation, cause much anger and animosity in almost all communities. This animosity is even directed against the authorities in charge of making the decisions about draft dispensation."[15]

• • •

During the first two years of the war, when the German army was achieving spectacular successes on the ground, the *Luftwaffe* controlled the skies of Europe, and the navy, particularly the submarine fleet, dominated the seas around Europe, Hitler could rightfully claim that he had the great majority of Germans behind him. During this period, the attitude of the German population was that of "us versus them." For many Germans, the period marked a return to patriotism, but a patriotism having more to do with traditional honor, virtue, and cultural chauvinism than with Nazi glory and ideology. The contemporary German mindset was much more intent on defending the fatherland than on expanding the German *Lebensraum* onto Slavic soil.

During this first phase of the war, the Nazi Party kept a low profile, allowing people's attention to focus on the military. Yet despite early upbeat reports from the various fronts, people remained uncertain about the future. Still, it was dangerous to doubt a German victory openly. Expressing doubts in public constituted a punishable crime, and if a Nazi informer was close enough to hear, the speaker could land in a concentration camp.

In 1941, a series of events radically exacerbated German doubts. The records documenting those doubts are not extensive, but they can be found in Gestapo reports that tracked attitudes of the German population. The attack on the Soviet Union on June 21, 1941, the entry of the United States into the war in December of the same year, and the first Soviet counter-offensive in the severe winter of 1941–42 in defense of Moscow all caused Germans to wonder in private whether the war would be won. Even though many who remembered Hitler's political triumphs in the 1930s still believed in victory, the general German mindset turned decidedly pessimistic. When Nazi authorities started a massive effort to collect heavy winter clothes for soldiers on the eastern front, many people began to question the war's progress out loud.

. . .

Eventually, the major disciplinary action for even a minor infraction by a soldier stationed in Western Europe was transfer to the Russian front. It was more than just a form of punishment, however; assignment to the Russian front had a brutalizing effect on those who fought there. The Nazi elite fighting units, particularly the SS and the army's police battalions, were engaging not in normal battle maneuvers but rather in mass murder. The German population at home was generally aware of at least some of the brutality, which they rationalized as a struggle against partisans. Rumors, partially substantiated by official military reports, spread that the stretched-out supply lines connecting the army deep in Russian territory back to Germany were vulnerable to partisan resistance. Detailed reports on partisan activities behind the fronts fed the old *Dolchstoßlegende* (dagger-thrust, or stab-in-the-back, legend), to which many Germans attributed their country's defeat in World War I. Propaganda reports from the eastern front also tended to conflate the partisans, Jews, and enemy combatants into one frightening Hydra-like foe.

Once bombs started falling on German cities and Germans could judge for themselves the military power of the Allies, doubts about eventual victory increased even further. Hitler and his propaganda machine tried every means at their disposal to keep the triumphalism going, continuing to trumpet German victories and explaining away reversals as strategic adjustments that would ensure the *Reich's* final, inevitable victory. People often whispered doubts as jokes. In German cities, for example, air raid shelters were marked on house fronts with a white arrow pointing toward the cellar and by the letters, *LSR* for *Luftschutzraum*. One common joke was that this abbreviation meant "Lernt schnell Russisch" (Learn Russian quickly). A more daring joke referred back to Hitler's 1933 unveiling of his first Four-Year Economic Plan, when he proclaimed to the nation, "Give me four years and you won't recognize Germany anymore." As German cities were bombed and transformed into ruins, the phrase took on a less utopian meaning. Now when Germans uttered it, it was in sarcastic reference to the destruction of the country that could land them in prison.

The Nazi leadership decided that since media reports about the war "still showed a strong tendency to stress [its] frightening aspects,"[16] heroism, rather than suffering, should be spotlighted. The younger members of my generation experienced the war, at least at the beginning, to a large degree through the reactions of their elders, especially the mothers, sisters, wives, and daughters of the men fighting. Fear for these men's lives, not pride in their martial deeds, was the overriding emotion. One of the most effective weapons the Nazis used to create positive feelings was the so-called *Wunschkonzert* ("wish concert," or concert with audience participation),[17] which was turned into a very popular radio program in which messages from soldiers at the front were read to their loved ones back home, interspersed with songs that listeners, whether at home or at the front, requested. Love, peace, the better world to come after the war, and best wishes to relatives and friends—these were the topics of the Sunday *Wunschkonzerte*, which were designed to relieve fears and further a sense of emotional normalcy.

THE BUREAUCRATS' PLAN
FOR THE HOLOCAUST

Following the initial slowdown of German advances and subsequent setbacks on the eastern front, the Nazis proclaimed a radical mobilization of all sectors of the German economy and society for war. It was within this context that the notorious Wannsee Conference took place on January 20, 1942. At this juncture, too, the old, incremental approach to eliminating the Jews was abandoned and the quantum leap taken to a "final solution" in the form of the Shoah. No top Nazis were present at this meeting; rather, representatives of the middle management were given carte blanche to take care of the "Jewish problem." The minutes of this meeting indicate that technocrats were at work—transportation experts and chemists—as well as members of the SS, who were well informed about the demo-

graphic distribution of the Jewish population throughout Eastern Europe. In the words of a Yale historian cited in the film
Shoah, the preparation for the genocide constituted a "revolution
of bureaucrats."

In a dinner conversation on January 23, Hitler kept his
remarks at the level of metaphor. "One has to act radically," he
said. "If you pull a tooth, you pull it all at once, and the pain
passes quickly. The Jews must disappear from Europe."[18] Just
four days later he reiterated, "The Jews have to pack up and disappear from Europe. Let them go to Russia."[19]

The bureaucrats in charge of the genocide had to be more
precise than Hitler to put their death machine into motion.
During 1942 they had to plan the technical details of the "punishments" to be meted out. To do so, they had to define different
categories of victims. Thus, Jews, Gypsies, Russian and Ukrainian criminals, and Germans who had received prison sentences
of more than eight years were lumped together as the group to
receive the most severe punishments, including execution. Any
uncertainty as to an individual's fate was resolved with brutal
clarity: "bei nicht genügenden Justizurteilen durch polizeiliche
Sonderbehandlung"—bureaucratic language which stated that
in cases where legal decisions proved insufficient, "special treatment," a standard euphemism for summary execution by the
police, was in order.[20]

In organizing the genocide, the Nazis perfected what they
had practiced so successfully from the outset, namely, the cam-
ouflaging of violence as an end in itself. With the genocide
moving toward a climax, one typical local Gestapo report, of
November 28, 1944, stated that of the last Jews evacuated from
Würzburg on June 17, 1943, fifty-seven had been sent to the

Auschwitz *Durchgangslager* (transit camp—an especially cyni-
cal euphemism), and seven to their new *Wohnsitz* (domicile) in
Theresienstadt. In addition, the report noted, 563 marks and 80
pfennig were taken during body searches.[21]

Many of my generation who attained draft age as the war
progressed were solicited to join the fighting units of the SS, the
Waffen (armed)-*SS*. The sense of foreboding at the prospect of
being so chosen was palpable. I remember vividly the day that
three SS officers in long leather coats held a recruiting session
at our school, and our collective relief when they left in dis-
gust, having failed to convince any of us to sign up. In another
instance, a memoirist recalls his class of draft-age youths culti-
vating silkworms to produce silk for army parachutes. The SS,
thinking these young, actively engaged Germans would make
good recruits, put them under great pressure to volunteer, evoking the image of SS soldiers as "real men, capable of leading a
German victory." No one stepped up; rather, the students all
insisted that their contribution to the war effort was best served
by their silkworm cultivation.[22]

As the Holocaust was put into motion, a growing fear, or at
least apprehension, began to color the Germans' mindset. I, as
well as some of the people I interviewed who also grew up in
rural Germany, remember Nazi authorities floating a vague
plan to relocate a certain percentage of Germans living in agricultural regions to the East, particularly to the Ukraine, in
order to germanify this Slavic region. The term *relocation* had an
ominous ring to it, because the SS and Gestapo used it also to
describe the fate of the Jews being transported to camps in the
East. Of course, this association was not discussed openly and
was perhaps not even well understood, but subliminally it con-

noted a loss of control over one's life, transportation under order to unknown places and an uncertain future.

In tandem with the movement toward total war, particularly as a German victory became less and less likely, SS and Gestapo surveillance of the German population increased dramatically, as did persecution and murder of non-Jewish German doubters. The German population harbored a justified fear of these organizations, with their black uniforms and sinister skull emblems. Anyone accused of making remarks considered "inimical to the war effort" had no recourse to a defense once the Gestapo had weighed judgment.

I still remember the sickening fear that settled over our family on one occasion. My father had been in England on business a few months before the beginning of World War II. I am in possession of the passport that permitted him to travel to Great Britain. Shortly after the war began, the Gestapo abruptly arrived at our home one day to interrogate him about the purpose of that trip. After an hour they left and did not return. Even my father, who had been a member of the Nazi Party since 1933, was shaken by this experience.

Anxious whispers circulated even among the simplest people. One member of the *Wirtschaftsgilde,* during a group discussion of the past, told about her family's maid, who feared the Nazis might take her mentally retarded child away from her in one of their euthanasia sweeps. The maid cleaned the house every week, all the time loudly proclaiming her hatred of the Nazis. The family had to warn her to keep her voice down so as not to get herself or the family in trouble.

During the war the Nazis posted warnings all over Germany stating that people should be careful what they said out loud, for "der Feind hört mit" (the enemy is listening in)—implying that the Allies had planted spies all over Germany. In fact, the "enemy" here included those Germans who simply uttered doubts about Nazi aims or the fortunes of the war and thus were "in league" with the Allies. Not mentioned, of course, was the fact that the Gestapo was listening even more closely than any purported spies. Effectively, they were saying, If you're not for us, you're part of the enemy out to destroy Germany. One German recalled an incident involving his grandfather:

> As I remember it, it was in 1944 when three Gestapo agents showed up to everyone's complete surprise at my grandfather's farm in Maibusch. My grandfather, the respected tailor August Becker, had a small brewery and tailor shop, where many customers visited him. It was early in the morning, and the Gestapo agents ordered all the apprentices to leave the shop immediately. Grandfather alone was to stay behind because they wanted to interrogate him without witnesses, as was their custom. We had heard rumors [about the Gestapo's methods]; that's why all members of the family were terribly afraid. What does it all mean? What was Opa accused of having done? Not until a day and a half had passed, interrupted only by brief pauses during the day and at night, did the Gestapo finally leave. . . .

The writer assumes the Gestapo interrogated his grandfather because he had illegally listened to the BBC, London. The report continues:

> Later on, Grandfather told us the most important aspects of the interrogation. As far as I remember, it really had to do with "political conversations" held at the workshop. Among other things, one of the customers, a respected citizen of the village of Hude, Herr Grüttemeyer, is supposed to have said something that could be heard throughout the entire shop: "What the GPU

[*Gosudarstvennoye Politicheskoye Upravlenie*, or Russian Secret Police] is for Russia, the Gestapo is for us here." . . . The Gestapo wanted a clear yes from my grandfather about this statement. But they did not really know my grandfather, who was a little smarter than these feared Gestapo agents. In spite of all the cross-examination to catch my grandfather in contradictions, he stuck stubbornly to his first answer: "I could not follow the conversation of the customers and the apprentices, particularly when several customers had to be served at the same time and I was busy taking measurements and finishing a piece of clothing rapidly. Besides, I could not imagine that Herr Grüttemeyer would say something like that against the state."[23]

To conclude this discussion of the relationship of the war to the Holocaust, I am compelled to ask once more and with renewed urgency: What in the end made the Holocaust, that enormous step beyond traditional anti-Semitism, possible? Among many factors, two stand out for me: (1) the gradual shift of executive powers from the SA, or Brown Shirts, to the SS and Gestapo in the 1930s; and (2) the existence of a particular kind of anti-Semitism, one that became horrendously virulent in the various European theaters of war, particularly in the war against the Soviet Union.

FROM THE BROWN SHIRTS TO THE SS AND GESTAPO

From the very beginning of the Nazi movement, the "big show" was effective, but it was only one part of the equation, the other part being violence and suppression of deviance, however the Nazis chose to define it. As their hold over Germany solidified, open, crude, obvious, public violence became less desirable. The street-brawling days of the Night of the Long Knives (Hitler's

1934 purge of SA leader Ernst Röhm and other political enemies) were replaced by subtler, carefully laid plans developed away from public scrutiny. In institutional terms, that meant that the more disciplined SS took over from the crudely violent Brown Shirts, whose well-known adage was "Und willst Du nicht mein Bruder sein, so schlag ich Dir den Schädel ein" (If you don't want to be my brother, I'll smash your skull in).[24] Of course, the SA returned in full force during the Night of the Broken Glass, November 9, 1938. But generally, as time went on, the key levers of power became concentrated in fewer and fewer hands within the Nazi elite. Law enforcement, for example, was taken away from the traditional police and given over to the SS and the Gestapo. Heinrich Himmler paid careful attention to this transfer of power, especially during the formative years from 1934 to 1937.

The thoroughness with which the SS and Gestapo controlled public life is astonishing. Not all aspects of public discourse could be as easily reined in as the press, of course; in their surveillance capacity, therefore, the SS and Gestapo relied on the NSDAP infrastructure—the centralized, hierarchical bureaucratic apparatus—down to every city and village. Each street block was assigned a *Blockwart* (block guard), always a local party member. The German province of Hesse-Nassau, for example, had 2,583,500 inhabitants; of these, 427,000 were Nazi Party members, 33,165 of whom were in charge of watching over the population.[25]

Since the SS and Gestapo operated by a combination of stealth and careful planning, only a few old SA street fighters made it to the top. One such was Heinrich Müller, who became head of the Gestapo under Himmler. He expressed his sentiments succinctly to one of his associates: "You see, I come from a modest social background and I worked myself up the ladder with a pickaxe and hard work. You, on the other hand, belong to the intellectual class. One should shove all the intellectuals into a coal mine and set off an explosion."[26]

As the 1930s passed, the lines between different kinds of deviance were deliberately blurred. This blurring enabled the SS and Gestapo to move comprehensively against criminals, political opponents, Jews, and homosexuals under the all-inclusive rubric *staatsfeindliches Benehmen* (behavior inimical to the state). As head of the SS, Himmler emphasized the need to transform the civilian police into an arm of the Nazi state police. In this newly designated *Reichspolizei,* all policemen who were Jewish, socialist, or communist or had politically centrist leanings were eliminated. This new police force under SS control had many tasks, two of which Himmler highlighted in a directive to the SS bureaucracy: "I would like to make you aware of two tasks: the FIGHT against the transgressions and crimes committed under paragraph 175 [law against homosexuality] and the FIGHT against abortions. With profound seriousness and the bitter insight that the spread or even the continued existence of these pestilences pushes every nation to the brink of disaster, we have persecuted these hideous atrocities without mercy."[27]

In the new structure, the Brown Shirts were relegated to the role of foot soldiers who collected party dues, participated in parades, and led the attack on the German Jews and their possessions. They were the "public works" part of the party that could be brought into play whenever needed. Because an aura of lower-middle-class toughness clung to the SA, the younger generation did not strive to emulate them. Rather than discussing a subject with anyone who disagreed with them, the Brown Shirts preferred to batter their opponents physically and get on with it. Particularly on the local level, everyone was aware of the modest social background of many SA members. On one occasion that I recall, at a meeting of all the Nazi organizations in Kleinheubach, an SA underling was given temporary command of the assemblage. He immediately jumped to attention, almost lifting himself off the ground, and shouted, "Alles hört auf mir!" (Everybody follow my commands!). We all snickered at his incorrect grammar (*mir* instead of the correct *mich*) and found him ridiculous.

While decreasing the active role of the SA, the Nazi leadership increased its symbolic value. The national hymn, "Deutschland, Deutschland über alles," was rarely sung by itself. Rather, it was usually followed by the "Horst Wessel Song," which celebrated the historical role of the SA and the "heroic" death of one of its members. The song began, "Die Fahne hoch, die Reihen fest geschlossen" (Raise high the flags, tightly close the ranks), and it concluded with a reference to the fallen members of the SA—shot by the Communist red front—who marched in spirit along with the living.

Despite their symbolic importance, Brown Shirts were generally not happy with their diminished power in the Nazi hierarchy. After all, they had done the dirty work, smashing heads to advance the cause. As the 1930s progressed and they were ordered to run sports clubs and other peaceful activities, there was a growing disquiet in their ranks. "Many members of the SA have told me," writes one historian, "that the lack of recognizable goals and the lack of greater tasks had a depressing effect on the membership.[28] In the end, however, the SS preferred to rely on the 32,000 highly efficient and secretive Gestapo agents that were available to them.

· · ·

While many informative explanations for the Shoah have been advanced since World War II, the dramatic jump from basic anti-Semitism to active genocide has not been sufficiently explained. In particular, too little emphasis has been placed on the different kinds of anti-Semitism that prevailed at the time. In spite of their common focus, it is useful to recognize that four different kinds of anti-Semitism were at work. The distinctions between them help us to isolate the most virulent strain, which was activated during World War II.

Religious anti-Semitism is more or less encoded in the notion that "the Jews crucified Christ." This variant, however, lost much of its punch with the advent of secularism and the Enlightenment in the eighteenth century. The Nazis rarely used it, since they did not want to rely on Christian notions for their ideology.

Ethnic anti-Semitism, which played a central role in Nazi ideology, can be summarized by the cliché that the Jews were racially inferior, radically different, and that they wished the Germans harm. It was the most comprehensive variant (and the most comprehensively studied after the fact), but in Nazi theory it assumed such extreme forms that most Germans could not possibly square it with their personal experience of their Jewish neighbors, who did not appear to them to be "subhuman."

It is unfortunate but not surprising that after World War II many scholars came to view ethnic anti-Semitism, with its strong emphasis on Nazi racial theories, as the main reason for the Holocaust, given that even before the Nazi regime it was openly espoused by the right-wing, reactionary intelligentsia in Germany, Austria, France, and England. These Western academics mistakenly assumed after the fact that if some members of the German intelligentsia propagated these noxious ideas, they must have reflected a broad consensus of the populace. What they failed to take into account is the fact that during the Nazi era opposing viewpoints could not be expressed or documented without enormous risk. Moreover, historians who never experienced the shared values of Jewish and non-Jewish Germans have neglected the importance of the everyday in their thinking and writing.[29]

Economic anti-Semitism increased dramatically during the 1920s and early 1930s, since Hitler made it a point to blame the Jews, among others, for Germany's economic plight. As the 1930s progressed, however, the role of economic anti-Semitism decreased for the obvious reason that the Nazis stole the wealth of the Jews and destroyed their livelihoods.

Cultural anti-Semitism emerged as the most virulent variant during the Nazi years. For one thing, in the later days of the Weimar Republic, when the Jews played prominent roles at the cutting edge of modernism, in the arts, sciences, literature, film, and music, the German bourgeois perceived avant-garde creativity—everything from Freud's psychoanalysis to Einstein's theory of relativity—as a threat to tradition. The Nazis carried on with this thinking, perceiving such creative productivity further as a threat to their ideology and so excluding Jews from these professions.

For a time, none of these variants of anti-Semitism alone was sufficient to fuel the well-organized genocidal furor that ultimately took place. As the war progressed, however, cultural anti-Semitism intensified, eventually becoming a force strong enough to make the Holocaust possible. An important aspect of this variant is that it had a geographical focus outside of Germany, encoded in the concept of *der Ostjude* (the Jew of Eastern European origin) and fed by the trauma of fighting a war of survival, as the Nazi ideologues portrayed it, against the Soviet Union. Many Germans considered the Communist Party, which had fought the Nazis in the streets of German cities and villages, a spearhead of this mortal danger.

In appearance, lifestyle, customs, and traditions, most Eastern European Jews bore only a passing resemblance, if any, to the Jews that Germans knew as their neighbors. *Der Ostjude* became the subject of virulent anti-Semitic caricatures in Julius Streicher's *Der Stürmer,* depictions that dehumanized Jews and made them appear totally alien. All Germans became familiar with these widely distributed, distorted representations of Jews who looked different and lived far away. It is therefore not surprising that the 1979 U.S. miniseries *Holocaust,* when aired in Germany, had a transformative effect on the population as a whole, because the Jewish *Familie* Weiß was portrayed as *Western* European in both appearance and lifestyle. Deeply moved by their fate as portrayed in that series, Germans said with surprise and dismay: They were just like us.

DESCENT INTO HELL

The genocide was slow to unfold. The son of a hairdresser in Silesia whom I interviewed recalled that at first when Eastern European Jews were gathered up for "relocation" to destinations such as Auschwitz, Sobibor, and Treblinka, the Jewish women, longtime customers in his mother's salon, came to have their hair done before starting their trip. Similarly, stories abound of wealthier Jews of Paris insisting on first-class train accommodations for their trips east to the camps. Few of them had the intuition necessary to predict the fate that awaited them in gas chambers. The German adage "Suppen werden nicht so heiß gegessen wie gekocht" (Soups aren't eaten as hot as they are cooked) allowed many to brush aside whatever concerns they might have had. Even SS orders to eliminate Jews were couched in euphemistic terms. One of many Gestapo reports, for example, calls the removal of Jews an "Abwanderung der Juden nach dem Osten" (emigration of Jews to the east).[30]

Even when the death camps were in full operation, primarily in German-occupied Poland, the Nazis were able to construct a nearly impenetrable wall of silence around them. The horrific secret was generally limited to the active perpetrators and their helpers, and in any case the sheer immensity of the mass exterminations made them virtually unbelievable. Two Slovakian Jews, Rudolf Vrba and Alfred Wetzler, who managed to escape from Auschwitz on April 7, 1944, had a hard time convincing the Jewish Council in Bratislava of what they had seen happening with their own eyes because the council simply couldn't believe anything on that scale *could* happen.[31] Anecdotal evidence that leaked out from the Polish resistance, close to the extermination camps, never succeeded in convincing the general German public that mass killings were taking place. As is now well known, by the summer of 1944 Allied governments had sufficient evidence of the genocide in hand, yet still no drastic action was taken.

How could the majority of Germans not have known about the death camps? How could crimes of such immensity escape being noticed? Perhaps a simple analogy is instructive. A seismologist recently explained to me that a tsunami is barely noticeable in the middle of an ocean. Creating only a small rise in water level as it races along, it would not even be perceived by passengers on an ocean liner. But as it approaches the coasts, where the waters become shallower, it increases in power until it hits the shore with violent force. The descent into hell started just as gradually, with many minor incidents and small steps, none of which garnered enough attention to mobilize resistance.

My generation was less aware of these incremental steps than our elders, who remembered the Nuremberg Laws of 1935 depriving the German Jews of their citizenship. The statutes did not touch most Germans personally, but a limited segment of the population, namely Jewish and non-Jewish marriage partners. In the 1961 film *Judgment at Nuremberg,* the main defendant, formerly a German judge, desperately pleads his innocence vis-à-vis the Holocaust; the presiding American judge, played by Spencer Tracy, replies that the first time the defendant convicted someone he knew to be innocent was the start of the path that led to genocide. The descent into hell, as I see it, was made possible on the psychological plane, by the Germans' lack of empathy for their Jewish compatriots or, to put it in legal terms, by a general undervaluing of and disregard for civil liberties.

A First Step

One of the Germans I interviewed recalled an incident that might represent a first downward step. Pupils in her history class, she said, were busily taking notes while their teacher lectured, when someone saw through the window that the synagogue near the school was on fire. The teacher stopped the class and took his pupils outside. There they saw Nazi thugs desecrating the religious site, and the SA had formed a cordon around the burning synagogue that prevented the fire brigade from extinguishing the fire. After a while the teacher said to his pupils, who were gaping at this unprecedented scene, "Und jetzt zurück zum Unterricht" (And now, back to our lesson). As ordered, the students returned to the classroom, picked up their pencils, and continued to jot notes about ancient history. The teacher resumed exactly where he had left off when the outside world inconveniently interrupted.

A Second Step

I perceive a second step in another story about a young officer in one of the elite SS divisions who, traveling through the countryside of central Poland, passed by rows of executed civilians, their corpses hanging from the trees that lined both sides of the road. Although initially shocked and sickened by this scene of wanton murder, the officer assuaged his conscience by recalling his duty to obey Hitler and defend the fatherland regardless of the cost. Many stories similar in structure have emerged from World War II, and they reveal how successful the Nazis were in separating morality from duty in their committed followers.

A Third Step

At a 2007 meeting of the *Wirtschaftsgilde,* toward the end of my interviews, I invited several of the participants in my project to join me for some unstructured free associations about moments from their past that they had not yet talked about. The sessions provided one more opportunity for this group of older Germans to recall memories they had in common. They happily shared innocuous aspects of their past lives that bound them together, almost as much, perhaps, as the large events in which they had been caught. After two hours, I felt that the mood of the group was relaxed enough to allow a spontaneous response. So I asked them, "Was there anything so extreme and strange in your experiences that you have never mentioned it to anyone before?"

An elderly gentleman sitting in the last row whom I had not yet interviewed raised his hand and related an anecdote that is almost impossible to narrate. Even after listening to it several times on the tape, I found it difficult to render it into English without losing the tone and impact of his matter-of-fact recall.

Yes, I have a strange story to tell. I was a research chemist at the IG Farben works in Ludwigshafen. Among us were several older chemists who were employed there during Hitler's period who had worked on secret chemical experiments. Some of the top researchers at that time were Jewish and were called "honorary Germans." They did not have to wear the yellow star. Sometime before my retirement, several of our older scientists were sitting around during lunch, and someone suggested that all of us might want to organize a trip to visit Poland as tourists and include a visit to Auschwitz on our itinerary. An elderly scientist sitting opposite me turned pale; he then said he wanted to have dinner with me.

During that dinner he told me that for one year he had been in charge of the chemical division of the huge Auschwitz-Birkenau factory. He told me that a chemist would hold this job for one year, then someone else would replace him. Everyone given that assignment was under strict orders to keep quiet and afterward was subject to constant surveillance, to ensure they never talked about their experiences. This older colleague told me that the chemists in Ludwigshafen were a close-knit group; they knew about each other's foibles, even about their extramarital affairs and the affairs of their wives. But this particular bit of information— about their one-year job relocation—they never shared with each other, let alone with the outside world.

As the elderly gentleman told this story, the phrase "Abteilung des Riesenbetriebs Auschwitz-Birkenau" (division of the huge Auschwitz-Birkenau factory) overshadowed everything else he said, even though it came and went as a simple fact, just as if he had said his colleague was temporarily in charge of the water-works in Berlin. I could not get around the complete absence of gravity in his voice, the matter-of-fact reporting. I looked out the window, unsettled. A silent bomb had been dropped right in the middle of the room, not so much by the story itself, but by the way it was told to the group. Perhaps this is what happens when a situation is beyond words. The language describing a situation *in extremis* fades into abstraction, as in this case, or it becomes ghoulish, as when the pilot who brought a nuclear holocaust to the city of Hiroshima gave his aircraft the chipper-sounding name of *Enola Gay*, after his mother. Both Krupp and IG Farben constructed chemical factories at Auschwitz-Birkenau. Although the Zyklon B pellets used in the gas chambers were not produced there, the chemical factories forced 405,000 inmates into slave labor between 1940 and 1945. Of these, 340,000 perished.[32]

A Final Step

Modern tools of extermination represented the final step in immunizing the perpetrators against their acts of violence. In planning the details of mass extermination, Himmler designed procedures that, on the surface, appeared both efficient and rational. In an order signed on January 6, 1943, he outlined how certain executions should take place: how many men were necessary for an execution squad; how many feet away from the victim they had to be posted; and how many cigarettes each victim was allowed, namely, three.[33] Aside from satisfying bureaucratic instincts for order, these procedural details confirmed for the execution squads that they were participating in a rational, well-defined, and therefore necessary process. Emotions and moral sensitivities thus became mere distractions from the specific tasks at hand.

Rudolf Höß described his promotion to commander at Auschwitz as follows: "There was no turning back. With strange feelings I entered my new range of activities, a new world, to which I was to be bound and chained. . . . I knew all about the life of prisoners. . . . But the concentration camp was something new for me." Finally, with the impending arrival of mass transports of Jews, Höß "felt relieved" that efficient gas ovens were to be used rather than the traditional method of mass shootings. "I was always appalled by shootings, particularly when I thought of the women and children. . . . Now I was relieved that we were going to be spared these bloodbaths. . . . Gruesome scenes are said to have taken place, the running away of the wounded, the killing of the wounded, above all, of women and children. The frequent suicides in the ranks of the execution squads, because they couldn't stand wading through blood. Some became insane."[34]

In the mindset of the Nazi ideologues, their elite SS units, and the military police battalions who spearheaded the war in the East, there evolved a growing unwillingness to differentiate between *Ostjuden,* Polish partisans, Soviet soldiers, and hostile Slavs whose lands the Nazis had usurped. In a limited way, this deadly perspective appeared in the ranks of the regular army as well. Any differences between these enemies mattered less and less to the Germans as they fought the war with growing ferocity. Moreover, by defining their war as a "war of survival," the Nazis lowered the threshold of civilization, thereby setting the genocide in motion. In the eastern theater, the geographic distance from Western Europe and the German population provided them with a *cordon sanitaire* to wage an unrestrained dirty war in near secrecy with military precision. I believe it was the genocidal thrust discovered in cultural anti-Semitism that removed the last vestiges of restraint in the execution of *totaler Krieg,* explaining, at least in part, the quantum leap to the Shoah.

This outline is of course too short to deal comprehensively with the intimate link between World War II and the Holocaust. Nor was that my intention. As Bernhard Schlink said in an interview about his novel *Der Vorleser* (The reader), "I wanted to write about my generation. I didn't write a book about the Holocaust."

THE CURTAIN FALLS

Hitler insisted to the very end of the war that Germany was invincible. His pronouncements about Germany's unshakable will, the undaunted bravery of the German armies, and the enthusiastic support of the home front were meant to keep the curtain raised over the Nazi stage as long as possible. Of course, all war propaganda stresses the prowess and virtue of one's own side, but in Germany this propaganda carried some weight because of the Nazis' success in rebuilding Germany in the 1930s. The military reports from the various fronts were masterpieces of creative imagination, what we today call spin. Serious battlefield losses, increasingly frequent as the war went on, that resulted in the abandonment of occupied territory were explained away as *im Zuge der Frontverkürzung* (a strategy to shorten the front). Such losses were presented as planned for better eventual counterattacks. This positive spin was kept up until the German army had withdrawn to the German borders, at which point the Nazis spread a rumor about a *Wunderwaffe* (miracle weapon) that would end the war in Germany's favor. Hitler's "miracle" was part of an imaginary arsenal that would be unleashed against the unsuspecting Allies when the moment was right. As Zarah Leander, a pro-Nazi Swedish star, sang in a song that was especially popular toward the end of the war, "Ich weiß, es wird einmal ein Wunder gescheh'n, und dann werden tausend Märchen wahr" (I know a great miracle will take place, and then a thousand fairy tales will come true). Some believed that this song expressed real hopes for winning the war, while others saw it as mere fantasy; still others were well aware of the underlying irony.

As the war progressed, a noticeable split grew within the German population. On the one side were the Nazi fanatics, who believed up until the last weeks of the war that a German victory would come. The rest of the Germans remained circumspect in expressing their views about the war prospects. All, however, remember hearing comments about the vast expanse of Russia and the sleeping giant, America. As the war wound down, a similar split occurred within the army. Increasingly,

German soldiers simply went AWOL, fleeing their fighting units and undertaking long treks through the forests and back roads of Europe to return to their homes and families. On the other side were those who, to exhibit their bravery and faith in the *Führer*, steadfastly defended bridges against overwhelming odds until they were killed.

As the Western Allies approached, women sowed white flags from bedsheets to wave as improvised flags of surrender. The timing of when to hoist these flags was important, because armored SS units sometimes made final sweeps through towns to hunt down any deserters from the retreating German army.

On May 8, 1945, it was all over. News of the collapse of the Nazi regime and of the horrors of the death camps reached most Germans about the same time. In my village, the American occupiers posted photos of mass graves of murdered Jews on the town hall billboard. Most of us were too worried about what would now happen to us, individually or as a community, to do more than numbly register the genocide. Questions of guilt and responsibility came later.[35]

AND LIFE WENT ON

By the end of World War II, millions of Germans had died, as soldiers in the battlefields and in Siberian POW camps, as civilians in the bombed cities, or as refugees attempting to flee the East. The first time Germans were asked to participate in an international event following the war, they didn't know how to present themselves. What anthem should they play? Obviously, the *Deutschland Lied* used by the Nazis was out of the question. To play Beethoven's "Ode to Joy" was also inappropriate.

The suggestion was therefore made to play the late medieval ditty "Oh, du lieber Augustin" (Oh, my dear August), which folklorists believe describes the life of a drunkard during the time of the black plague. Everything is gone, so the song goes, and August ends up in a pit filled with victims of the plague. But lo and behold, the alcohol in his veins protects him from the deadly disease, and he climbs out of the pit unharmed to carry on.

The folk song made the rounds because it expressed the state of mind of the surviving German population. My paternal grandmother could certainly understand the meaning of the ditty, which told of improbable survival against all odds. In a letter that reached me in the early spring of 1950, after I had returned to the United States, she described her situation after the war in a few sentences. At the end of the war, she was sixty-nine years old. Her husband, my grandfather, was nearly blind due to a World War I injury. One of her sons was missing in Romania, and rumor had it that he had died there. Another son, my father, was in a prisoner of war camp in England. Her third son had survived the war but was penniless and without work. The youngest son returned from Russia mentally disturbed and with both of his feet partly frozen off; he had been a machine gunner east of Smolensk and participated in the army spearhead that made it to the gates of Moscow. Her eldest granddaughter, then pregnant, had suffered through the last month of the war in Berlin, and her second grandson was either dead or in a prison in Russia.

From my grandmother's letter, it was clear to me that the psychological wounds had not healed and the damage to the family was far from resolved. Traumas fade away slowly, if ever, particularly when no one talks about them. But at the end of her letter, she expressed a positive thought about life, which is still engraved in my mind. "Now the snow is beginning to melt," she wrote, "the worst of the winter is over, spring is not far away. Carnival season is here, and the young will join in all the fun and have a fine time. Good for them. I am going to cheer them on." Yet such attitudes are not universal. As Manfred Fischer, a member of the *Wirtschaftsgilde*, told me as recently as November 2006, "The fear of war has reverberated through all generations of Germans and is present in every German family in some way even today."

A DANGEROUS MYTH

Total war ultimately engulfed every part of Hitler's Reich. Some have claimed that what happened at the end of the war in Nazi Germany was the fulfillment of a vague, collective, fateful Teutonic desire for destruction. As the war climaxed, this belief *was* turned to flesh, made real in the death camps and in the smoldering ruins of the cities. The myth of a final, apocalyptic destiny that had appeared sporadically throughout German cultural history—in early-nineteenth-century Romanticism, where night was preferable to day, and in the fantasies of Richard Wagner in his Ring Cycle, which concludes with *Die Götterdämmerung* (Twilight of the Gods), an opera that Hitler passionately loved—had become reality. This myth gained strength in the twentieth century through Oswald Spengler's influential work *Der Untergang des Abendlandes* (Decline of the West).

During their twelve-year rule over Germany and Europe, the Nazis saw themselves as the answer to a fateful cultural decline. It is well documented that Hitler's view of the final struggle between good and evil, as he defined it, was also fed by a fascination with death and destruction. This fascination was linked to the myth of a battle between civilizations and the life-and-death struggle between superior and inferior races. This is a dangerous cultural fantasy in any age, for the belief in a clash of civilizations may become a self-fulfilling prophecy. History is not like a Wagnerian opera, nor is it like the biblical Armageddon, although it may have seemed so—and still may seem so—to many people gifted with a flair for mythic flights or motivated by an attraction to violence and hatred of "the Other." This is the way Hitler saw history, and many who have tried to understand the Nazi movement (or were part of it) accepted this *grande ligne d'histoire*. But what ultimately happened at the finale of the Nazi's big show—in the war and the Holocaust—inflicted horrendous misery and caused the death of tens of millions of individual human beings, each one suffering his or her own pain, agony, or gruesome death.

·   ·   ·

A case can be made for almost all the known theories, singly or in combination, for the rise of Nazism: anti-Semitism; the collapse of the German middle class during the Weimar Republic; the harshness of the Versailles Treaty; fear of Bolshevism; Bismarck's notion of the state as protector; authoritarian family structures; economic depression; Prussian militarism; a myriad of cultural explanations ranging from Luther's separation of the value of the individual from the public sphere, to Meineke's analysis of mass movements since the French Revolution, to Thomas Mann's notion of *machtbeschützte Innerlichkeit* (inwardness protected by power); and Hitler's brilliant use of modern tools of communication (this last explanation plays an important role in *my* understanding of the Nazi rise to power). But even when taken together they do not add up to a critical mass sufficient to explain the Nazis' breathtakingly rapid rise to absolute power over Germany.

CHAPTER FOUR

In Search of Individuals

The individual responsibility to history is to tell the truth, to tell one's own truth, which always leads to complexity; it always leads away from categories to the individual story.

    Eva Leveton

BREAKING THE SILENCE

There I was in bed in the evening. It was after an air raid. The city was all engulfed in flames, and the houses on the opposite side of the street also were burning, and finally collapsed with much noise. I still see the flames shooting up high and flickering, and I remember the terrible horror and I shouted for my mother. She came in and sat by my bed. It calmed me greatly. And she told me, "Turn your face toward the wall, then you won't see anything, and close your eyes tight." I hoped she would stay, but she left. As she left she said, "You have seen nothing."[1]

It is very hard for my generation of Germans to revisit the time before the collapse of the *Reich* in the spring of 1945. For mere physical and psychological survival, it was necessary for us to look forward; to look back meant facing a wall too high and formidable to be easily scaled. When I began recording the stories of my older friends and acquaintances in the *Wirtschaftsgilde*, I realized that none of us seemed to have kept a diary of our traumatic early years. Only one member, Siegfried Spiecker, had made an effort to record a brief episode in his life as a young soldier fighting on the western front between the Rhine and the Vosges Mountains of France. As the front moved ever closer to Germany in 1945, his army unit was ordered to attack an Allied position. He knew that such an attack had no chance of success, but they had to follow orders. He feared for his own life and realized that if he were killed, no one would ever know what his life had been like. Many of his comrades were killed, but Siegfried was taken prisoner on April 4, 1945, by the Americans. As a prisoner he retained his desire to record his war experiences, and although he had a pen, the only paper he possessed consisted of small pieces of American cigarette paper. He has kept his tiny scribblings about the final battles in which he participated to the present day. They have faded over the years so that much of what he wrote is barely legible.

A wall exists not only between the present and those times, but also between the present and the fading memories and aura of guilt. Some participants in that history have shut down access to parts of themselves. Yet the sense of group solidarity I witnessed in the basement of that resort hotel in the Italian Alps, when they opened up to each other about their war experiences, in time also benefited me. I gained their trust, and they told me their stories. I was struck by their openness and, except in a very few cases, by the absence of subterfuge.

Once the interviews began, I was impressed by the variety of the approaches individuals took to recall their pasts. One person

I interviewed had obviously told his story in great detail before, because the recall was neatly structured and interspersed with moral reflections. Others built their recollections around a defining moment, usually a catastrophic event. One person with great imaginative gifts seasoned the description of her flight from the East with picaresque anecdotes. Some poured out their anxieties about what they had experienced, while a few shaped their memories as self-justifications against accusations that I neither uttered nor implied. Some recalled the most traumatic moments in their lives with a mere throwaway phrase, so that if I hadn't paid close attention I would have missed them. Some interviewees wanted to exculpate a close relative. Others gave simple accounts of what they knew or were told about the complicity of a family member in the Nazi movement.

In my own story, as narrated in *An Uncommon Friendship: From Opposite Sides of the Holocaust,* I refer to an uncle who had been a member of the SS in charge of a refugee camp. After the war, surviving inmates hanged him.[2] What I didn't mention in that book was that this Uncle Ludwig saved my life when I was six years old. I had decided to hook my toy steam engine up to electricity and was just about to stick a wire into a 220-volt wall outlet, when this uncle leapt across the room and tore me away, saving me from a jolt that might very well have killed me. For a long time, I simply repressed the fact that someone who must have caused misery and death in a refugee camp had saved my life.

Many of the narratives had a picaresque quality. The prototype for picaresque narratives of war in German culture is Grimmelshausen's *Der abenteuerliche Simplicissimus Teutsch* (The Adventurous Simplex). In an epic sweep, the baroque novel published in 1668 portrays the horrors of the Thirty Years' War of 1618–48. Subjected to overwhelming forces, its protagonist is swept this way and that by a fate that is fearful, unpredictable, and beyond his control. The story is full of tragedy and gruesome humor as Simplex fights his way through days, months, and years in a chaotic, precarious world devoid of social and economic stability. The protagonist stays faithful to himself while seeking out small openings that allow for some measure of individual initiative. In normal times this hero would have been a master of his life; here, he is reduced to mastering strategies for his survival.

Survival strategies came up often in the recollections of my interviewees. But an additional narrative pattern emerged that I would best describe as *Protestant* accounts of the past, based on inner moral conflicts. Both these patterns—the picaresque and the confessional—characterize many of the stories I heard. In spite of the fragmentary nature of what the interviewees told me, the integrity of their stories, which spanned both sides of the 1945 divide, provides a reliable key as to who they were before the war and who they became afterward. Not all of the stories I gathered came from members of the *Wirtschaftsgilde* organization. Stories I include of the nonmembers help explain a range of German voices that have not been heard in the United States—among them, from letters soldiers wrote home from the various fronts, as well as eyewitness accounts from the thirties and the forties recorded in archives in Berlin and Munich.

EBERHARD WEINBRENNER

Eberhard Weinbrenner comes from a family that he describes as *gut bürgerlich,* which is to say, solidly middle class. He counts a number of architects among his ancestors. His father broke out of this mold as a young man, joining the colonial civil service of Imperial Germany in Cameroon, one of Germany's African colonies. Later on, he became the mayor of Weinsberg, a southern German town. This was a happy time for Eberhard's father—until 1933. The picturesque town, nestled among its vineyards, is best known for the legend of the faithful wives who were permitted to carry their most precious possession out of town before it would be leveled by King Conrad III's army in 1140. The wives decided to carry their husbands out on their backs. Ever since, the story of the "Faithful Wives of Weinsberg" has symbolized marital loyalty and devotion.

Under Hitler, Weinsberg was more than memorable legends, good wines, a gentle landscape, and an industrious citizenry. It became a town deeply split between the Nazis and those who opposed them, while the majority of the inhabitants stood quietly on the sidelines, fearful that any form of opposition might land them in jail, or worse. This ideological split weighed heavily in the Weinbrenner family. Eberhard's father was in constant opposition to the regime. But Eberhard himself, who in youthful enthusiasm was attracted to Nazism, moved to the other side of the divide. Thus, his youth was marked by conflict, one that ran through his family and his own soul. I was moved by the honesty of the account he gave of his life during the Nazi regime.

Eberhard's earliest memory with political significance has his family huddled around the radio on January 30, 1933, listening to the ceremonies in Potsdam when Field Marshal von Hindenburg handed over executive power to Adolf Hitler. Eberhard's father, a sympathizer with the conservative Peasant Party, worried that he might be arrested, and his anxiety was evident even to his young son. The eight-year-old could eavesdrop on his parents' uneasy conversations because the wall between their bedrooms was thin. He caught snatches of what they said and realized quite early in his life that his parents were against the Nazi regime. Their opposition cast its shadow into the public sphere. One of their closest friends, the head of a famous school for vintners, was openly attacked in the notorious anti-Semitic newspaper *Der Stürmer* as someone who neither condemned the Jews nor signed up for the Nazi cause.

Eberhard felt close to his parents and admired them, yet he soon became devoted to the *Jungvolk*. He developed into a first-rate athlete, winning praise for his skill in competitive sports. He began to participate in camping trips organized by the *Jungvolk*. At first he felt tentative during these outings, torn between timidity and ambition to prove to his superiors how good and brave he was. Gradually, these trips became more and more important to him, and Eberhard, who was tall and blond, seemed destined for a leadership role in the Nazi movement.

At the same time, his father's opposition to the Nazis became public knowledge, particularly following an open fight with the Nazi Party district leader. Although the split deepened between Eberhard and his parents, he now believes that his father's popularity in Weinsberg protected him from persecution. Meanwhile, Eberhard's loyalty to the *Jungvolk,* his athleticism, and his budding leadership abilities assured his rapid advance in the organization's hierarchy.

Despite such success, Eberhard was troubled by something that didn't fit the mold of the ideals he was raised to believe in. He couldn't reconcile the differences between a close family friend, a venerable vintner with a quiet, dignified demeanor, on the one hand, and the SA thugs "with their fat stomachs" who pestered this man, on the other.

As time went on, his conflict with his parents intensified. They were devout Christians and defended their Protestant church against attacks by the Nazi Party. Eberhard's conflicting emotions—his enthusiasm pitted against the firm resistance of his parents—finally became unbearable and culminated in an argument with his mother. The incident still agitated him on the day of our interview. "I lay crying on the couch," he said, "because I simply could not deal with this family conflict.... This ideological quarrel was the underlying pattern of my early life."

The differences between parents and son spilled beyond the walls of the family home. In middle school, a Nazi teacher gave him the assignment to memorize a poem that glorified Nazi ideals, desecrated weak people, and made fun of the church. Eberhard's father forbade his son to memorize it, whereupon the Nazi teacher accused the father of interfering with his son's education. Eberhard was caught in the middle. The matter was dropped when the school's principal sided with the father. The teacher, however, did not give up trying to pit Eberhard against his parents. He told the young believer that by resisting his parents he exhibited true *Heldenmut* (heroic courage).

This experience sharpened Eberhard's sense of political differences, so that when he entered *Gymnasium* he noticed the depth of the split in the teaching staff. There were those teachers who hung on to conservative cultural traditions and saw the Nazi movement for what it was—a right-wing revolution that cloaked itself in the mantle of defending traditional German values. Other teachers were convinced of the new revolutionary cause the Nazis advanced. Eberhard told me, "We knew exactly

Figure 1. Eberhard Weinbrenner (seated third from left), Karls-Gymnasium, Heilbronn, 1943, shortly before class was disbanded for military service.

who was pro and contra. We had no doubt about that, and we had a certain respect for the contras, who maintained the courage of their convictions against overwhelming odds." He remembered an instructor, a 150 percent Nazi, who decided to devote a course to Nazi indoctrination. When his son died in the war, the instructor dropped the course and withdrew into his shell. "We actually felt sorry for him then," Eberhard remarked.

With his tall, athletic physique, blond hair, and a proven track record in the *Jungvolk,* Eberhard was a prime candidate for the SS. His father was vehemently opposed, and even Eberhard's own enthusiasm did not go so far as to be attracted to this ominous Nazi force, with their frightening uniforms and sinister aura. In fact, the SS was not particularly popular with most of his fellow *Gymnasium* students. When the SS organized a presentation to attract the boys at his school, one student evaded the event by climbing out of a bathroom window—an act for which he could have been harshly punished had he been caught.

Eberhard explained that a particular encounter with an older friend—I will call him Hans—prompted him to take a second look at the regime to which he was so devoted. Hans had been his leader in the *Jungvolk,* and Eberhard looked up to him. Hans joined the SS, became an officer, and received the *Ritterkreuz* (Knight's Cross), the highest medal of honor bestowed by the Nazis, for bravery in battle as a tank commander. When Hans came home on furlough from the eastern front, Eberhard was eager to see him and hear about his glorious and valorous deeds. When they met, Eberhard was stunned to see before him a broken young man, not the hero he had imagined. The friend had completely changed. When Eberhard asked him what the matter was, Hans told him, "We are doing terrible things in the East, horrible acts. I cannot talk about them. I cannot put these things out of my mind. They depress me. I have lost all my ideals."

A few months later, Eberhard found out that his friend had died in battle on the eastern front. His last encounter with Hans and the fact of his death sowed the seed of broader perspectives in Eberhard. He began to look at the world around him with a skeptical eye and to notice things that had escaped him before. He followed closely the proceedings of the infamous Nazi trials of the conspirators who attempted to assassinate Hitler on July 20, 1944. He came to the conclusion that they were not traitors at all, but that they had risked and lost their lives to defend ideals that seemed noble to him—his parents' ideals of uprightness and honor not rooted in the Nazi creed. From that moment for-

ward he harbored doubts about the commitments he and many
of his peers had made to the Nazi cause.

Toward the end of the war Eberhard volunteered for a sabo-
tage mission in the German navy that involved two-man U-boat
crews. Why did he do so, since he no longer believed in Nazism?
His explanation made sense. At this stage in his life, and this
late in the war, he was motivated by a mix of patriotism and the
desire to enjoy the thrill of a last, daring adventure.

Eberhard Weinbrenner, now a distinguished, award-winning
architect, is one of the most imposing figures of the *Wirtschaftsgilde.* He was a member of the jury that selected architects to
construct key federal buildings prior to the German government's move from Bonn to Berlin some years ago. He backed
the design that "embodied the openness of a democratic society,
an accessibility of its citizen to those in power, and above all, a
design without pathos." As he told me this, Hitler's master architect Albert Speer came to my mind, and the long road Germany
has trodden since World War II.

VOLKER SCHÄTZEL AND
ANNEMARIE GEIL

The Schätzel family has lived near the Rhine River for several centuries. Now over eighty, Volker Schätzel is the oldest
member of this family of vintners, whose genealogy goes back
to the Thirty Years' War. Early family records document ancestors from a line of lower nobility with roots in the famous wine
village of Rüdesheim. Until the beginning of the nineteenth
century, the Schätzel family held their land in feudal tenure for
the archduke or the Catholic archbishop, but Napoleon's vast

secularization process allowed the family to buy the land out-right. While there is great variety in the taste of the various grapes Volker and his son grow in Rheinhessen, their wines all blend tartness with a flowery bouquet in a unique way. Over the centuries these wines have been enjoyed by medieval knights, merchants on their way to the large cities, bishops, dukes, Prussian generals, Napoleon's soldiers marching east, the Kaiser's grenadiers marching west, Hitler's *Wehrmacht,* the French who occupied the region at the end of World War II, and, today, people all over Europe to whom the winery delivers its products.

"For seven hundred years, we had an unbroken chain of vintners in the family," Volker told me as we walked on the crest of a hill covered by neat rows of vines that reached all the way to a small river in the valley below. I realized that wine regions do not instigate wars. Volker Schätzel was proud not only of the family winemaking tradition, but also of the progressive political ideals that have prevailed over the past two centuries in many of the German regions west of the Rhine—traces, perhaps, of the liberating effect the French Revolution and Napoleon had on this part of Germany. They not only helped this family buy land, but also influenced their political beliefs.

Nazi propaganda of *Blut und Boden* (blood and soil) distorted the lives of German peasants to ideological ends. The Nazi vocabulary became filled with *völkisch* (tribal, in this case Germanic) terms, intended to impart a new meaning to words and phrases such as *Erde* (earth), *Scholle* (clod of soil), *Bauer* (farmer, peasant), *auf dem Acker* (in the fields). By linking people to their soil in an unbreakable bond, *Blut und Boden* was used to justify war to defend German lands. It also provided a blueprint for the acquisition of foreign territory in Eastern Europe, to be followed by colonization and germanification by settling German farmers from the *Reich* there after the expected victory.

The history of Volker Schätzel's family would seem an ideal example of the Nazi's blood and soil notions. But nothing could be further from the truth. Those who grew up in agricultural regions of Germany and who toiled in the fields knew instinctively that this propaganda was an invention, a virtual reality constructed by a Nazi bureaucrat who probably sat at a desk in a comfortable office in Berlin. No one who came off the fields at the end of the day would have created a magic link between Germany's manifest destiny and his own backbreaking labor from sunrise to sunset. Volker Schätzel knew this. His reality had no place in Nazi propaganda.

Unfortunately, neither was his reality recognized by those who came to judge Germans after the war. There were many men and women like Volker and his wife, Annemarie, who had no voice under the Nazis. And afterward they were forced into silence or simply ignored. So it happened that some of the finest cultural traditions of Germany were shoved aside as tainted or simply irrelevant.

As we walked over his hills, we talked about the German writer Carl Zuckmayer, a native of this region whom Volker admires greatly because they share the same values. In his play *Des Teufels General* (The Devil's General), Zuckmayer describes the Rhine region as the wine press of Europe, where for many centuries people from a great variety of ethnic and cultural backgrounds lived, drank, made love, and had babies—Romans, Huns, Germanic maids, Jewish merchants, soldiers from all over Europe, and adventurers from many corners of the world. This was the region that produced Goethe, Beethoven, and

Gutenberg, concluded the author. For both Volker and myself, this passage is one of the moral high points in German literature. By the time we finished our walk, we knew we would be friends, and I knew Volker would entrust me with his story.

The advent of Nazism in Germany was a calamity for the Schätzel family. It was not that their opposition to the Nazis was based primarily on politics; older family members were not active in any party that opposed Hitler. Their conflict with the Nazis was of a more fundamental nature, one that could not be settled by force in the streets or by parliamentary strategies against the new rulers—which was impossible after 1933, in any case. Their opposition was rooted in cultural traditions and social values based not on armed defense but on the quiet consensus of an agrarian society, on established customs, a simple faith, and civil manners.

Although many decent Germans were taken in by Hitler's claim that he had their values in mind when he gained power in 1933, many were not—among them, the Schätzel family. Volker was close to his father, Albert Schätzel, who was his role model. One of Volker's earliest memories of his family under siege involves blatant graffiti some Nazis painted on the side of their home: "This German citizen still buys from the Jews." The Schätzel women wanted to wash this Nazi attack on them off the wall, but the father insisted that it be left as a badge of honor.

Albert Schätzel was deeply involved in the governance of his local region as town councilor; however, it became increasingly obvious to him that he would have no influence under the new regime. Since he did not want to legitimize the Nazis with his service on the town council they now controlled, he resigned. He was fortunate that, because he was an established vintner, his opposition did not have immediate financial consequences for his family. The same was not true of many Germans of his generation and social status, who as civil servants depended on their jobs and could not afford to resign.

While on business in Frankfurt, Albert Schätzel witnessed the Night of the Broken Glass first hand. Volker remembers exactly what his father said when he returned home: "We have to be ashamed to be Germans." Volker adds that he and his father had a unique personal relationship, which made his father's judgment in all matters very important to him. It was based not only on the father-son bonds of a traditional family, but also on an attitude of responsibility that his father inculcated in him; the father often said to him, when Volker was confronted with a choice, "Die Freiheit hast du" (You have the freedom to make your own decisions).

What was at work here was not paternal authoritarianism of the sort the Nazis used for their own ends, but solidarity based on a stable tradition that was life enhancing and inclusive of others. But then the war came, putting an abrupt end to the peaceful years of winemaking. Everyone was swept up and tossed around by that deadly combination of whim and fate that marks times of mayhem. One of Volker's uncles was killed in Stalingrad. Volker's father was ordered to act as a regional air raid warden and by 1943 had joined the army to avoid being drafted into the SS. At the same time, young Volker became a soldier, leaving the fields of grapevines for the fields of death. Before departing, he asked his father, "Wie soll ich mich verhalten?" (How should I behave?). Volker does not remember his father's answer—and what would it have mattered anyway? He was now a part of the war machine, and his ability to make his own decisions was reduced to ducking so as not to get killed, and

Figure 2. Volker Schätzel at eighteen as a reserve officer candidate, 1943.

obeying orders so as not to be executed. While in Italy, however, Volker did not duck at the right time, and shrapnel pierced his lungs, a piece of which remains inside him to this day.

He told me that lying naked in an Italian hospital, he held a woman in his arms for the first time—not to make love, he added quickly with a chuckle. He was in no shape for that, and besides, he kept his chastity until he married his wife, Annemarie, years later. The nurse lifted him up and held him tight in order to drain pooled blood out of his chest cavity. His military duties on the fields of battle were over, but he was still a simple foot soldier in the army. That was fine with him, since he harbored no heroic ambitions. Besides, a local Nazi leader had told his father that Volker should forget ever becoming an officer, because "we in the Nazi Party now have something to say about these matters."

For a time, his wounds kept Volker away from the fighting. But as he began to recover, he feared he would be sent back into the direct line of fire. Guns really only interested him for hunting deer and shooting fowl. He made the best of his hospital stay and plotted his return home—by legal means, with all the proper papers, if possible, or if necessary, by illegal means, through the use of persuasion.

New Year's Eve 1944 found Volker Schätzel at a party with other wounded soldiers and nurses. Wine, music, and the faint hope that someday life might be completely different were punctuated by Goebbels's staccato, singsong voice on the radio pronouncing his vision of victory for the *Reich*. At about the same time, his nurse took Volker to see the film *Baron von Münchhausen,* whose fairy-tale flights of fancy into fame and valor provided a brief escape from the grim business of war and survival.

Volker soon decided the time had come for him to return to his vineyards, and so joined countless other AWOL soldiers who abandoned their fighting units to make their hazardous way home, begging for food at isolated farmhouses or from women, children, or old men at work in their fields. Before the *Stunde null* (zero hour, the German term for the immediate aftermath of World War II), they had to make sure that the SS did not catch them, for that would have meant a swift execution on the spot.

After the zero hour, being caught by the Allied forces would have meant a POW camp. The closer Volker got to home, the more he was caught up in the shifting combat lines, and the chances of being shot or captured increased from day to day. But all he could think of was getting home.

He made it to the house of an uncle, who advised him to lie low and stay put: "Bleib bei uns, die Amis sind schon in Hanau und es ist bald vorbei" (Stay here with us, the Americans are already in Hanau and it will soon be over). Since Volker still suffered significantly from his shrapnel wound, his uncle was able to get him admitted to a local hospital. But the hospital was not as safe a haven as his uncle's home. Volker realized that the Americans were so slow in coming that the danger remained acute the SS might catch up with him and hang him in public as a warning to others. He thought it safer to put his uniform back on and be treated officially as a wounded soldier. This should work, he reckoned, as long as he did not have to present any official papers to explain his distance from his fighting unit in Italy and his proximity to his home.

At long last the front line passed by, and he was in American-occupied German territory. Although he "felt liberated," he heard rumors about brutalities in some of the American-run POW camps. Jaundice saved him from such a camp, however, and he was admitted to an American field hospital, where he was fed well. A month after the war ended, the U.S. Army released all those from the hospital who were farmers and sent them on their way home with proper papers. These lucky farm boys were not provided with transportation, though, so they had to find their own means of locomotion. Volker knew the way. He first jumped on a freight train filled with coal, then hitched a ride on a milk truck. Eventually, as he approached his native village of Selzen on foot, he saw children out in the potato fields collecting potato bugs. One of his cousins recognized him and ran ahead of him through the village, announcing as loud as she could to everyone in earshot, "Volker kommt!" As he told me this, tears came to the eyes of my vintner friend, and our interview came to an end.

Hitler's mayhem did not permanently break the ancient pattern of life as Volker's family had known it for generations. The Schätzels continued to grow and harvest grapes, which they then turned into wine that they sold near and far. The family never sought recognition for its open opposition to the Nazis. After all, that was simply a matter of common decency. While he preferred the tools of winemaking to guns, Volker could now return to guns for hunting. That sport became his passion beyond the vineyards and brought him decades later to Alaska for a big-game hunting trip.

On another visit a few years ago, as we walked in his fields, Volker pointed out some wild pheasants huddled on the ground. He told me it was against the law to shoot them when they were not in flight. I thought that this must be very frustrating for a hunter, but he replied, "By no means. All you have to do is to have someone clap his hands loudly while you hold your gun at the ready. As soon as the pheasants take to the air, they are fair game." We had a good laugh and made our way back to his home for dinner—taken, naturally, with several different bottles from his well-stocked wine cellar.

•   •   •

Annemarie Geil was born in 1926 on the Rhine, where some of the best German white wines are made. The daughter of a vintner, even as a young girl she wanted to study viticulture, preferring this option to the old-fashioned expectations for young German women: marriage and child rearing. Full of pride, she told me she was the only woman in an all-male viti-culture course, in which she did very well. She brought to the school a reputation for intelligence, focus, and knowledge of winemaking—from tending the vines all the way to bottling the wine—even before she read books on the subject.

Annemarie's reputation as the only single, professional woman in the field came to the attention of Volker Schätzel. Located in the small village of Selzen, the Schätzel estate is now run by one of Volker and Annemarie's three sons. It exudes comfort, hospitality, and an atmosphere of hard work and good living. From the winegrowing regions of the globe—including those in Germany—emanate peace and a taste for pleasure rather than a desire for power.

Annemarie is not talkative, but when she speaks, she is to the point and interesting. When we sat down together for our inter-view, I saw sad eyes and a troubled face that I had never seen before. It was as if someone had taken a heavy burden from her shoulders and placed it between us on the table. I could not help noticing a change in her as she laboriously told me what had been on her mind most of her life.

Her story was not her own, but that of her best friend—I will call her Sophie—whom she had gotten to know more than fifty years earlier, when they were both young women work-ing near Munich. Sophie's story begins after the war, in 1946, in the Czech city of Karlovy Vary, known in German as Karlsbad, one of the famous spa towns during the heyday of the Austro-Hungarian Empire. Sophie's father was hospitalized there, too ill to be moved back to Germany, so Sophie obtained a visitor's permit from the Czech authorities to tend to him. While in Karlsbad, she was suddenly arrested and falsely accused by Czech authorities of attempting to smuggle a rare Stradivarius violin out of Czechoslovakia. In jail she was raped by one of the Czech guards. A month later she realized she was pregnant. To accuse her attacker was useless. She was, after all, a German and therefore outside the protection of the law.

Pregnancy at least gained her release from prison, and she made her way into one of the German refugee camps in southern Germany. Going from one menial job to another, she survived a brutally cold winter. Nine months after her arrest, alone in a hospital with no one to lend her moral or financial support, Sophie gave birth to a boy. She raised him by herself, as well as she could, shunned by her own family because of the shame of the infant's illegitimacy. Finally, a rich man married her. She had five children with him, and she tried her best to live a normal life in West Germany.

Her husband, however, mistreated her, never letting her forget that her eldest son not only was born out of wedlock but also was the result of a prison rape, which in his moral judgment weighed against her. The only way Sophie could raise her six children, keep the house in order, and take care of her husband's daily needs was to suffer her humiliations in silence. But what really broke Sophie's heart, Annemarie said, was that her eldest son turned against her because she had conceived him in prison. Annemarie, the only friend to whom Sophie told the entire story, silently carried the heavy burden of her friend for more than fifty years, while she raised her own children and participated in the rich and fulfilling seasons that wine growers and the merchants of their vintages experience. I was struck by the dark presence of this cloud in Annemarie's life half a century after the fact, and the high wall of silence that the two life-long friends built up around the secret one shared with the other—a suffering away from the public sphere.

Annemarie was deeply rooted in her Christian faith, which shaped the Schätzel family's anti-Nazi views, known in the village and the region, during Hitler's reign. It was her faith that enabled her to empathize with Sophie's suffering, but neither of these women felt, in spite of their faiths, that there was any kind of redemption in Sophie's fate, simply because they knew that she had committed no sins in need of redemption. "The meek shall inherit the earth," the Bible says. This hope was never further from being realized than in the period of Nazi rule in Europe. But one thing can surely be said about the meek, wherever they live: They usually suffer in silence. When Annemarie and Sophie were young, their voices and other voices like theirs were never heard, whether they were herded into gas ovens, firebombed in cities, or raped in prisons—and most of these victims were women.

A half year after my interview with Annemarie, my wife and I were lecturers on a Rhine-Mosel cruise organized by Bear Treks (now called Cal Discoveries), the tourist branch of the University of California Alumni Association. Before we boarded our ship at Mainz, we visited the Schätzels at their winery to arrange a wine tasting on board. It was a pleasant, sunny evening in early autumn around harvesttime. We sat on the veranda of the restaurant at their winery and, after tasting a variety of wines, selected three whites to take on board. Annemarie sat next to me. When she sipped the wine, I could tell she was not only judging its quality but also, simply, enjoying it.

WALTHER CAMERER

The story of Dr. Walther Camerer reminded me of an encounter I had several years ago with an elderly acquaintance, Franz Morgenroth, in my village of Kleinheubach. In spite of their different social backgrounds—Dr. Camerer came from a line of distinguished physicians, while Franz was the son of a laborer—they had, in a profound way, much in common.

I met my village acquaintance near the church, where he stood on the street in the middle of the block. I wasn't surprised, because it seemed that every time I visited—about once a year—I found him in the same place, looking up and down the street watching the occasional car drive by. He had lost a leg in Russia during the war. This time I asked him how he came to pick this particular spot from which to observe the world. He looked at me for some time, wondering perhaps whether I, a former villager who for years now had lived in California, would understand his reasoning. But then, raising his cane to point to his right, he began in the local dialect so familiar to me: "You see, I was born on that end of the street many years ago, and now I live on the other end of the street"—he raised his cane to point to his left—"where I will die." He then pointed down to his prosthesis. "And the one time I had to go somewhere else, to Russia, I lost my leg."

Like the laborer's son, Herr Morgenroth, who lived twenty miles down the Main River, Walther Camerer had a deep attachment to his picturesque town of Wertheim-am-Main (now a stopover for luxury riverboats on the Budapest-Amster-dam itinerary), where several generations of his family have resided. Walther Camerer and his father and grandfather before him were all distinguished medical generalists who took pride in caring for the sick. Now Walther's son continues the tradition. If you watch the elder Dr. Camerer slowly make his way up to the church on a Sunday morning, you have the feeling that he is familiar with every cobblestone and with all the uneven surfaces of the street. He has the air of an elegant senior, with polite gestures. You can easily imagine that in his youth, the adult men still wore top hats on festive occasions. His old-world manners are quite natural to him, learned not in school but in the comfort of a stable, well-to-do home. In the life of his family, the present had always been stable, the future pre-dictable, and the past proof that God was in his heaven and all was well in an orderly world. Only the river inundating the low-lying sections of Wertheim every once in a while brought reminders of destructive disorder into the everyday lives of the townspeople.

I knew that Walther Camerer had spent more than five years after the end of World War II as a prisoner of war in various Soviet camps in Siberia. When we met for our interview, he launched right away into a lengthy discussion of the medical research projects he had been involved in over the years. I think he would have preferred to remain on this subject, which he comprehended so well. This was the area of knowledge and expertise he claimed as his own, over which he had control—the parameters defined by facts, not fantasies. After a while, I pressed on with my agenda, and he told me, by way of intro-ducing himself, that after the war a former Jewish inhabitant of Wertheim, now a citizen of Israel, had come to visit him to thank him officially for what his father had done to help the Jews. Then he added, as if he felt a need to justify himself, that the rumors he had heard on the eastern front about mass executions of Jews, he took at the time to be propaganda. During one of his leaves from the front, however, he continued thoughtfully, he noticed that all the houses owned by Jews in his native town stood empty.

It took him some time to get around to telling me about his hellish experiences in the Siberian camps. When he finally began, he relied on the language that doctors use to describe and analyze medical symptoms. In a way, he became his own patient, whom he approached with sympathy but also with the distance necessary to be as dispassionate and objective as possible. He began his story in the Siberian camp, as if his fighting before as a soldier was unimportant. In fact, for a while it seemed to me almost as if he had not had a life before his Siberian imprisonment at all, the harshness of these memories having obliterated everything else for him. It is often said that individuals have one or two traumatic (or charismatic) periods in their lives that cast a shadow over the rest and shape their identity and their understanding of the world. Dr. Camerer's beloved Wertheim, the family pedigree, his days in uniform, and his return home—all this faded during the hour of our interview in the face of his five years of captivity.

His status as a doctor helped him greatly in these prison camps. Because there was virtually no medical care available for the POWs, at least none that could truly be called "care," the Soviet doctors were primarily interested in preventing epidemics, which could affect the guards as well as the prisoners.

"Bugs know no borders," Dr. Camerer said with a grin. When several of the guards contracted a rare skin disease for which the Soviet doctors had no cure, a high Communist official came to Dr. Camerer and asked for his help. "They had pus all over their faces," Dr. Camerer told me, "and I found a cure for it." From then on his reputation in the camp soared, and he was given more medical responsibilities. For a time this role gave him a small measure of immunity against the bone-chilling cold, gnawing hunger, dark hatred of the guards, and sense of hopelessness about a future life.

This situation changed drastically after an imprisoned SS officer asked him to prepare a small medical kit for him, because he planned an escape. Camerer prepared the kit and wished him good luck. But the escapee did not get very far and was quickly caught by the Soviets. When the medical kit in his pack was traced back to Dr. Camerer, the camp commander threatened to execute him. But Camerer argued that the authorities had told him to use medications from his own private pharmacy to help inmates if they needed it, and that is exactly what he had done in the case of the escapee. The commander seemed to believe him—sufficiently, at least, to commute his death sentence to twenty-five years of hard labor.

When Walther Camerer entered the *Straflager* (penal colony), he realized that no one could survive there for very long. He initially worked at carrying heavy stones, and broke three ribs doing so. He was not allowed time to heal, but was switched from carrying stones to breaking up clay clumps, which was still excruciatingly painful work. I interrupted him to ask whether such work was forced upon them for no other purpose than to cause suffering. He didn't answer my question. He did not want to discuss motivations and attitudes. He was only interested in events as he remembered them.

His skill as a doctor got him out of this particular hell. The wife of a Polish engineer, a colonel and a Jew, had fallen desperately ill. When all other medical efforts to help her failed, he turned to Dr. Camerer. She had had a cold and then a severe earache. After a short time, the earache disappeared, but the patient remained ill. Dr. Camerer diagnosed septic fever and concluded that the infection had turned inward. He wrote up his diagnosis and delivered it to the colonel. She was taken to a hospital in Swerdlovsk, where, on the basis of his diagnosis, the medical staff drained the infection from behind her ear. She recovered. As an act of gratitude, the Polish colonel had the German physician transferred from the penal colony to a prison hospital filled with tubercular German POWs. Dr. Camerer commented to me with a glimmer of pride, "You see, we Germans had a good reputation as doctors in Russia!"

In the prison hospital Dr. Camerer witnessed "the strangest event of my life." One of the German soldiers had been in the camp since the beginning of the war in 1941. The Russians had captured him as he lay in the snow with shrapnel in his lungs, left behind for dead by his German compatriots. Later on, a new POW who came from the same town as the first inmate arrived at the hospital, and they naturally began to talk about their hometown and their youths, sharing the sights and sounds of their particular corner of Germany in their own local dialect, which the others understood but could not speak. As Dr. Camerer recalls, the conversation provided them a small sense of comfort, despite their immediate environment of barbed wire, dull defeat, and hopelessness. In the course of their exchange, the new arrival said he had recently married a war widow, whose husband had died at the Russian front at the beginning of the war. He mentioned her name. His hometown compatriot fell into a stunned silence, and then said, "You married my wife!" Walther Camerer remembers that the two prisoners stared at each other for a long time. What to do?

They decided that if they both survived the war, they would go home but stay in a nearby village, inform the woman about their return, and then let her decide whom she wanted as her husband. Camerer shuddered at the brutality of this choice for the woman, but he added that the older inmate had such an advanced case of tuberculosis that it was very unlikely he would survive to make it home. He did not know how it all came out, he said, adding, with a smile and a faint motion of his hand, that life could be stranger than fiction. When he finished his story, a strange silence possessed our interview room, as if after Siberia life for him was always shadowed by those years and that his POW life *in extremis* had remained a constant, if hidden, challenge to his normal, everyday existence.

The last time I saw Dr. Camerer was on the occasion of the eightieth birthday celebration of his old friends Prince Alfred-Ernst zu Löwenstein in the autumn of 2004. The elderly physician had become quite frail. Yet he walked firmly up the cobblestone street and the paved incline leading to the entry of the Lutheran church of Wertheim, greeting friends and acquaintances. I imagined him standing among a gathering of friends—several lifetimes ago—the men in cylinder hats bowing to kiss the gloved hands of ladies.[3]

HELMUT HERRMANN

Helmut Herrmann was the oldest person I interviewed. Born in 1915, he was eighty-seven when he told me his story. When Hitler came to power, he was old enough to be drafted, and when World War II ended, he was a thirty-year-old major in the German army. At the time of our interview in 2002, he was still in robust health. He had a keen mind and a clear recall of past events without any ideological overlay. The only time he deviated from telling his personal story in a simple, straightforward way was when he complained that the past was "shaped by the clichés of those who have a particular axe to grind."

A German Boy Scout in pre-Hitler days, he remembered campfires, long hikes through forests, and singing. His peers were young and full of idealism. After Hitler gained power, the Boy Scouts were taken over by the Hitler Youth. He and his friends thought that this new organization would carry on in the same spirit as before. After all, many of the songs were the same, and so were the campfires, he told me. But as time went on, they began to notice a change. "We thought it would continue as always, but we were wrong." Soon his Boy Scout troop split up. Seven of the boys joined the Hitler Youth; six, including Helmut, did not.[4]

Helmut wasn't interested in discussing his political reasons for not joining the Hitler Youth. But in his telling of his story through the 1930s, I noticed that his political attitudes were shaped by the leaders he met and who they were as individuals, quite aside from the roles they played in Nazi organizations.

Helmut didn't believe his lack of interest in the Hitler Youth would have consequences for him. But when the time came for him to receive his graduation certificate from secondary school—the all-important *Abitur-Zeugnis*, which remains the key to success in German society—the cultural ministry in Stuttgart balked, saying that he had the grades but his refusal to join the Hitler Youth weighed heavily against him. A history teacher intervened on his behalf, however, and in the end he was granted the certificate.

It was 1936, and he began his long stint in uniform that would not end until May 1945. At first he was assigned to a workers' brigade, led by two men he despised. One was a drunkard and a failed student, who bombarded them with "lessons about the New Reich." The other, an unemployed laborer, lorded his new-found leadership position over the better-educated underlings assigned to him. After six unhappy months, Helmut volunteered for the army, his favorite branch of the military, and joined the *Gebirgsjäger* (mountain troopers), an army unit specifically trained for fighting in mountainous terrain. Not long after completing the required two years of military service, he was ready to start his university studies. But the war broke out in 1939, and he was one of the first soldiers back in uniform. Unlike the Hitler Youth or workers' brigades, the army emphasized military discipline over political propaganda, as he recalled.

When World War II began in 1939, there was none of the enthusiasm that had marked the launch in 1914 into World War I, which was supposed to be the war to end all wars. Helmut Herrmann's army unit marched through Slovakia and Poland all the way to Lvov, without encountering much resistance. They had barely arrived, however, when they were ordered to turn around and march back toward the German border for two days. Like others whom I interviewed, this German soldier was given little information about what was happening in the world at large. Later on, the soldiers found out that Stalin and Hitler had decided to divide Poland between themselves and that the eastern part of Poland would be taken over by the Soviet army.

On their long march back, leaving Soviet-occupied Poland in the autumn of 1939, Herr Herrmann remembers being joined on the paths on both sides of the main road by a long stream of Jews carrying their belongings. The Jews, remembering the pogroms of the past, were more afraid of the Russians than of the German army, to whom they looked for protection. Herr Herrmann added, "Little did they know—and we, for that matter, did not either—what was in store for them at the end of the road."

Helmut Herrmann's road led from one European battlefield to another. The only constant in his soldierly existence was the regiment to which he was assigned. His regiment was transported to Romania, and from there it marched through Bulgaria to the Greek border. When the British landed in Greece, it marched on, all the way to Athens. From there it was ordered to go to Crete, because German paratroopers were unable to hold their ground against the British on that island. Not much later, Hitler invaded the Soviet Union. Herrmann's unit was first ordered to the Arctic, but since the battle around Leningrad required more German troops, it was sent instead to the Baltic, where Herrmann stayed for eighteen months.

At this point, Herrmann's fluid narrative suddenly grew halting—the only time it did so. I asked him what the matter was, and he said that the hell of it all had suddenly struck him. The hellhole that was the eastern front is a theme that ran through many of the recollections I heard as well as the letters of soldiers that I read.

In 1943, Helmut Herrmann became not only the adjutant to the commanding officer of the regiment, but also his friend. They talked openly with each other, and Herrmann clearly remembers one of their many private conversations—after Stalingrad, in 1943—when the commander said, "You know, of course, Herrmann, that this war is lost." Helmut remembers asking, "In that case, what are we still fighting for?" "Honor" and "duty" were mentioned, with little conviction, as possible reasons for fighting on. He also recalls how they viewed with mocking irony the war propaganda that assured them glorious victory. They finally concluded between themselves, "Perhaps we have to save Germany from the Russian Communists."

From the Baltic, Herrmann's unit of mountaineers was transported briefly to France and then, finally, to Italy to fight against the Allies as they advanced up the Italian peninsula. By 1945, Herrmann was a major in the divisional staff. When he told me this, he lit up visibly and became quite animated in his recall. In spite of the temporal wall that separated us from the war years, there was little doubt in my mind that he saw the end of the war less as a defeat than as liberation. The German army staff in Italy made contact with the Americans, whom they met secretly in Switzerland; there they agreed that as soon as Hitler was dead, they would immediately stop fighting. The war ended for Helmut Herrmann and his divisional staff when the American officers invited them all to a dinner party, at which Herrmann tasted his first American whiskey. Since he had a clean record, he was soon sent home.

As a soldier, Helmut Herrmann did his duty from 1939 to 1945; he always marched on—through Slovakia, Poland, Romania, Bulgaria, Greece, Crete, Russia, France, and Italy. He never joined the Nazi party.

LORE ZIERMANN

A heavyset woman in her seventies, Lore Ziermann, née Brzit-wa in 1933, had to walk with the help of two canes when I interviewed her. Although she was not born or raised in Bavaria, she has lived in Munich most of her life and now speaks with a noticeable Bavarian accent. I knew from her son that she fled Silesia at the end of the war. During her interview I learned that Lore Ziermann is apolitical and has no axes to grind. She is not a revisionist.

I already knew something about the German refugees and their trek westward after being chased out of the eastern German provinces that became part of Poland after World War II. More than a million of those refugees lost their lives to starvation, murder, or illness. The fate that befell them is to some degree chronicled, and after the war, many of the surviving refugees joined political parties, particularly the *Bund der Heimatvertriebenen und Entrechteten* (BHE, or Union of People Evicted from their Homes and Disenfranchised). For a while, they represented a revisionist potential as they sought to reclaim their lost homelands. Eventually, however, this group became integrated into the emerging civil society of the Federal Republic of Germany.

But the stories of their suffering were overshadowed by the Holocaust, and although the documentary evidence of their plight is now available, it has not had an impact on the

German public sphere. Here in the United States, their stories are not generally known, and those who do tell them may not be able to escape the suspicion of seeking to revise the history of World War II.

In most traditional German families, the man was the master of the house, but authoritarian structures largely disappeared after the war, since many of the men were killed or imprisoned, and the women, by default, became the head of the household. War or no, Lore was probably born to be a matriarch. She has a strong sense of self. She knows her likes and dislikes and is not reluctant to express them. She devoted her life to raising her children, most of whom hold high positions in scientific research, banking, or private industry.

On the occasion of her son's fortieth birthday, her family members converged on Moraga, California, from far-flung parts of the world for a reunion. Her son, a naturalized American and a scientist with the California branch of a German pharmaceutical giant, was a friend of ours, and we were invited to the festivities. Conversations ranged all over the map, and you sensed that these people were as comfortable in Rio de Janeiro as in Munich. Each of Lore's children has a unique personality, and it is clearly evident that they had all been encouraged to develop their individual talents. Lore sat in the middle of this family festivity, sunk low into a comfortable couch. When anyone wanted to talk to her, they had to bend down. It was her diminished mobility as much as her imposing presence that placed her at the center of the birthday celebration.

Her son told me that the entire family knew only the barest outlines of her early life because she had always remained silent about her past. As they were growing up, whenever the children would ask about her days as a refugee from Silesia, she would change the subject. After a time they gave up asking. She knew of my interest in unrecorded German memories from the Nazi period, and to her son's great surprise, she agreed to tell me her story.

A few days after the birthday party, I interviewed Lore Zier-mann. It was not so much what she told me as how she introduced her story that impacted me most. Her first words sounded like an apology. "Why do you want to hear my story? It's really not worth listening to, and besides, I don't want to burden you with something that has to do with my past." I realized that to reveal her past to me called into play a sense of shame. She brought to mind a vivid memory of my youth: Frau Sichel, one of the Jewish residents of Kleinheubach, sauntering up the cobblestone street in 1938 after the Night of the Broken Glass as if nothing had happened, attempting to hide her humiliation over what Nazi thugs had done to her and her property. Both my friend's mother from Bavaria and the Jewish woman from my village had been made into objects by violence. Although these two women experienced radically different fates—one had her life cut short in a death camp, while the other made it to West Germany and lived a full life—neither one had control over what happened to her during that period. Outside forces decided not only their fates, but also the nature of their everyday lives. And most days were lived under the threat of violence.

It was not easy for Frau Ziermann to tell me her story. The self-assurance she had as the matriarch of a large and successful family had vanished. She is by nature talkative, and her spon-taneous charm makes her most likable; but now she sat across from me seeming exposed and defenseless, as if at risk. Before she began, she said something in German that told me how difficult it was to turn me, a relative stranger, into a confidant, an accomplice in a tale she had never told before: "Du weißt nicht, ob Sie das überhaupt interessiert" (You [familiar] don't know if it will even interest you [formal])—a strangely ungrammatical sentence in which she switched between the familiar *Du,* used among friends, and the formal *Sie* customary when talking to strangers. The silence with which she had surrounded her past had evidently acted as a safety zone that protected her from intruders and unnamed dangers. Clearly, the lack of any collective context in which she felt comfortable to articulate her past experiences made it extraordinarily difficult for her to bring down the massive wall of silence she had maintained for decades. Who would be interested in her story as a German refugee? She had never been interested in *her* fellow refugees, because many of them had axes to grind, while she did not.

Finally, she began to talk. Outside the window, a big SUV full of suburban American kids slowly drove past. Inside, for us, it was spring 1945, in Silesia, the day the war in Europe ended. Lore was twelve years old, and her half-brother a few years younger. Her stepfather was a medical orderly at the local military hospital. (Lore's birth father died when she was quite young, and Lore's mother had remarried a man named Langner). Not long after the end of the war, Soviet orders came that her family would be relocated to Prague, in Czechoslovakia.

Their train was crammed full of the wounded and the hospital's medical staff and their families, among them Lore Brzitwa Langner's family of four. The food the Langners took along was scant because the swiftness of the evacuation didn't allow for much planning. En route to Prague, the train suddenly jerked to a stop in the middle of open fields. Part of the mass of humanity pressed into the train was taken off and made to stand near the tracks. The selection had been random and everyone wondered what it meant. That became clear in a few minutes. Shots rang out, then more shots, until the entire group taken off the train lay dead—old and young women, children, wounded soldiers, old men. Lore believes that the authorities in charge of this transport decided that the train was overcrowded and that killing some of the occupants would solve the problem.

When the survivors arrived in Prague, they straggled under heavy guard through the city. Because of what German soldiers had done to the Czechs during the Nazi occupation, the townspeople jeered at them. They were all guilty, simply for being German. They finally were deposited in a school building. Lore saw Russian soldiers drag many younger women downstairs with ropes to rooms where they raped them undisturbed. The road of sorrow did not end there. The Czechs herded the Germans together and drove them, women, children, and old men, through the streets of Prague, where onlookers taunted them. As they crossed Wenceslas Square, as Lore recalls, she saw a woman's corpse hanging by a wire from a lamppost, her stomach slit open.

They ended up in a camp with large barracks. In the middle of the camp was a crematorium where corpses were burned. The victims—German women, children, and elders—had not survived the ordeal of starvation and forced evacuations from the German provinces ceded to Poland. "Leider hab' ich gesehen, wie sie verbrannt wurden," she said dolefully (Unfortunately, I saw how they were incinerated). Then, as she was about to continue, her voice wavered and she came near to tears, although it took only a few seconds for her to tuck her emotions away again. Her stepfather, she said, was suddenly hauled off before their eyes. They thought they would never see him again, but he survived several POW camps in the Soviet Union. Nor did he know at the time that his wife, Lore's mother, was pregnant.

But then Lore, her mother, and her brother experienced some good luck: they were selected for a work detail to help local farmers with their chores. Assigned to a chicken farm, they slept in the chicken coops. At least they were beyond immediate physical danger at this point, and the food was better than the cabbage soup and wet bread they had received in the camp.

As time passed, her mother's stomach grew larger, as Lore put it, and she wondered whether the baby would be born in a chicken coop. But luck was on their side once again. Since the Czechs wanted nothing to do with a pregnant German woman, they released her family at the end of November and sent them by train back to Germany. By way of Pilsen, the Langners made it to Würzburg, which lay in ruins.

On December 10, 1945, Lore's second brother was born. In spite of the total destruction around them, their miserable living conditions, a newborn baby to care for, and little to eat, all she remembers is a feeling of freedom. The war had ended and her trials in the East were over.

Eventually, Lore's stepfather returned, barely alive, from Soviet captivity. When I asked about their life after the family was reunited, she recalled one simple fact: they never talked about what had happened to them, what they had gone through. I suggested that her mother and father may have talked about their experiences of misery out of earshot of their children, but she was quite convinced that they, too, had maintained a total silence. I then asked her whether she had discussed with her younger brother the random shooting of the train passengers, the corpses in the crematorium, or the woman hanging from a lamppost. She answered that they had never exchanged a single word about these things. Perhaps her brother hadn't witnessed all of these horrible events, I suggested, but she countered, "Oh no, he was there, always by my side." I inquired whether she had ever discussed with her brother the psychological effects of their experiences in the East, avoiding perhaps the specific traumas. Again she demurred and insisted that no personal, let alone intimate, conversation had ever taken place about their shared traumatic events. She added that her own children knew only fragments of her history, just the barest minimum to satisfy their basic curiosity about their mother's past.

This ended the interview, and again, as at the beginning, she apologized for having told me all this. It was clear to me that sharing her burden with someone else seemed to her an imposition of sorts. For over fifty years she had carried these memories in silence. I later wondered what effect this unearthing of her past might have had on her, a woman who, as the mother of adult children who are very much part of the world at large, seems to live fully in the present.

Her son's California birthday party, long by American standards but normal for Germans, who love to celebrate well into the night, was relaxed and spontaneous. As I said good-bye to Lore, she took my hand and said, "Ich bin stolz, ein Deutscher zu sein" (I am proud to be a German). There was not a trace of defensiveness in her voice, and I came away convinced that she had become who she was because of the rebirth she experienced after the war, raising a family in West Germany and enjoying

Figure 3. Lore Ziermann, 2006.

her children's successes. The German as sufferer was not part of her worldview.

The weight of her many good years and the fullness of her life had made it possible for her to bear the burden of her youth, which, over the years, grew lighter as she became accustomed to keeping it buried inside. I felt it inappropriate to ask whether bad dreams and nightmares haunted her. And I sensed her gratitude that I had listened.

HANNELORE REBSTOCK

I didn't know Hannelore Rebstock (née Mehnert in 1924) very well before I interviewed her. But I knew that she had survived the bombing of Dresden, when the ancient city on the Elbe River, with its baroque architecture and Saxon charm, was turned into rubble and more than 100,000 people perished—burned, melted, and blown apart by incendiary bombs. The destruction took place the nights of 13–14 and 14–15 February 1945, a little less than three months before the end of the war. The bombing came as a shocking surprise; as the war had begun to wind down, the inhabitants of Dresden were feeling safer and hopeful that they would be spared destruction, since the city didn't seem to have any strategic importance.

At the time of its incineration by the British air armada and the U.S. Air Force, the population had grown rapidly, expanding by more than half a million refugees from the East who were fleeing the Russians. Ever since Kurt Vonnegut published *Slaughterhouse-Five* in 1969, the destruction of Dresden has been widely known. Chronicles of those two nights have been compiled, and the town's destruction has become part of the epic sweep of violence that characterized the end of the war. I had known about those two nights ever since I sat glued to the radio in Kleinheubach, listening to live reports of the bombing of Dresden. I was initially hesitant to undertake an interview with this survivor. Her husband had told me that she had never told her story to anyone.

When we met, I introduced myself to the frail, elderly woman with a handshake across an empty table. It was immediately apparent that her horrifying encounter with violence had made her life radically different from mine. My first dinner with Bernat Rosner, my friend who had survived Auschwitz, came to mind. In both cases, it was the awareness of difference that challenged me to understand and to empathize as much as possible. I knew that only a dialogue had a chance of bridging the differences between these survivors and me. In both cases, my intention was not to add to facts and circumstances already well chronicled by historians, but to narrate the experiences of two individuals. I hoped to retrieve and thereby save the most traumatic experiences in their individual lives from the leveling effect of the violent storm that engulfed them.

It is one thing to read books and monographs about World War II and Dresden, and quite another to sit with someone willing to recall the darkest moments of her life for you. At first, we were caught by our immediate surroundings: bare white walls, a large table and several chairs, green trees outside the window, and the muffled sound of footsteps in the hallway. I fiddled with my tape recorder, tested levels, and fiddled some more until she remarked, "Wir sitzen hier in einem kahlen Raum" (We're sitting here in an empty room). I agreed, and posed my first question. In an hour we were done. I had scheduled several other interviews that day, but I had to cancel them. I couldn't go on as if nothing had happened during that hour with Frau Rebstock, when her burden to some degree became mine. I heard later from friends of hers that she felt a great sense of relief after the interview. I was glad for her sake.

It was Tuesday in Dresden, she began, not quite a normal day, because it was carnival season, and even that late in the war traditions had not been entirely discarded. That afternoon, boys and girls had been running around the streets dressed as pirates, Indians, cowboys, witches, clowns, and the usual bevy of princesses and angels. But darkness came early in winter, and eventually the youthful apparitions disappeared from the streets and returned to their homes.

Sometime after nine o'clock that evening, the radio announced that a large armada of airplanes was approaching Dresden. The usual large flares appeared in the sky—*Weihnachtsbäume*

(Christmas trees), as the Germans called them—lighting it up. Searchlights from the ground briefly illuminated some of the aircraft—British Lancaster bombers, as Hannelore remembers. She hurried down to the air raid shelter beneath her house, a knapsack of supplies on her back. She had barely arrived there when the ground beneath her heaved, and she threw herself down in the fetal position. The earthen floor beneath her rolled like a series of waves as bombs fell on the city. Then the bombing stopped, and the attack seemed over.

She and her mother and neighbors decided to have a look, and made their way out into the open. What they saw was a city engulfed in flames. They knew they had to be very careful, because the sirens warning the population of impending air raids had ceased to function. Sure enough, half an hour after midnight the second wave of bombers arrived. She said that with so many buildings in flames, the pilots must have seen the city below them clearly. She was right. A pilot from the fifth fleet of the Royal Air Force described what he saw from the air: "The eerie glow seen 320 kilometers away became brighter and brighter as we approached our goal. Even at the height of 6700 meters we could recognize details on the ground illuminated by a ghostlike glow—details that we had never seen like that before. And for the first time after all my air raids over Germany, I felt sorry for the population down below."[5]

Hannelore Rebstock suddenly lowered her voice and seemed to talk more to herself than to me. "The burning city during the second wave turned into an inferno," she said. Refugees and soldiers had amassed in the square in front of the main railroad station, as fire and destruction rained down on them. Dresden had not built large air raid bunkers as most other German cities had, she explained, because everyone assumed that that treasure trove of baroque art and architecture would be spared.

Hannelore and her immediate family survived the bombings. Her worse nightmare began afterward. Initially, her immediate surroundings mattered most, as her actions focused on personal survival. But in the days and weeks that followed, she began to see and feel the larger effects of the orgy of violence that had turned her city to ashes. Streets had become huge piles of rubble. She and other survivors spent many hours digging out the dead from underneath the collapsed houses. But what stood out most in her mind after all these years was the sight of what they thought were tree trunks, from broken-off trees, that turned out to be human beings shrunk into grotesque shapes from the firestorm. This, and the fact that every day for many weeks carts were continually filled with corpses and dragged to the cemetery, where charred remains were buried in mass graves. She sat in silence for a moment. Then she continued: "You know, as time went on, you just became dead and rigid inside. I joined many other women carrying bricks, day in and day out. We all were survivors, but no one ever spoke about what we had gone through. We just worked side by side not saying a word about those two nights, and so it was for many years afterward. No words spoken. But nightmares about being caught in caves pursued me. These nightmares did not get better until I had children, then they faded somewhat, but they've never really left me completely."

She concluded by saying, "You know, there is only one person who completely understands about my days in Dres-

Figure 4. Hannelore Mehnert as a nurse in training, 1946. (All her childhood photos were destroyed in the bombing of Dresden.)

den." When I asked her who that was, she said it was a man her age who had survived Auschwitz. "We share our horrors and we understand." I nodded, grasping what she meant. Then she added something that I did not understand—that the color purple caused intense panic in both of them. She told me this with quiet intensity, as if I would naturally know what she meant.

I didn't know, though, and I didn't dare to ask, as I sensed such a probing would invade the privacy of certain emotions I had no right to access. I remembered when my friend Bernie told me about the Yiddish plaint the inmates sang at nightfall in the barracks at Auschwitz. He spoke every word of the song in perfect Yiddish, but I did not ask him to sing it. It was his to remember or forget, and not for me to hear. So it was with Frau Rebstock. She told me her story and expressed some of her deeper feelings about her experiences, hidden for so many years from others. But whatever secret linked the color purple in the memories of these two survivors remained with them.

· · ·

In the spring of 1945, Siegfried Spiecker, a young soldier recently recruited into the *Wehrmacht*, became a POW under the control of the U.S. Army. In July 1945, two months after the war had ended, he was interrogated by an American GI during a foot trek from Munich to Frankfurt-am-Main. The American wore a trim uniform and spoke fluent German; Siegfried was haggard and worn out. One was the victor, the other the vanquished. The German soldier without rank had no important secrets to hide, and the American had many other prisoners to interrogate, so the questioning was routine. But there was a strange twist to their encounter. The American was a Jew born in Germany who had fled just in time, and the German was born in the United States, but his parents had returned with him to Germany in 1927 when Siegfried was one year old. At the end of the interview, the American GI shook his head and said, "Just think of it! I was born in Stuttgart, and now I'm an American soldier, and you were born in Philadelphia, and now you're a German prisoner!" Moved by his recall of the event long ago, Herr Spiecker had to fight back tears as he remembered that the GI shook his hand in a friendly way, spoke with regret of the "crazy war," and then left him with a shrug of his shoulders, saying, "That's the way it goes—the roll of the dice."

The roll of the dice also applied to two German pilots I came to know. Klaus Conrad was shot down over England early in the war. The other, Johannes Kuhn, tried to fly the last fighter plane, an ME 109, out of Berlin at the very end of the war. They both crash-landed and survived, and those traumatic moments shaped the rest of their lives.

KLAUS CONRAD

Klaus Conrad was born in what was known as the Polish Corridor, claimed by Hitler from Poland. For generations the Conrads had been farmers. They were considered "Polish citizens of the German nation," a confusing characterization for all those who lived on this historically contested land. Klaus Conrad's forefathers had helped Poles, Russians, and Germans in the fight against Napoleon's armies. Legally, young Conrad was considered a potential recruit for the Polish army. To avoid being drafted by the Poles, he attended the Berlin Olympic Games in 1936 and never returned home. Without dwelling on the subject, he informed me that his father "perished miserably at the hands of the Poles."

In 1941 Conrad was a lieutenant in the *Luftwaffe*. On a bombing mission over Liverpool, his Heinkel III plane was hit by anti-aircraft fire over the coast of England, but he managed to bring it down safely in a field. As he ran away from the airplane, it exploded. He did not get very far before someone shouted at him, "Hands up!" At that moment, as Klaus told me, "The war was over for me."

An interrogator spent considerable time with this German captive, because the British wanted to find out details about a device the Germans had developed that gave them greater accuracy in pinpointing targets. Klaus did not go into this, and I, as a layman, would not have understood a technical explanation. What mattered to Klaus Conrad was that the encounters with

Figure 5. Klaus Conrad as a pilot in the German air force, 1940.

his British interrogator had a profound effect on him. "He was a very likable person," he said, "and he really did not press me all that much for information." Instead they went on rides in the countryside, ate dinners together, and all the while discussed a variety of subjects. The bonding worked. Conrad started reading British newspapers, and after a while the British officer suggested that there might be another way of looking at the war aside from the German point of view. "That comment began to preoccupy me," Klaus confessed. Eventually he was shipped to North America for six years as a POW, but before he left the two promised to meet after the war.

The young German lieutenant did not settle down behind the barbed-wire enclosures of the various Canadian and American POW camps he experienced. Rather, whenever he saw a chance to break out, he took it. Each time, he was recaptured and put in a camp where the surveillance was tighter. But this did not deter him. At one point, he and another escapee headed for the east coast of the United States in the vague hope of boarding a neutral ship that would take them back to Germany. For him, escape was less an act of patriotism, and even less an expression of solidarity with the Nazi regime, than something more fundamental—an urge to get out of prison and return home.

In spite of his reputation as a prisoner prone to escape, Conrad got to know some of his captors personally, and one POW camp commander became a close friend. After the war they paid visits to each other. Klaus came away from his Anglo-American experience a bona fide cosmopolitan, and went on to develop an extensive network of acquaintances and friends ranging from Australia to the British Isles. As he reminisced on the many contacts that grew out his POW years, he remarked, "So klein ist die Welt, so nett sind die Leute" (The world is so small and the people are so nice).

Perhaps the most improbable part of his story is that he studied geology and forestry while in a Canadian prison, then graduated from the School of Forestry in Eberswalde, Germany, in 1944. I asked him how it was possible to earn his degree while the war was raging in Europe and he was a POW on another continent. "It was not all that hard," he replied. "I received the study material from Germany via the Red Cross, and the written exam was held under supervision. The degree was confirmed before the war's end." He went on to earn his doctorate in 1948.

JOHANNES KUHN

The dice landed differently for Johannes Kuhn. The son of devout Christian parents, he was deeply religious as far back as he can remember. His mother was known to feed the poor in her village, and when the Jews were openly persecuted, she provided them with baskets of food and little tokens of support. (Johannes remembers once delivering some of these small gifts to the Jewish citizens while wearing his Hitler Youth uniform.) It is not so much that the family resisted Nazi ideology, but rather that they lived by the principles of conscience that Luther had preached. On the Night of the Broken Glass, Johannes remembers that his father quoted Zechariah 2:8 from the Old Testament: ". . . for he that touches you, touches the apple of his eye." Like millions of other German families during Hitler's reign, the Kuhn family clung to a quiet faith and a religious inwardness that they believed would protect them from outside forces. As it turned

Figure 6. Johannes Kuhn (far left) on a JU87 Stuka wing, 1944.

out, such beliefs could not withstand the onslaught of violence that engulfed all, believers and nonbelievers alike.

Johannes told me several times how much he loved flying— "to hover over the clouds far from the ground," as he put it. When he attained draft age, he volunteered for the German air force and became a fighter pilot. Stationed in northern Germany toward the end of the war, he was in the middle of the final battles around Berlin. As late as April 1945, he raced through the burning capital to get to an air force hangar, his orders being to fly an intact Messerschmitt to the western front. Despite every kind of firepower targeting him from the ground, he managed to get the plane out of Berlin by flying low over the rooftops. "You know," he said, "I always possessed a deep confidence in my inner strength, in my *Lebensvertrauen* [trust in life]."

As the Russians were approaching the Elbe River, the commander of Kuhn's squadron assembled the pilots and, with all the Nazi fanaticism he could muster, exhorted them to prove their valor for the fatherland by crashing their planes, kamikaze-style, into the bridges spanning the Elbe. The pilots listened, and then they told the commander that if he would lead them in this final sally, they would follow suit. The commander changed the subject.

While Klaus Conrad spent the last weeks of the war reading newspapers from the other side and engaging in conversations with his captors, pilot Kuhn spent them in dramatic action, where life and death were decided by split-second decisions or violent, unforeseen events. Cities beneath him burned, long streams of refugees filled the roads, tank columns advanced toward Berlin from all sides. Johannes knew it would all be over soon. Yet he loved to fly, and knowing that after the war he would no longer be able to do so, he savored every moment he was not in battle and could soar over the clouds "like a bird."

An incident during those final weeks of the war defined who Johannes Kuhn became afterward. He and his squadron of fighter planes had been ordered to bomb a bridge that the Soviet army had built. Yet as he was diving toward the target, the bomb release mechanism failed, and the bomb didn't drop. As hard as he tried to get rid of it, nothing worked, and he was stuck with the bomb in the belly of his plane. By this time his crippled plane had lost so much altitude that he could no longer use his parachute and he was forced to crash land. He knew that even if he survived the crash, the impact would probably set off the bomb, but he had no choice.

Figure 7. Pastor Johannes Kuhn preaching to pilgrims on Mt. Tabor, Israel, 1989.

He managed to bring the plane down, jump out of the cockpit, and run away from the aircraft, which indeed exploded behind him. As he recounted this incident, his face was covered with perspiration. He seemed to be back there in the spring of 1945. Then, after a long pause, as if recalling the exact moment of the insight that would shape the rest of his life, he said quietly, "I did not ask *why* I survived, but *for what purpose*." As he stood watching the burning wreckage, he made the decision to become a Protestant minister. After the war his reputation as a pastor grew, and he became well known through his popular radio broadcasts in southern Germany. His many books witness his deep faith and conviction that people are put on this earth for a purpose.

At the end of our interview, Johannes handed me two old photographs. One showed him and other *Luftwaffe* pilots lying on the wing of a Stuka dive-bomber. The other showed him praying with a group of German pilgrims on Mount Sinai.

MANFRED FISCHER

Manfred Fischer was only eleven when the war ended, but he had already been taught how to shoot a rifle and throw a hand grenade, in case he was needed to defend the fatherland. The Americans were slow in coming to his town of Plochingen, near Stuttgart, and the family sat in the cellar and waited. Finally, his mother got tired of waiting. Ordering her children to stay in the cellar, she went up to the kitchen on the ground floor to prepare a tub of Swabian potato salad.

As she told her family later, she finally saw American GIs rounding the corner of their street with weapons at the ready, their fingers on the triggers. She walked outside, holding the tub of potato salad in front of her to show the curious GIs that it contained something good to eat. This action, undertaken on the spur of the moment, changed the family's immediate fate and in due course became an important stepping-stone in Manfred's future life and career.

With one exception, all the Germans were removed from their houses in that upscale street to make room for the American soldiers. Only the Fischer family was allowed to stay in one room of their house, which became the U.S. Army's headquarters in Plochingen. Frau Fischer continued to cook for the soldiers every day, with the GIs supplying chickens and other provisions that seemed the stuff of fairy tales to this German family used to the deprivations of war. Meals were distributed to the soldiers at the entrance of the Fischers' garage. This arrangement lasted for several weeks, during which Manfred came to love the GIs. The potential grenade thrower had been given back his childhood with the potato salad his mother cooked and the chickens the American guests in uniform brought to their shared meals.

That was not the end of it, however. Two years later Manfred was chosen, together with three hundred other young Germans in their early teens, to participate in a tent camp organized by the American army to introduce young Germans to the ideals and practice of democracy. Manfred remembers how delighted he was to be picked up in an army truck and delivered to the campsite. Good food, fireside meetings, talks about America, and simple interactions with the American soldiers in charge of the youth camp filled the days.

The physician of the camp, Dr. Carleton Gajdusek, selected a few of the brightest youths for special instruction. Years later,

Figure 8. Manfred Fischer on his mother's lap and his brother Hans, near the entrance to their garage, 1936.

in 1976, Dr. Gajdusek received a Nobel Prize in medicine for identifying the bacterium that causes kuru, a disease prevalent among the natives of New Guinea. Manfred and the physician became friends for life. Dr. Gajdusek even tried to coax Manfred with several research stipends to come to the United States, but Manfred decided to stay in Germany. There, he eventually became a professor of physics at the University of Stuttgart and director of the German space program. Throughout his life, Manfred has retained a deep affection "für Amerika und Amerikaner." To this day, he loves the American openness and can-do attitude vis-à-vis the problems of science and living. What's the moral of this story? It helps to be born at the right place and live at the right time—and to have a mother who makes potato salad at the right time for the right people.

GERHARD NEIZERT AND
HELGA STURSBERG

At nineteen years of age, Gerhard Neizert found himself a draftee in eastern Prussia, a remote part of Germany, on a day he would never forget: June 21, 1941, the day Hitler attacked the Soviet Union.

Gerhard recalled the mild night before, when the sun's faint glow never completely vanished but only faded to gray during the small hours of the next morning and the contours of the trees and bushes remained illuminated until daybreak. The mood of that quiet night was etched in the soldier's mind for more than half a century—and he brought it back to life for me in recall: a still pond, wisps of fog drifting over its surface; a few ducks that flew past; and a large bird, probably a crane, flapping its wings as it landed in the high grass at the far edge of the pond near the forest.

His unit had been stationed in eastern Prussia for several months, cut off from news of home and the war. Their officers had told them that plans were being worked out between Stalin and Hitler to allow the German army to move quickly through southern Russia to assume control over Middle East oilfields under British control. The spoils of that surprise strike would then be shared between the Russians and Germans. As Gerhard lay in wait with the other soldiers, he did not think much about that information. East Prussia was far from home, particularly for one born and raised in the Rhine region of Germany. The moments ticked past in silence. Yet the utter peace of it all was pervaded with a sense of doom.

Gerhard has a special talent for recalling the past, doing so with anecdotes that evoke events in a lively, coherent way. I heard his particular German voice clearly, and it conjured up for me the experiences of many individuals—millions of Germans in uniform. In the lull before the storm, most of these young men did not think primarily of the *Reich* that they represented, but rather of home, where they would have preferred to be.

"And then, at three in the morning on June 21," Gerhard said, "all hell broke loose with a massive German artillery barrage," and the invasion of the Soviet Union began. He now realized with a flash that he was part of a giant machine with all of its wheels churning and no private space left. A Nazi song was composed to celebrate that event in which he was now a participant; it glorified enthusiastic German troops as they jubilantly moved eastward, with "freedom as their goal and victory as their flag." But Gerhard thought of neither freedom nor victory; rather, like

Figure 9. Private Gerhard Neizert in East Prussia, before the invasion of the Soviet Union, 1941.

all those ordered to march into the vast expanses of Russia, he thought of only one thing: getting out alive.

Although Private Neizert was not in the first wave of the German attack, the peace he felt during the hours before the storm was not to return for years. His column of tanks and armored vehicles moved slowly across the border into Russian territory. After several hours they reached their first Russian village, where the column stopped. There was a fountain, and they were very thirsty, but they didn't dare take a drink because they had been told that the water might be poisoned. Thirsty, they waited and listened to the roar of the war ahead of them in the distance. Suddenly, a peasant opened the door to his house and peered up and down the street and at the armed column. Then, with two empty metal pails, he made his way gingerly through the stopped military vehicles and filled his pails with water from the fountain before hurrying back indoors. The soldiers were filled with relief. Now they knew they could drink all the water they wanted before continuing their eastward advance.

Before long, Gerhard saw his first dead soldier, a Russian lying at the side of the road. He was to see many more, both Russians and Germans. And soon thereafter he was in his first skirmish. As a member of a unit of four, he set out in a rubber boat to cross the river Luga. Having arrived on the other side, he and his unit were ambushed. In the fog, they had lost their sense of direction and had wandered into the Russian line. Of the four, only Gerhard made it out alive.

As the soldiers marched deeper into Russia, they all hoped it would "go fast, like in France." Gerhard described the various incidents of the Russian campaign, and they began to blend into one: ducking, running, eating, sleeping, marching, shooting, and more marching through the endless expanse of Russia, most of which lay ahead of them. His months and years of fighting became stations on the way to Russian captivity. "Your senses began to dull after a while, and the atrocities you heard about passed you by, or you repressed them, focused as you were on your own survival. We became small cogs in enormous machinery. Somehow you lost your sense of individuality, you were disenfranchised as a human being," he said, his distinct voice now a whisper.

I asked him whether he saw any Jews while he served in the East. "Once," he replied. "On the way home for furlough, we stopped in a town in eastern Poland and we left the train for a break, and there, near the railroad station, were women and children with the yellow star who offered to polish our boots for a few coins." I sensed Gerhard's reluctance to recall this strange scene, which he obviously found unsettling.

One day the fighting was over. Yet it was only after several years of Russian captivity that Gerhard Neizert could say he had survived World War II. I got the impression that during the war itself he had hunkered down inside as a coping mechanism. Furthermore, there was something different about his manner of recall. As his time in Russia seemed to grow as infinite as the expanse of the territory itself, as the daily fight for survival—of efforts not to be killed, or to kill, and not to be captured, not to freeze to death in winter—took over, his initial ability to make past moments become present began to fade. Thus, the very style of his storytelling—and he was by far the most gifted storyteller of my interviewees—reflected the loss of individuality this contemplative young soldier suffered after leaving the quiet piece of earth in East Prussia on that midsummer's night in 1941.

.   .   .

Helga Stursberg, the woman Gerhard Neizert would eventually marry, was eleven years old on June 21, 1941, living in her parents' comfortable villa in Neuwied on the east bank of the Rhine River. When I spoke with her, her pride in her family was palpable. Her grandfather and father had worked through World

War I and the Great Depression in the 1920s to make a success out of the Friedrich Boesner factory, which produced nuts, bolts, screws, and other metal fasteners for cars, trucks, and, during the war, military vehicles. Helga was particularly proud of her father, whom the entire family admired. A modest, soft-spoken man, he was interested not only in manufacturing but also in art, philosophy, and music. "My father was highly respected in the community," Helga told me. She still loves to recall the long walks her family took on Sundays as the high point of her youth, when she learned more than she did in school—a love for beautiful things, a respect for ethics, and an interest in the world at large.

Helga remembers her mother, who was fifteen years younger than her father, as unconventional, imaginative, and unpretentious. She told me that her mother went shopping in old clothes and the clogs that she wore to work in the garden and fields around their villa. Her mother even tended the family's own little farm, to supplement their food supply as the war wore on.

Over the years, the family business brought the Stursbergs in contact with many Jewish families who lived in the Rhine Valley. Jews had lived in that region of Germany as merchants and artisans for almost a millennium. Helga was a member of the *Bund Deutscher Mädel,* the female equivalent of the Hitler Youth. One of her close girlfriends was Jewish, and Helga was disappointed when she learned that her friend couldn't join because she was Jewish. The BDM leader even reprimanded her for wanting her friend in the organization, saying, "Ein Deutsches Mädchen hilft keinem Juden" (A German girl does not help

Figure 10. Helga Stursberg, 1939.

a Jew). Helga remembers the exact words of this reprimand, which was meant not so much to correct her personal behavior as to make a statement about a "natural law," about what could and should not happen.

By early spring of 1945, the American army had reached the left bank of the Rhine River, and the daily artillery barrage increased as the days went on. When the bombardment grew worse, Helga's family decided to move into the spacious cellars beneath their villa, where they had food supplies and even a small kitchen and bedroom. There they could wait out the war—or at least the passing of the battle lines beyond the Rhine. "Yes, yes, we lived for three weeks down in the cellar; we had a stove, food, enough to eat—potatoes, jars of vegetables prepared for the winter—and all the utensils you needed to run a temporary household." Then, her voice not changing in tone, she said: "We children slept in the cellar located in the middle of the house, our parents in the front cellar, where they were killed. The first American soldier I saw after we were occupied was . . ." Dumbfounded, I stopped her. "Wait a minute, Helga, what was that about your parents?" Ignoring my question, she tried to continue her story, but I didn't let her. "I want to know about your parents."

She finally gave in and, almost with a touch of embarrassment, answered me. "My parents decided to move to the front of the cellar to take a nap, because it was more comfortably arranged. An artillery grenade hit that part of the house. They were killed instantly. If they had stayed in their normal bedroom upstairs, they would have survived." It was March 1945, and Helga was fourteen.

Helga's grandmother then cared for Helga and her brother, who was two years older. One evening, a few months after her parents were killed, Helga went to the graveyard to visit their crypt. An American soldier followed her with "sex on his mind," as she said. He approached her and asked what she was doing there, and she replied, "My parents lie here. They died because of an American grenade." The soldier lowered his head, apologized, and left.

Gerhard and Helga, who were distantly related, met in 1950 at a wedding. They married eight years later. For one thing, Gerhard had to get used to the "new world," as he called it, that he encountered back in Germany after five years as a Soviet POW. He also attended university. Helga told me that he was a shy young man, having spent nine years cut off from women. After marrying in 1958, they worked hard and raised a large family that now includes great-grandchildren.

PRINCE AND PRINCESS
ZU LÖWENSTEIN-WERTHEIM-FREUDENBERG

Even the most imaginative soothsayer could not have conjured in his crystal ball the years that lay ahead of Alfred-Ernst, Prince zu Löwenstein-Wertheim-Freudenberg, and his eventual wife, Ruth-Erika von Buggenhagen, when Hitler took over Germany in 1933. The upheavals of war and the postwar chaos brought them together by chance. Alfred-Ernst, or Butz as family and friends call him, belongs to the landed aristocracy in the province of Franconia, with roots via the noble house of Wittelsbach all the way back to the twelfth century. Ruth-Erika, or Eka as she is called, comes from nobility as well, in her case from a long line of Pomeranian Junkers. One of her forefathers was a close friend of Martin Luther. Stability and permanence have historically characterized Butz and Eka's social class. The mobility of the middle class was not theirs as a given, nor did revolution and radical social change belong to their values. In a way, their aristocratic families had more in common with the peasantry, with whom they shared a devotion to stewarding the land on which they lived and an expert knowledge of crops, forests, underbrush, deer, wild boar, birds, seasons, fires, and droughts.

One strong trait of the German nobility is patriotism and a belief in the country's time-honored traditions—which were a far cry from the principles espoused by the Nazis in their nationalistic revolution. In the end, twenty cousins of the extended zu Löwenstein lineage perished fighting Hitler and his usurpers.

For me, Butz's and Eka's stories of coming home begin with the death of a young lieutenant, Ruth-Erika's brother, Hans-

Bernd von Buggenhagen, the last surviving male member of their ancient family. His letters from the front reveal his conviction that he would die in Russia. In a farewell letter to his parents, he wrote: "Should this letter ever reach you, then I will already have died in battle. I believe I will not come back and I will perish before the enemy. . . . With me our proud family lineage will end, and I will try to die faithful to the tradition befitting a Pomeranian nobleman. I am not sad, but I will give my life in loyalty to the greatness of my fatherland."[6] His last wish was that his remains be brought home and buried on the family's land under trees that he so dearly loved.

The von Buggenhagens made many futile attempts to have his remains returned to them. Hans-Bernd's father, overcoming his distaste for Hitler, pleaded for reburial in a letter addressed directly to the dictator. His desperate request was declined by one of Hitler's adjutants, in a brief note filled with empty bureaucratic slogans of the type that had served the Nazis so well since 1933. Coming home was denied Hans-Bernd, dead or alive. For his part, Hans-Bernd's father, whose health had been compromised by a World War I chest wound, seems to have lost interest in life after the death of his only son, and he succumbed to pneumonia in 1943.

For the rest of the von Buggenhagen family, the ancestral home wound up being lost to them as well. And therein, perhaps, lies the gist of Ruth-Erika's story of the war.

Before the collapse of the Third Reich, Ruth-Erika was a young woman employed as an orderly in a hospital close to the Polish border. When the Russians came, she fled west, back to her home, and found 105 refugees crammed onto their estate; they were lethargic and lacked all initiative. Soon, her family had to prepare its own flight. They hid their valuable china, but freshly poured concrete betrayed the hiding place and marauders ransacked the property. Their silver they hid with the help of a farmhand, who stole it after their departure, they later learned. The mother, Ruth-Erika, and her two sisters packed whatever necessities they could carry and joined the endless trek of Germans fleeing westward to escape the advancing Soviets, but the Russian army was faster and overtook them. Rape, murder, and plundering followed. Ruth-Erika and her younger sister disguised themselves as old women to avoid being raped, but their mother did not escape a severe beating. The damage to one of her knees made walking, let alone marching long distances, excruciatingly painful. They decided it was safer for them to walk at night and in the early morning hours, since most of the Russian soldiers were drunk at that time. Once they slept in the loft of a large barn and had to witness the rapes of young women on the floor below. After that they preferred to sleep outside in potato fields, no matter how cold and wet.

The family, though slowed down by the mother's injury, limped forward, trying to keep each other's spirits up. They had money and managed to buy a horse. Abandoned carts were everywhere, so they took possession of one and were thereafter able to move with greater speed. While they were on the move, they dealt with the fate of all refugees: "Wir standen vor dem Nichts" (We faced an empty void).

Hunger gnawed at them. On one occasion they were lucky to be given a dead rabbit. Gypsies they met on the road had provided them with a knife, so they were able to carve up the animal, cook it, and share it with their temporary companions. Despite the mayhem, Ruth-Erika also remembers bright moments, as when a Baron Tschernikov, extravagantly dressed and accompanied by two pages, appeared out of nowhere to join them. He introduced himself as an opera singer and proceeded to bellow arias across the north German plain, providing convincing proof of his profession. Ruth-Erika was glad for his two male companions, whose presence assured that the baron left the women alone.

The family was relieved when they finally reached territory under British control, but an English officer was under order to turn all refugees back. The four of them refused to turn around, telling him in broken English that they would rather be shot. The officer, saying he couldn't do that, reluctantly allowed the four to continue on their way.

They finally reached the Elbe River and were able to cross it on one of the few intact bridges. On the other side they found bicycles, which they rode in the direction of Lüneburg, where they had relatives. En route, one of their bicycles broke down, and as they tried to fix it, a large man approached. They did not dare look up, because stealing was so common, particularly from defenseless women. When the man finally stood next to them, they realized that he was their cousin. They were safe.

West of the Elbe, the women obtained permission to work on a farm and were assured they wouldn't be sent back to the East as refugees. A hay-filled barn became their domicile, and backbreaking farm work earned them enough food to survive. They had little time to think of what they had left behind—their land, their estate, and the history of their family now uprooted from their home. On one of Ruth-Erika's birthdays, someone wrote a poem to her suggesting that one day she might live on her land again.

Eventually, Ruth-Erika became a helper in the Bremen home of a distant relative of her future husband, the young Prince Alfred-Ernst zu Löwenstein-Wertheim-Freudenberg. The family received generous CARE packages from another relative, Hubertus zu Löwenstein, a Catholic theologian who had fled to the United States after Hitler came to power. Ruth-Erika's fortunes were to improve, although she did not yet know it, when she was asked to present herself in Amorbach in southern Germany to work for the Count of Leiningen. That was where the son of the then Prince zu Löwenstein-Wertheim-Freudenberg showed up on his bicycle one day for a visit. Later, when she worked in Würzburg, Alfred-Ernst continued to ride his bicycle the considerable distance to see her. She later learned that his father had remarked that the friendship must be serious if the lazy young man would undertake such a long, strenuous journey on a bicycle. His father eventually requested that she get a driver's license, but she didn't have the money to pay for it. It was not easy for her to admit to him that she was, despite her aristocratic lineage, now a destitute refugee.

The Nazi assumption of power in 1933 cast its shadow on the baroque castle of the Prince zu Löwenstein and his family in Kreuzwertheim on the Main River. By rights and tradition, the family played an important social role in the region; it was therefore quite naturally in the crosshairs of the Nazis, determined as they were to build a radically new world. Alfred-Ernst remembers three Nazi visits to his family home. The first came when the newly elected mayor of Wertheim, a believer in the *Reich*, insisted that he and his wife be invited to dinner at the castle, so that he could introduce himself as the local Nazi authority. When the old prince saw the mayor and his wife amble up the street for the occasion, the mayor in his fancy SA uniform and his wife dressed in a long evening gown, he became enraged. Though also upset, his wife tried to calm him down. As the unwelcome guests rang the bell for the servants to let them in, Alfred-Ernst's mother recited, half in jest and half in desperation, a famous line from Bach's Christmas Oratorio, "Wie soll ich dich empfangen, und wie begeg'n ich dir?" (How shall I receive thee, how shall I meet thee?), and everyone burst out laughing. The unwelcome dinner went on as planned. The mayor and his wife were satisfied, because they could then tell everyone they had dined at the castle.

Two other visits had nothing to do with Nazi ceremony. In these instances the guests were Gestapo agents. At the first visit, they wanted to know details about the international organization of girls residing in Geneva for which Alfred-Ernst's mother was the chair of the German section. The second, more ominous meeting had to do with one of Alfred-Ernst's uncles, Dr. Richard Merton, a Jew who had converted to Christianity and married into the zu Löwenstein family. At issue was the confiscation of his property. This uncle was imprisoned in the Buchenwald concentration camp, but family connections facilitated his release and he was able to flee to the United States. Alfred-Ernst was young at the time, but he vividly remembers the unpleasant luncheon meeting and the fact that the two Gestapo agents would not touch any food until the family members at the table had tasted it. He realized then that those who feared being poisoned were capable of poisoning others.

Alfred-Ernst was drafted in 1943 into the workers' brigade and later into an elite army division that specialized in counterespionage. Admiral Wilhelm Canaris (who later spied for the

British and was executed by the Nazis) was in charge of counter-espionage. Heinrich Himmler, who had always been suspicious of this special unit not subject to SS control, later managed to have it transformed into a regular fighting division used for special assignments.

The young prince's aristocratic background was both an advantage and a disadvantage, as Alfred-Ernst told me. On the one hand, while he was in training two of his sergeants took great delight in subjecting him to especially hard drills. His connections, on the other hand, helped him get assigned to duty in southern France, rather than to the Balkans.

The SS, however, dissatisfied with the elite unit's efforts to contain the French resistance, took all initiatives away from them. As Alfred-Ernst related his story in a slow and deliberate fashion, carefully searching for the proper phrase or word, his dislike for the SS, which he had learned at home, was apparent. He called them a *Sauhaufen* (a rude bunch of pigs). His unit's assignment was to send coded messages to the German army headquarters in Berlin, but it was an exercise in futility, he said, because no one in Berlin trusted their messages. He remembers in particular one message that warned of the impending Allied landing on the coast of southern France. The answer came back that a landing was not possible—yet it indeed came to pass.

Of all of the Germans I interviewed, Alfred-Ernst came across as one particularly ill suited to fight, spy, or simply have weapons in his hands intended to kill other human beings. He showed little interest in discussing his life as a soldier in occupied France, which seemed to have left him with few memorable impressions. His narrative came alive, however, with graphic detail, when he recalled the withdrawal of German forces to the *Reich* and his own road home to the Main River as soon as he thought it prudent, as he put it, to "take the law into my own hands."

After moving into Germany from France, his unit was stationed atop a hill near Darmstadt, and he was able to observe American tanks crossing the Rhine near Worms in great numbers. What he saw contradicted the headquarters' radio broadcast from Berlin—that the Allied attempt to cross the Rhine had been prevented. On the contrary, the American tanks were rolling by so fast that his small army radio unit soon found themselves in no-man's land. That suited the country prince just fine. After all, the Germans were retreating in the general direction of his home. He and his comrades loaded their belongings onto a small truck and took off. But Alfred-Ernst did not want to sit on the truck, so he took a bicycle and rode alongside, holding on to the truck on level and uphill stretches and passing it on downhill stretches. In spite of a strafing attack by low-flying American fighter planes, they reached the Main River just a few miles from Freudenberg, a village that provided his family with part of its name.

Going home was all that mattered to the young prince. He almost made it to the castle at Kreuzwertheim, where he could have hidden in one of its many nooks and crannies until the end of the war, but German military police caught him and put him in prison across the river in Wertheim. An officer with the rank of major, who knew Private Alfred-Ernst zu Löwenstein to be a prince, interrogated him. In the interview, the major, who could easily have ordered his execution, addressed him as

"Your Highness." The interrogating officer even granted him a twenty-four-hour furlough to visit his parents.

The furlough passed, but the war was not yet over. Alfred-Ernst was still in the uniform of a German private, and he joined up with a unit of soldiers who were heading from Wertheim to nearby Rohrbrunn, at the same time that the entire German army was in a general retreat from Allied forces. This small group managed to steal official stamps and forge marching papers that enabled each of them to find his way home as best he could. When Alfred-Ernst returned to his family's castle, some towns and villages in the Main River Valley, Wertheim among them, were hoisting white flags to greet the American victors. Rumor had it, however, that the SS would take revenge on any towns that surrendered. The zu Löwensteins decided to defend themselves against a possible SS raid, distributing guns to family members and servants and coming up with a battle plan. It never came to a showdown, but the rumor about SS reprisals was true, as I learned many years later from a UC Berkeley colleague, George Leitman, a Jewish German-American who served as an interpreter at the Nuremberg Trials. When Leitman's army unit liberated Aschaffenburg, which lay between Wertheim and Frankfurt on the Main River, they were horrified to find the corpses of ten teenage boys hanging from lampposts. The boys had hoisted white flags and were strung up by the SS shortly before Leitman's unit arrived.

Despite Alfred-Ernst's best efforts, the Americans eventually captured him. He spent a few months in an American POW camp, where the treatment was harsh. But unlike his brother-in-law, Hans-Bernd von Buggenhagen, whose fate willed that he

Figure 11. Princess Ruth-Erika and Prince Alfred-Ernst zu Löwenstein-Wertheim-Freudenberg, 2007.

die in Russia, Alfred-Ernst finally came home, and civilian life resumed for him. On a visit to relatives in the Odenwald in the fall of 1947, he met his future wife, Ruth-Erika. They became engaged in secret, though his father decreed an official engagement date of June 26, 1948.

The hectic period of Nazi hysteria was finally gone from their lives, and the slow pace of aristocratic life emerged again. Butz and Eka did not marry until 1954. They then raised a large family in the castle he inherited, and developed a wide circle of friends. For decades following the war, they played an important role in the local German-American association, consisting of Germans and primarily American military personnel, and they remain life enhancers to the present day, touching everyone who comes in contact with them, regardless of background or status, with their straightforward, kind manner and good humor. Their nobility is one of the heart, something the war and the Nazis couldn't destroy.

THE BERTSCH FAMILY

What I initially knew about the Bertsch family was overshadowed by one stark fact: the patriarch, Walter Bertsch, had worked for a while with *SS-Obergruppenführer* (Senior Group Leader or SS General) Reinhard Heydrich, the key organizer of the Holocaust. Even though his son, Werner Bertsch, defended him, saying that as an economist on Heydrich's staff his father was not involved in planning and executing the genocide, I was tempted to dismiss this family as morally tainted by its association with the architect of the genocide. Did I really need to know more? In time, though, I decided that my moral condemnation was blinding me to history. And indeed, there was much more to the family than I had assumed.

By the time I interviewed Werner Bertsch for the second time, in April 2005, I had been acquainted with him for several years. A tall, friendly man, with striking angular features, he

Figure 12. Werner Bertsch, 2007.

met me near the famous cathedral in his hometown of Ulm. He was eager to tell me about the city, with its proud history, explaining that it was an important center of commerce during the late Middle Ages, as well as the birthplace of Albert Einstein. As director of an important local bank, Werner had raised money to reconstruct a side gate of the cathedral that once allowed artisans and workers to enter the holy site while it was being built. He suggested an insider's tour of the cathedral before our interview, which I readily accepted. As we entered the cathedral, Werner noticed that I was cold. It was only a few degrees above zero, and inside the cathedral it felt clammy and damp. He removed his thick wool scarf and wrapped it around my neck to keep me warm. He wouldn't take it back until we entered his apartment.

As we got started, he seemed to be struggling with the most appropriate way to begin his story. Eventually he said, "Ich beginne mit meinem Vater, Walter Bertsch" (I'll start with my father, Walter Bertsch). He then traced the history of a man who had a "brilliant civil service career as a legal expert on economic issues," which led him from pre-Nazi days in southern Germany to an appointment in Berlin in 1936 to work in the Nazi regime's ministry of economic affairs. The upward trajectory of his career gained him an important post in the German-occupied territory of Czechoslovakia in 1939, in the *Hauptabteilung Wirtschaft* (central office of economic affairs). His boss, *Freiherr* (baron) von Neurath, was the one responsible for bringing him to Prague. Werner Bertsch wanted me to know that von Neurath had been a former foreign minister, respected by the British. The notorious Reinhard Heydrich replaced him in 1941, shortly after Germany attacked the Soviet Union, because the Nazis considered von Neurath "too soft" on the Czechs, who, as fellow Slavs, supported the Russians. Heydrich kept Bertsch on because, as Werner explained, "he respected my father highly for his exceptional qualifications as a civil servant."

Walter Bertsch's job was to select Czechs to work in the German war industry. Initially, Werner said, Czechs applied for work in the *Reich*, but as the war progressed and conditions worsened for "foreign workers" in Nazi Germany, qualified Czechs workers were forced to go there. Werner avoided the term *slave labor*. A German newspaper article of January 1942 announced the promotion of Dr. Walter Bertsch to the ministry of economics; another article on the same page talked about the need for greater productivity in German industry for the war effort.[7]

Werner's father eventually became the German liaison to the Czech puppet government. In his oversight functions, Walter

Bertsch was charged with making sure the economic policies of the *Reich* were carried out by the Czech regime. I was struck by the steady climb of this career civil servant up the ladder, beginning in pre-Nazi Germany and continuing on into the vortex of the genocide.

After the war, the Czech government sentenced Walter Bertsch to life imprisonment. A number of key witnesses at his trial, although officially opposed to the Nazi regime, spoke out on behalf of his moral uprightness and testified that he was a "decent man, and always correct in dealing with the Czechs." Werner employed the term *correct* several times. "My father always acted correctly," he said, "and he never sent a single person to any concentration camp." Werner tried very hard to erect protective insulation around his father, to distance him from his boss. Yet, he admitted with a sad ring in his voice, "I guess his ambitions got the better of him, and he became entangled in the regime"—though perhaps, he speculated, the charismatic power of Heydrich's personality left Walter Bertsch little choice. He quoted a statement his mother made about Heydrich after the war: "He possessed the kind of personality that would make it possible for him to sign someone's death sentence with one hand and present flowers of deep regret to surviving family members with the other hand." In other words, he was a sociopath, who maintained a screen between his private sense of self and his public actions.

The family stayed in Prague almost until the end of the war. On April 4, 1945, Werner, his mother, and his younger brother finally fled west. Before their departure, Walter Bertsch told Werner, then fourteen, to look after the others and himself. Thus, as a young teenager, Werner was cast into the role of the man of the family, its protector and its hope for survival. Although his parents no longer believed in a final victory, Werner, in his youthful naiveté, still did. He felt ambiguous about their flight because of the potential embarrassment he would suffer if they were ever to return to Prague, where he might be accused of cowardice by schoolmates who had stayed and whose families, too, believed in a final victory. The family never saw their father again, for he died in a Czech prison in 1952. Werner's mother, however, never wavered in her loyalty to her husband and kept a candle burning next to his photo until she died. And Werner came to see himself as the defender of his father's decency, in spite of his father's proximity to Heydrich.

Werner Bertsch then added a twist to his family's history that surprised me. "I did not know until after the war that I had an uncle, and that he was married to a Jewish woman. If I had known it, it would have thrown me into an inner turmoil." His mother had not told her sons that she had a brother who left for Palestine in 1933. The Nazis in essence cut the family ties to various members who had taken wildly divergent paths. Yet as soon as Hitler was gone and the war over, both sides of the family—Walter Bertsch's widow, her brother, Max, and his Jewish wife, Dola—made contact and met at the Swiss-German border.

The amazing turn in the Bertsch family's history is that their Jewish relative in Israel, Dola, happened to be the daughter of Eliezer Ben-Yehuda, one of the founding fathers of modern Zionism and an early advocate of Hebrew as the official language of Israel, even prior to the creation of that state. Werner's son, Matthias, born in 1966, was Dola's favorite nephew. When she died in November 2004 at the age of 102, Matthias, a bright,

Figure 13. Dola Ben-Yehuda Wittmann and Matthias Bertsch, in Israel, 1995.

articulate, upbeat journalist, represented his family and spoke at her funeral at the Hebrew University in Jerusalem.

During several long-distance phone calls, Matthias filled me in on some details about the German-Jewish marriage in his family's past. His maternal grandmother's brother, Max Wittmann, was to inherit the family's factory in Germany. In 1931, Max met the daughter of Ben-Yehuda in Paris. They fell in love and married. When Hitler came to power, the Nazis advised Max to divorce his Jewish wife; otherwise, he would have difficulties keeping the family's firm in business. Max Wittmann refused to divorce the woman he loved. But at the same time, he did not want to destroy the family's firm. His only choice was to leave Germany, which he and his wife did in 1933, settling in Palestine, where they lived out their lives.

Matthias met his great-uncle Max and Max's wife, Dola, when he was eighteen, on a visit to Israel as part of a student exchange program. About ten years later, as he was about to finish his university studies, he met with Dola a number of times during another visit. His parents supported his interest in Israel and helped finance his trips.

Matthias now became curious about his grandfather, Walter, and especially about his activities in Prague. Walter had always been a strange and abstract figure for him, someone Matthias regarded as a *Nazi Täter* (Nazi activist or perpetrator) but without attaching any particular feelings to him. To this day, Matthias still wonders what the exact duties of his grandfather were, beyond selecting Czechs for work in German factories, first on a voluntary basis and later as victims of forced labor. Vis-à-vis his father, Werner, Matthias, as a politically radical younger German, at one time had trouble accepting his father's "commitment to capitalism," tempered though it is by a commitment to social equity derived from his Protestant faith.

Young Matthias's best friend at this writing is Jewish-American. This close and abiding friendship has nothing to do with expiating the sins of his forefathers. Rather, Matthias told me how unburdened and free he felt as a teenager during his first visit to Israel, and how much he enjoyed his camaraderie with the Israeli participants in the youth exchange program. His easygoing and communicative personality came out even through our telephone conversations, and I wasn't surprised to learn that Matthias possesses friends all over the world.

Werner finished our session by telling me of his family's fate after the war. He initially became a stonemason to support the family; only later was he able to study law as the foundation for a career in finance. It struck me how closely the careers of the two older male members of the Bertsch family matched on the level of professional expertise, yet how differently their careers played themselves out within society as a whole—the older Bertsch as an executive in the Nazi reign over Czechoslovakia, and the younger Bertsch as a contributor to the economic miracle of the new, postwar Germany. Werner admitted to me that it was Matthias, the youngest Bertsch, who convinced him that his father's entanglement in the Nazi regime could not be ignored.

After our interview, as we again walked through the streets of Ulm, I felt in good company, knowing that a fine human being driven by high ethical ideals walked beside me. The day before my departure, Werner gave me a large envelope of printed and typed materials and photos that illustrated his family's history in the twentieth and twenty-first centuries—a history situated between the mass murderer Reinhard Heydrich and a founder of Israel, Eliezer Ben-Yehuda. In the envelope were, among other things, newspaper clippings about Walter Bertsch's promotion to minister of economics in the Nazi puppet government of Czechoslovakia, photos of Matthias with Dola Ben-Yehuda, and copies of funeral orations from Hebrew University that celebrated her life.

DIETER VON LERSNER

Anyone acquainted with the city of Frankfurt will have seen the *Römer*, the three Gothic step-gabled houses that were once Frankfurt's city hall. One of the three houses is the ancient seat of the illustrious patrician house of Limpurg, which, closely tied to the fortunes of the city, has been involved in international

finance and commerce throughout its modern history. The Limpurg family was known not only for its wealth and social status,
but also for its charitable work on behalf of the poor, old, and
sick. This tradition of charity continues today, under the watchful eye of the current head of the family, Dieter von Lersner. My
wife, Sally, and I got to know Dieter and his wife, Ruth, on long
walks in the snow of the Italian Alps during several of the yearly
conferences of the *Wirtschaftsgilde,* to which we all belong. Before
I began research on this book, we had conversed primarily about
religion and capitalism. Like many Germans of his generation,
Dieter believes that the profit motive should be tempered and
controlled by ethical considerations that take into account the
disadvantaged. We never talked about the Nazi period, at least
not until I began work on this project. Even then, he was one of
the last people I interviewed.

Since I held many interviews in the alpine hotel, I needed a
large, comfortable room that was easily accessible. Dieter offered
his room, because it was centrally located. When I finally turned
on my tape recorder to interview him, I could not believe what
I heard—that Dieter and his family had believed in the righteousness of the Nazi cause to the very end of the war, in fact
until May 8, 1945, the day of the official capitulation of the *Reich.*
I could not square this with the impression I had gained of a
kind, modest, thoughtful man. I now recorded his memories. He
told his story in a straightforward manner, without excuses or
subterfuges of any sort.

He had been an ardent member of the *Jungvolk,* where he
advanced to the high rank of *Jungstammführer* (a Hitler Youth
leader), in charge of 480 boys between the ages of ten and fourteen. (To retain his title and influence, he did not join the Hitler

Youth but stayed in the *Jungvolk*.) As he moved up further in the *Jungvolk* ranks, he was chosen to attend several indoctrination camps that would prepare him to become part of the young Nazi elite.

Dieter is one of the few Germans I know who actually read Hitler's autobiography, *Mein Kampf.* The central message he carried away from Hitler's creed was that the strong win. His father had been an ardent member of a World War I veterans organization and helped drill this into him as a powerful mantra. In his history lessons at the time, the Vikings, who were presented as an example of a powerful people who ranged far and wide to conquer and rule, particularly impressed Dieter. He and his like-minded compatriots inherited what they considered a duty to keep alive that Viking spirit and to translate it into twentieth-century terms. Dieter related this to me with a strange air of detachment, suffused with sadness. Recalling the intoxicating feeling of control his rank bestowed upon him, he said, "There is no way to explain to someone raised in the spirit of democracy what it means to a sixteen-year-old to lead 480 young Germans and to march in front of them in a parade."

Dieter von Lersner lived with his family in Potsdam near Berlin. At the time, a German officer and member of the *Oberkommando des Heeres* (High Command of the German army) was stationed in their house, and he became a family friend. Dieter was proud that a man of such distinction lived under their roof. But the family went into shock when, on July 20, 1944, they learned of the attempt on Hitler's life and, the next day, July 21, an SS squad car arrived to arrest their houseguest—Captain Friedrich Karl Klausing, one of the conspirators in the plot against Hitler. Klausing's job had been to keep at the ready an airplane for Claus von Stauffenberg, the head of the conspiracy, who had placed the bomb next to Hitler that failed to kill him. The Nazis brutally executed the von Lersners' houseguest.

The resultant confusion in the von Lersner household was total. All Dieter can remember is a phrase that his family repeated over and over again: "That young kid, that young kid . . . *[Das Jüngelchen, das Jüngelchen . . .]*, how could he, of all people, have done this?"

At the beginning of 1945, the Russians were closing in on Berlin. Dieter von Lersner was drafted, and one of his recruiting officers said to him that the war would be lost. Dieter asked his mother for her reaction to this prediction. "Let's hope that this is incorrect," she replied, "because if it were to be true, what would happen afterward?" A future after the collapse of the regime was simply unimaginable for this family.

Dieter was wounded shortly before the end of the war. On the day of the *Reich*'s capitulation, he wrote in his diary, "We have certainly been betrayed."

After our interview, I told my wife, Sally, about his honest account of his past as a teenager in Hitler's Germany and how hard it was for me to connect the Dieter I knew with the youthful Dieter. She mentioned to me an exchange she had had with Dieter on one of our snowy walks several years earlier, when he told her that he could forgive neither himself nor the Germans for what they had done. I felt moved by his remorse but also puzzled. How, I wondered, could this soft-spoken, kind, and decent man, who for many years taught history to young people, who came from a distinguished family that represented some of the finest German traditions—how could he have been taken in by the Nazi movement? The standard answers—poverty; anti-

Semitism, no parental guidance—did not apply. Dieter's parents were not poor; anti-Semitism does not seem to have played a role, though the chaos of Weimar may have had an influence; and Dieter's parents set a pattern of belief that Dieter followed. There was of course the heady seduction of the Hitler Youth. But Dieter's circumstances do not explain the level of the family's commitment to the Nazi regime.

One clue may have lain in the personal beliefs of the young von Lersner. The family did not drop their Christian faith to follow the pagan, Teutonic religion espoused by Nazi ideology but remained active churchgoers during Hitler's Germany. In fact, many Germans, their roots deeply embedded in Christian ethics, were originally attracted to Nazism because of the movement's broad-based social program to help the poor and provide medical care for the sick.

After the war, while a graduate student at the University of Tübingen, Dieter wrote a master's dissertation, "Die evangelischen Jugendverbände Württembergs und die Hitler-Jugend, 1933/1934," about the interface between the Protestant youth organizations and the emerging Hitler Youth in the southern German state of Württemberg from 1933 to 1934.[8] In it, he detailed the slow demise of these Christian youth movements as they proved unable to maintain their own identity and still cooperate with the Nazis.

Dieter cited a revealing incident that took place in the small town of Blaubeuren, when Protestant youths tried to march through the street carrying a swastika, and Hitler Youths took the flag away from them, declaring they had no right to identify themselves with the Nazi flag and the Hitler Youth. It was just a matter of time until the Hitler Youth swallowed up and per-

verted the causes of the Protestant and Catholic youth movements, as well as the many German Boy Scout organizations.

These historical explanations go only so far in explaining Dieter's path to leadership in the Nazi youth movement,
however. Apparently he was simply carried away by a sense
of idealism. Once inside the system, very few possessed a sufficiently strong, independent self to resist, or at least to reflect
critically on their political commitments. Instead, leading several hundred young German boys provided a sort of intoxicating legitimacy.

Most of Dieter's life, of course, was lived after the Nazi
period. He has always been a proud member of his illustrious
family, with its roots in Frankfurt. Over the decades, the family has grown, and its members have been successful in the new
Germany, contributing to its wealth and welfare. At this writing,
the family is in the process of creating a private trust fund of
30 million Euros to finance the construction of a hospital.

KLAUS TIEDJE

In my mind, the story of Klaus Tiedje, born in 1926, is paradig-
matic for an entire generation of Germans, with his experiences
echoing those of so many of us. One of Klaus's earliest memories
is of the cold winter of 1929, when the Rhine River froze over. He
remembers a group of shivering men who were singing around
a piano on a street in Cologne, trying to earn spare change with
their music. Also etched in his mind was an unemployed book
dealer who arrived at the Tiedjes' home to beg for soup. The
phrase "Hurrah, wir haben Brot!" (Hurrah, we have bread!) still
echoes positively in his mind.

A peaceful world seemed to surround the young boy during the 1930s. He and I both heard phrases from our elders that stuck with us: "The state cares for the poor"; "Thank goodness we're no longer at war"; "No one goes hungry anymore"; "Let's collect pennies for the poorest among us." Klaus and his upper-middle-class family enjoyed the thirties as "die Sommer unserer Unschuld" (the summers of our innocence), and that is how many of my generation remember it as well. The phrase does not just reflect nostalgia for the bygone days of youth; it also suggests that times were improving, dark confusion and stark poverty being left behind, thanks to the rise of the National Socialists. And of course, for young Germans there were the drums, fifes, campfires, and songs about the great world that Germany would build and its youth would inherit.

Aside from the innocence of youth that most of us experienced in the thirties, Klaus recalls an incident that impressed on him the strange link between aesthetics and power. "I remember—I was approximately eleven years old at the time—when I sat in a streetcar opposite a youthful, blond, very elegant SS officer. His legs, clad in stylish boots, were crossed casually, and he stared absent-mindedly into the distance. He was quite aware of the impression he made. The cold distance coupled with elegance was fascinating and captivating. At the same time, it also signaled an indistinct danger. This uncanny feeling has stayed with me to the present day."

In August 1939, when he was thirteen, Klaus's peaceful world changed toward the end of his family's summer vacation. All of a sudden, his family broke off their holidays at the Elbe River delta on the North Sea and boarded a train south. En route, they changed trains at a station where his father and uncle met up.

Figure 14. Klaus Tiedje, standing apart from companions in the mountains, 1943.

The two men had an intense conversation out of earshot of the others. Klaus remembers their serious facial expressions and the ominous atmosphere that enveloped the family as it stood on the platform waiting for the next train. He knew that something important had happened. Less than two weeks later, war was declared.

In 1943, Klaus was seventeen and part of an anti-aircraft gunnery near Stuttgart. "I wanted to be a soldier." However, when he tried to remove the armband swastika worn by the Hitler Youth and don military paraphernalia instead, he got into a fight with one of the Hitler Youth leaders. By the next year, the danger of being drafted into the *Waffen-SS* was real, and to avoid this possibility he volunteered for the mountain troopers. "We were taught that bravery was everything; they never told us that the enemy had bigger and better weapons than we did."

Klaus Tiedje's father was a renowned architect who played a role in the construction of the *Autobahnen*. In this capacity, the father had contacts with Nazis in charge of labor, industry, and economic planning, but he avoided joining the Nazi Party until 1940. Although Klaus more or less embraced the Nazi regime as he grew into his early teens, he first became critical when, as a soldier, he had the opportunity to take a good look at the castlelike fortress of *Ordensburg* Sonthofen. Something about this school built by the Nazis to train the next generation of leaders unsettled him. He concluded that the spirit behind this architecture was unkind, even hostile.

During the final days of the war, Klaus was lucky to have an army superior who was not a Nazi fanatic and who assured the young recruits that, if he could help it, none of them would get killed. By then, Klaus had had enough. He abandoned his unit and slogged homeward throughout the waning winter days of the war until he reached the house of their family's servants. Assuming he was safe, he entered the house. He was greeted, however, not by a familiar face, but by a French officer. Klaus Tiedje immediately became a POW of the French army and was shipped off to Bayonne and a harsh incarceration. There he was confronted with photos of Nazi atrocities committed in the concentration camps. Assuming it was Allied propaganda intended to break their spirits, at that time he did not believe what he was shown.

The French authorities organized a "camp university" for the inmates, and Klaus was eager to join. The officer in charge of the camp noticed his enthusiasm and had him help prepare lectures. By nature curious and eager for personal contact, Klaus jumped beyond the walls of hostility to approach an officer with a straightforward admission of his desire to get to know France in a better way than through the camp. The French officer gave him the kind of pithy reply for which the French are known— "An excellent idea." A few questions and answers followed. Then the French officer suggested to the young German that he write the Sorbonne for their admission requirements. In due time, and even though he didn't know much French, Klaus received a positive reply from the university, with the proviso that he show evidence of a German exam corresponding to the French baccalaureate. With the Sorbonne letter in hand, he returned home in June 1947.

It took him a long time to gather together the necessary paperwork and obtain a visa for France, but Klaus did not give up. From Germany he wrote to the home address in Oran, Algeria, of the friendly French officer, and he also contacted another officer in charge of Franco-German cultural exchanges organized by the French Allied occupation army. To his great surprise, French occupation authorities in Stuttgart contacted him and informed him that he had been accepted to study law and economics at the Sorbonne. With the financial help of an aunt in New York, he became a student in Paris in September 1949. There he had a reunion with the French camp officer, and he deepened his ties to France, its people, culture, and history. Later, those ties extended beyond him to the lives of his children. One of his sons married a Frenchwoman and settled in the Alsatian region of France. Of his seventeen grandchildren, three are French, he reports proudly, and two Norwegian.

Toward the end of our interview, I asked Klaus Tiedje what attracted him most to France. His answer was specific: early Gothic architecture, particularly the cathedral at Chartres. The twelfth-century France of Abelard and Bernard de Clairvaux represents for him the high point of European culture. He added that viewing the Chartres cathedral for the first time was an epiphany for him. Thus, two monuments of European architecture—the Nazi *Ordensburg* Sonthofen and Notre-Dame de Chartres—helped define Klaus Tiedje's life. Both experiences are still very much with him today: the intuition that there was something hostile in the façade of the Nazi castle, where the party's future elite was indoctrinated, on the one hand, and the beauty and inspiration that he saw in the soaring, structured ascent of the Gothic church, on the other. For Klaus Tiedje, the road from one to the other was long and tortuous. Yet it was also the road that Germany took back to Europe from the xenophobic isolation of Nazism.

HANS-BERNHARD BOLZA-SCHÜNEMANN

My final interview was with Hans-Bernhard Bolza-Schünemann. We sat by a window in his home. Outside, an icy wind dusted snow off of bare tree limbs in his winter-white garden. A trim, dapper man of eighty at the time of our interview, with hardly any gray hair, he still speaks with a north German accent, although he lived most of his life in Würzburg, northern Bavaria. He reminded me of the quintessential uncle we all knew when we were little, the one with the ready smile and the candies in his pockets. But the city beyond his wintry garden held other memories.

Würzburg was almost completely destroyed during the last few months of the war. Streets were turned into low hills of rubble and pockmarked by craters, making parts of town you knew well just a few weeks earlier completely unfamiliar. But this past didn't seem to carry much weight as we began our interview. Now retired, Dr. Bolza-Schünemann has been a man of action. The present and future were always more interesting to him than the past.

Born Hans-Bernhard Schünemann in 1926, he, like all Germans of his generation, had a history before 1945. While his story is very much his own, a thread runs through it that I found in many of his contemporaries' stories. He was, of course, a member of the Hitler Youth, and he collected stamps that celebrated various triumphs of the Nazi movement. He heard the propaganda about the Germans' lack of territory—*ein Volk ohne Raum* (a people without space): we all knew that slogan, with its claustrophobic subtext. From his elders, he heard about the shame and suffering the Versailles Treaty had caused Germany after World War I. And then, there were the Olympic Games of 1936 in Berlin. Bernhard was lucky to have a grandfather who lived near this grand happening, so he saw it all firsthand—the enthusiastic crowds, the applauding visitors from abroad, the flags and fanfares, the athletes marching into the stadium that Hitler had built to celebrate the new Germany.

Since he had always been interested in the sea, Bernhard joined the marine division of the Hitler Youth. His father and stepfather had taught him early on how to sail and how to tie sailor's knots—as he remarked in the slangy dialect of his youth, "Da haste was von" (That's something useful). Toward the end of the war, Bernhard was drafted. He manned the *FLAK* or

Fliegerabwehrkanonen (anti-aircraft artillery) aimed at the Allied planes that bombed the city of Bremen. He remembers the firestorm in Hamburg that reduced thousands of civilians into horrifying charred stumps. With a shudder he told me, "I saw an entire hospital explode," adding in his straightforward manner: "I was furious."

His father owned a printing company, but since he refused to join the Nazi Party, he was demoted and allowed to work only as a technical director in his own firm. A Nazi was put in charge, since independent printing presses had been outlawed. Bernhard remembers how the firm celebrated an anniversary in 1943. Although he had contributed nothing to the success of the firm, the Nazi bureaucrat gave the keynote speech, while Bernhard's father, the real owner, businessman, and engineer, had to sit and listen. Afterward, there was to be a reception at the Schünemanns' villa, and Bernhard vividly recalls the fit his grandmother threw before the guests arrived. "Ich will die braunen Scheißer nicht sehen" (I don't want to see these brown [Nazi] shitheads), she shouted. Full of consternation, his father pleaded with her: "You must be quiet this very instant. You are causing us great difficulties!" Bernhard remembers the exact words.

At that point—he was seventeen—there were serious tensions within his family. The family had lost control over the firm they had built up over many decades, yet they wanted to preserve their presence in it to the degree possible. The battle lines were therefore drawn between those who wished to behave in an accommodating manner toward the Nazis and those who did not. Bernhard reports this without elaboration, but it seemed quite clear to me that the family's split over tactics vis-à-vis the

Nazis was more traumatic for him than the fact that his parents had divorced a few years earlier.

Bernhard was eventually assigned to a special radar unit of the German military, where he could apply the knowledge of high-frequency technology he had learned in an elite school in 1943. The Germans had some success with this technology, which enabled their anti-aircraft weapons to zero in on Allied bombers during their runs over Germany. After a while, however, the Allies camouflaged their planes by releasing aluminum strips high in the sky, a tactic that made them all but invisible to surveillance equipment.

Toward the end of the war Bernhard was drafted into the regular German army, and he immediately volunteered to help repair a high-frequency installation that the Dutch resistance had destroyed. He had barely arrived in Holland when he was captured, "on a fine, sunny spring day," he said with a smile. He was nineteen when Hitler's "Thousand-Year *Reich*" came to an end. The sense of defeat that he, like most Germans, felt had less to do with the collapse of Nazism than with the defeat of his country. But within a decade, Bernhard's real life took off—in America. As he related this part of his life, the entire tone of his narrative changed.

At the zero hour, Bernhard was a young man with huge promise. In 1951, the engineering skills he had learned in his father's firm in Bremen landed him a job with Koenig & Bauer, the oldest, most prestigious German printing press manufacturing firm in Germany, founded in 1817. There he designed a new type of printing press. When a company in Dayton, Ohio, placed an order for one of these presses, he begged his managing director, Dr. Hans Bolza, a great-grandson of one of the firm's founders, to allow him to assemble it himself. He made the request, he said, not only to help the company gain a foothold in the United States, but also to get to know America firsthand.

He became quite animated as he related the story of his first trip to the United States, which poured out of him as if it had just happened. "Das war eines der großen Erlebnisse meines Lebens" (That was one of the great experiences of my life). When he left for the New World in 1955 to begin his adventure, most of Würzburg was still in ruins. After finishing his business in Ohio, he flew west to Los Angeles, taking in the huge landscape beneath him, the cornfields of the Middle West, the Rockies, the dry deserts, deep canyons, more mountain ranges, and finally, the vast Pacific. This was for him the land of unlimited possibility, not as abstract ideology, not as a utopia of the sort touted by the Nazis in his youth, but one that had to do with personal challenges and the opportunity to develop all of one's talents—"to make it on your own." It was the first of many business trips Bernhard would make to the United States, but as such, it always remained special, as an adventure into an enticing world with open doors and minds.

In 1959 he traveled by train from Chicago to Oakland on the *California Zephyr*. For two days he took it all in slowly from the ground—Iowa, Nebraska, the North Platte River . . . Only an occasional train whistle suggested a railroad crossing somewhere in the vast expanse of land. America. He fell in love with this country—the young German engineer, who a few years before had struggled in the ruined cities of his homeland.

The expansiveness he saw in the American landscape also shaped his professional ambitions. As an inventor and engineer, he soon became the right-hand man of Hans Bolza, who was rebuilding his venerable firm out of the ruins of the war. His American business partners respected Bernhard Schünemann for his expertise and can-do attitude. With the principle of printing "faster and more" inspiring him to design ever-better machines, he made a success of the American branch of his firm. Eventually Koenig & Bauer had become a large multinational corporation, with 85 percent of its business done outside the borders of Germany, not only in the United States and Canada, but throughout the entire world.

One day in 1960, Dr. Bolza summoned Bernhard Schünemann to his villa for a conversation. "The old man," as Bernhard calls him, announced: "I want to adopt you." Bernhard did not at first understand. He replied that babies were adopted, but not grown men in their thirties whose parents were alive. When he got home, he reported to his wife, "Something funny happened today at my boss's villa."

Bolza had no sons. One was killed in the war and the other in a car accident. Of his three daughters, one was married in France, a second suffered from infantile paralysis, and a third was interested in neither engineering nor business. Herr Bolza had done his homework. After the war, German adoption laws were liberalized in an attempt to aid the many orphans and widowed mothers with children. They also helped Hans Bolza adopt an heir who was capable of owning and managing his prestigious and time-honored enterprise.

All members of both families had to agree to the adoption. Bernhard's own father encouraged him, saying that if Bernhard were to return to Bremen to run the family printing press business, he would spend his life printing small orders of calling cards or labels for cans of herring. Dr. Bolza's firm, in

Figure 15. Hans-Bernhard Bolza-Schünemann, 2005.

contrast, was the wave of the future. So it happened that Bern-hard Schünemann became Bernhard Bolza-Schünemann, chief engineer and inventor, as well as owner and chief executive. This greatly increased his effectiveness in dealings with American clients, because he could sign contracts on the spot.

Bernhard's adoption signified the new Germany that emerged after World War II, in which individualism and talent replaced genealogy and the blood that had occupied such a deadly place in the Nazi arsenal.

Before I left Würzburg, Bernhard and I spoke about the future, with its gathering clouds since the turn of the millennium. Bernhard is not given to abstractions, so he started to talk about his family. One son, who is now the CEO of Koenig & Bauer, is so pro-American that he built himself an American ranch-style house in Germany, importing the wood from the United States, as well as the carpenters, plumbers, and electricians to build it. The result is a home that is American right down to the doorknobs and toilet seats.

When Bernhard mentioned the generation beyond, his face was animated by a big smile. "Oh, yes, I have smart grandchildren too, including one particularly intelligent grandson." When I asked what interested this grandson, his answer came quickly: "Computer science and the Chinese language."

CHAPTER FIVE

German Soldiers Write Home

From my mother's sleep I fell into the State,
And I hunched in its belly till my wet fur froze.
Six miles from earth, loosed from its dream of life,
I woke to black flak and the nightmare fighters.
When I died they washed me out of the turret with
a hose.

Randall Jarrell, "The Death of the Ball Turret
Gunner," 1945

Kurt Weidemann left his wartime diaries locked up for over
fifty years. He told the German journalist Marlis Prinzing that
when he finally opened them, he feared he might encounter a
Nazi soldier in his younger self; instead he found a patriot critical of the Nazi regime but interested in defending his country.[1]
In 2002, these writings were published under the title *Kaum ich*
(Barely myself). In it, he shows himself to be an observant, sensitive writer. On June 3, 1941, for example, stationed near the
Soviet border, he wrote: "I am sitting on an old wooden beam.
Two calves are looking up at me with curiosity. The storks above
me on the roof have curled up their necks and placed their beaks

on their breasts. Far away, I can see meadows, forests, rows of trees . . . and the open evening sky. It is lonesome, cool and still just right for loving this land."[2]

How is it that this soldier, like so many others, believed he was performing a patriotic duty to defend his country in World War II, while fighting alongside him was a fanatic minority of young men who were willing to lay down their lives for the Nazi cause?

THE FATAL HANDSHAKE

On March 21, 1933, not long after the crucial election that installed the Nazis in power, Field Marshal Paul von Hindenburg, in his capacity as president of Germany, shook Hitler's hand in congratulations and so bestowed on the upstart chancellor a symbolic stamp of approval. Despite the defeat of imperial Germany in 1918 and the harshness of the Versailles Treaty, von Hindenburg had continued to earn Germans' respect as the head of the German army under the *Kaiser*. And during the economic and social collapse that plagued the Weimar Republic between 1918 and 1933, he represented, for better or worse, stability. Significantly, the fatal handshake did not take place after the German parliament, on January 30, 1933, chose Hitler and the Nazis to form a government, as required by the Weimar constitution; rather, it came on the heels of the devastating election results of March 5, 1933, and the trauma of the burning of the parliament building in late February. March 5, in effect, spelled the end of German parliamentary democracy.

For the majority of Germans, the handshake, in a supreme stroke of irony, legitimized Hitler—in actuality a right-wing and radical revolutionary from Austria—as a defender of stable German values and virtues. The Nazis knew how to translate this symbolic act into an effective propaganda tool. *Das Hitlerbuch der deutschen Jugend* (The Hitler book for German youth) describes the scene as follows: "March 21. Beginning of spring! Trees and bushes already display fresh green colors, primroses and crocuses bring joy as harbingers of the coming splendor of blossoms. The primeval life force rises triumphantly out of dead rigidity. . . . There, from afar, the carriage of the Field Marshal slowly makes its way through the throngs. Again and again the ancient Field Marshal raises his staff to thank the masses for the infinite love that surges toward him on this fine morning." After describing the foreign and domestic dignitaries in attendance, this panegyric quotes Hindenburg: "During the March 5 elections, the German people, in a clear majority, have provided the constitutional basis for this government to which I had [previously] entrusted power [to form a government]." Significantly, the centerpiece of Hindenburg's address was not Hitler, but rather the legal election process. The propaganda book also quotes Hitler's response, both his carefully balanced revolutionary cant about "the life force of the people as the guiding principle of Germany's future" and his assurances about established values: "We want to nourish in humble humility the great traditions of our people, its history and its culture."[3]

Hitler's success in creating a dual role for himself as representative of the new Nazi ideology, on the one hand, and of time-honored cultural traditions, on the other, was reflected in the German army that fought World War II, which consisted in essence of two ideologically defined groups of soldiers—a minority of Nazi enthusiasts and a majority of Germany patriots—as well as a significant percentage of Germans who had to go to war simply because they were drafted. At the outset of the war, most Germans believed Hitler's claim that Germany had been forced to defend itself against an unprovoked attack by Poland. Citizens had no way of knowing that this was a lie—that the attack was preemptive, initiated not by Poland but by Germany. Anti-Bolshevist fearmongering similarly justified Germany's preemptive assault on the Soviet Union later in the war. By and large, soldiers who accepted these fabrications sincerely believed they were fighting to defend their country.

POINTS OF VIEW

One could easily select a large number of letters out of the 80,000 letters at the *Feldpostsammlung* in Berlin that would reflect a single point of view, to support a particular thesis. But after working in this archive, I came to agree with a soldier named Toni K., who observed that the "German solder fighting in Russia did not exist. Rather, millions of such soldiers existed, and each one had his own fate."[4]

Letters home were subject to censorship. Company captains had the primary responsibility for censoring letters, but they seem to have used this prerogative only to a limited extent, for the simple reason that the task of fighting, particularly on the Russian front, left little time or energy to read letters. Above the company level, general censorship was limited. When it did occur, it focused primarily on military details of specific army units—their geographic location, tactics, and the like. Strategic information was generally not available to the soldiers and their immediate superiors in the field anyway, and the letter writers often complained that they didn't know what was happening beyond their immediate horizons. Their not infrequent ideological criticism, particularly from the eastern front, seems quite daring until you realize that the writers faced death on the battlefield almost daily, and they knew that the Nazi leadership could ill afford to punish their military "assets" simply because of what they wrote home.

More than ideology, however, the letters are dominated by everyday concerns and experiences—details about daily life at the front, on the order of "We have become adept at building livable abodes in a hole in the ground." The soldiers ask reams of questions about life at home, then often end with a guarded reassurance such as, "Dear parents, considering the circumstances, I am still okay, although our manner of living is completely different [from what I am used to]." The overriding sentiment of the letters, however, concerns hope for a life after the war: "And if the Lord grants it, we will live with each other in better times ahead." Throughout history soldiers have written similar letters from many wars and many fronts, regardless of the causes for which they risked their lives—with one difference: most of these German letter writers died in World War II, and their letters were kept by relatives for half a century.

The letter collection in Berlin reveals differences in education, attitudes, and values. These young men's first encounter with the East—Poland in 1939 and the Soviet Union in 1941—elicits an ingrained cultural chauvinism in many of them, who object to the dirt and poverty. In a letter of February 28, 1940, Franz B. writes, "As for the rest, there is unbelievable, Polish filth everywhere." Another soldier comments on June 14, 1941,

"Everywhere there is dirt and filth. The Poles walk around barefoot. I surely would not want to touch any of them. The houses and abodes are worse than our pigsties." But as the war dragged on in the East, soldiers began to talk about their *eigener Dreck* (own dirt).

Not all were so judgmental, however. Upon arriving in the Soviet Union, Hermann S. writes on July 10, 1941, simply: "You cannot imagine the degree of poverty we encounter here." And Johann P., writing from Poland on June 24, 1941, has a more differentiated view: "On first sight, these people are not likable. But I cannot really allow myself to pass judgment, since I don't really know these folks on a personal level at all. Perhaps if one got to know them better, one might come to a different conclusion."

The anti-Semitism found in some letters is linked to a specific kind of cultural chauvinism toward the East. The pictorial caricatures of the *Ostjude* (a Jew from Eastern Europe) frequently found in Streicher's *Der Stürmer,* with hooked nose, long beard, sidelocks, and skull cap, shaped the first impressions some soldiers recorded shortly after the invasion of Poland. In referring to the Jews he encountered in Poland, Friedrich M. writes on September 13, 1939: "Most of them could have been taken straight out of *Der Stürmer.*" Soldiers also commented on personal acquaintances, such as individual Jews whom they employed. Harald F., for example, writes to his wife, Ursula, on September 7, 1941, about a woman he paid to clean his quarters:

> This time it was not a prisoner who came but a Jewish woman, who somehow had been drafted to do this work. She wears the *Judenstern* [yellow star] on her sleeve and has an ugly Jewish face, one of the unpleasant kinds, so that a photo of her could perfectly well be

reprinted in *Der Stürmer.* Jews are trained here to work for us. Our Sara, as I call her, was glad to be able to do housework. For that she gets a midday meal, for which she is very grateful. She speaks a broken German, like all Jews from the East, but when she starts talking to the woman of her race working on the floor above, I cannot understand a single word she is saying. As I said, she has that typical Jewish face, which is rather unpleasant for me to look at. But she does good work. She thoroughly cleaned our room with wet rags, and in particular, she removed the dead flies from the windows so that our room has become almost a little jewel. She even washed down the door, which had become quite dirty, with warm water. Gradually, we feel more and more comfortable here.

In a few cases, virulent anti-Semitism emerges. On October 10, 1939, forty days after Germany invaded Poland, Ernst Z. writes home: "In the cities there live an awful many Jews, and they are well dressed when compared to the poor Polish folk in their rags. How will this problem ever be solved? R. ["R." is not identified by the letter writer] simply says, 'Kill them,' but 3,000,000? On the other hand, they are the cause of this war." Other soldiers disapprove of the violence perpetrated against Jews in language ranging from criticism to condemnation. One soldier even questions the legitimacy of the war because of its anti-Semitic excesses. Striking is the fact that the violence mentioned invariably takes the form of stories the soldiers have heard, not events they have witnessed. Soldiers encounter more Jews in Poland and the Ukraine than in the Soviet Union, but when they mention them, it is usually in neutral descriptions lacking ideology.

A surprising number of letters contain ideological opinions that differ from Nazi dogma, underscoring the fact that the picture painted by Nazi propaganda about the German army's glorious marches through Europe was a far cry from the reality on the ground. On March 24, 1943, Erich S. writes from Italy with bitter irony:

> The soldiers are numbed by speeches about soldiering, the joy of following orders, about pride, human dignity etc., while in fact we are being educated to behave in subhuman ways. All I have to do is to look at the simple infantrymen. They don't really know anymore that they were once human beings. . . . I hope this letter will be opened so that the appropriate authorities have something to laugh about and they can see that some of us want to preserve our humanity. *"Die Welt ist voller Sonnenschein; es ist so schön Soldat zu sein"* [The world is full of sunshine; it is wonderful to be a soldier].

Some letters were sufficiently ambivalent to allow a pro-Nazi interpretation of their meaning, had a censor discovered them. "Maybe," writes Michael G., "the German people have to stand once more in front of smoking ruins and carry what is most dear to them to the grave, before they wake up from that thoughtlessness and stupor . . . which still characterize those who have not yet experienced war. And out of those who emerge from this misery cleansed, a new German people will arise and a time of peace will reign." Others, however, openly and unambiguously condemn the Nazi system, as in the following sarcastic epistle by Martin D. from June 31 *[sic]*, 1943. Perhaps he feared the censor less than he feared dying in battle.

> All feelings for the homeland are taken from you, even if they say in the newspaper, "Germany is becoming larger and more beautiful." Here you have the total insanity of it all miraculously before your very eyes. You can see how things are getting more and more beautiful in the Ruhr area [the industrial region of Germany], and there will be no stopping until we have reached the pinnacle of beauty when it will stink everywhere of smoking ruins and corpses. All

of our magnificent youths must devote themselves to this "glorious fateful battle" and pay homage to those insane and "asocial" types and their call for destruction and mass murder in battle. . . . Many human beings suffer now and no one does anything to stop it. How could we have become so stupid? You begin to wonder whether people who don't stand up against all this deserve any better. We call ourselves the crown of creation, because we are endowed with reason. But half of us are subhuman. We should hate them, and I do so to the hilt.

June 21, 1941, marked the day when the war changed radically, not only for German soldiers but for Germany as a whole. On that date early in the morning Hitler's *Reich* declared war on the Soviet Union and thereby began a *Zweifrontenkrieg,* which most Germans feared, remembering World War I. Before that fateful day, talk was still heard of a settlement and an end to the war. But now it turned into an all-engulfing conflagration, with tens of millions killed, gassed, wounded, or driven from their homelands. Winning or losing became a less important concern than living or dying. Survival was now the highest priority.

While the previous major campaigns of the war had been short—Poland was subdued in two weeks, France in six—the same was not true of Russia, and the dangerous and haphazard flow of daily duties now demanded soldiers' undivided attention. Their immediate surroundings determined who they were as soldiers and human beings, and what they did as well as what they knew. Only when writing letters or standing guard during a long night watch were they able to let their minds drift away from the war.

On June 26, 1941, a soldier named Harald H. writes from Russia: "What an immense expanse of land lies before us as we enter

Russia, full of ancient mysteries and, now, a modern, brutal Soviet state." With a sense of realism and curiosity, Jakob P. contemplates a war with Russia before its outbreak: "The thought of Russia is not at all a pleasant one, but perhaps it won't come to pass. Even one winter in Poland, Moscow, or Siberia would not really be for me. Yet Russia holds a mysteriously hidden darkness that attracts me. Well, let's wait and see."

The reality of war put an end to such reveries and self-absorption. For some, things had already changed long before the Russian invasion and shortly after the conquest of Poland. "Am I too young, or too soft?" wonders Simon F. on November 11, 1939. "Well, just grit your teeth. Already, after two days into the war, I made a Polish soldier bite the dust—not out of any murderous lust. Rather, a sense of duty and steely calculation determined and guided my emotions. This is war. A gentle boy turned into a hard soldier."

From abject fear to a battle-hardened acceptance of killing was only a short step for most soldiers. On his eighteenth birthday, December 15, 1940, Kurt Weidemann writes about his initiation into the business of killing:

> Once you get beyond that threshold of fear, your mind clears up and becomes circumspect, and a steady calm comes over you. Then you still face the act of shooting. To see a life in front of you—your eye, gunsight, and this life in motion lined up in one straight line—and then to eradicate all of this, to turn it stiff and cold, a mourning family . . . but stop. I will not pursue this line of thought—impossible. Self-preservation drives me, and when I see someone fall beside me, the face of a brother underneath the gray helmet that makes us all the same, my heart!! Then courage and the lust to attack overcome me, the enthusiasm to give everything and to preserve everything.[5]

As the war progressed, the fight against partisans is mentioned in letters more and more frequently, as are references to its brutality. "We had the partisans encircled," writes Bruno L. on September 1, 1942; "we killed 50 persons, men, women and some children, and then we took their weapons as booty." Letters about partisans—or, as the Germans sometimes called them, "terrorists"—arrived home not just from Russia, but also from the Balkans, from Italy and France. If they were captured, the young men explain, partisans were summarily executed without mercy. From Italy, Christian S. writes on September 29, 1942: "As fast as the partisans came, they were gone. The partisans never engage you in an open battle. They create confusion through surprise attacks." Yet despite draconian laws against them, the partisans' strength did not diminish.

The German population knew and sometimes talked openly about the harsh retributions that their military meted out to partisans. The matter-of-fact tone with which soldiers discussed these acts is striking. "Snipers from various houses in the small village where we are now stationed shot at us," writes Johann L. on July 8, 1941, near the Duna River. "So we went ahead and incinerated the entire village, and in front of me I see a huge ocean of fire."

It was often difficult to distinguish friendly, or at least peaceful, civilians from those who might turn into armed partisans at night. As Joseph T. writes on December 3, 1943,

> The situation at the front remains unclear. The only sure thing is that there are an awful lot of partisans around here, whom we are now supposed to fight. After dark you cannot leave the town; the villages are also dangerous. The streets are mined, and individual vehicles are attacked. It's pretty uncomfortable. For the time being

we have set up temporary quarters in a village. It is another one of those muddy little burgs, but our quarters are quite fine. . . . The population is very friendly and fulfills all our wishes—whether out of fear or for other reasons, or perhaps because they have a bad conscience, I don't know. And I really don't care. For the time being, I enjoy this agreeable setup.

The merciless execution of partisans became a matter of routine, as phrases from many letters reflect: "Again, a few partisans are hanging from gallows"; "We really have no language for this"; "First Lieutenant M. sets fire to the barn. The Russians inside are burned alive. The weather is calm."

As the fight against partisans continued and the brutality of the war increased on the eastern front, casualties mounted in the German army. German soldiers on the front lines frequently observed as well how little concerned the Russian army command was for its own soldiers' lives. Many letters home describe Russians storming toward the German lines in waves; as one wave was cut down by machine-gun fire, the next wave arrived. One of my uncles was a machine gunner in one of the spearhead divisions east of Smolensk, heading for Moscow. He described such terrible scenes to us, ones that traumatized him for years after his return from Russia.

In the latter stages of the war, the brutal acts of violence the Soviet army perpetrated against the civilian population as they invaded Germany were pandemic. Describing the scene in one village that the Germans had retaken from the Soviets, Hermann H. writes on October 28, 1944: "The men and women who were unable to flee from the Soviets in time were all butchered like animals. God save Germany from ever falling into the hands of these beasts." Four days later, on November 1, he writes further of "the corpses of violated women, gruesomely murdered children, and old people. Well, the Russians may be able to kill 1,000 or 10,000 Germans, but they will be unable to kill 80 million."

Quite clearly, selective awareness was often at work, with soldiers criticizing the atrocities of the enemy while either ignoring their own atrocities or justifying them as retribution against partisans. Yet their fight against the partisans was only one aspect, and not even the most important one, of the soldiers' lives at the front. For one thing, the war was lived within extremely restricted parameters on the front lines, which usually consisted of a daily routine of fighting the Russian army, ducking their bullets, digging trenches, resting, and, above all, marching, and then marching some more—first to the gates of Moscow in 1941, and then back to the Brandenburg Gate of Berlin in 1945. The burdensome routine of marching weighed on some of them already early on, as in the case of Waldemar W., who writes on June 23, 1941, only two days after the invasion of the Soviet Union: "The time passes extremely slowly in these campaigns. You lose touch with yourself and all that is left of you is an eternal marcher, although we have been on the road for only four days." "A long road," "always that distant horizon," "a landscape under a blazing sun," "the sound of guns far away or close by"—these are the phrases in so many letters that produce an iconography of the vast country to the east.

Aside from complaints about routines suffered by any soldier, these letters also describe the harshness of the Russian winter (famous in history books since the days of Napoleon) and the resultant focus on personal survival—the fight against frostbite, diarrhea, exhaustion, lack of sleep—and, especially, worry about home. With the exception of the fanatics, Nazi slogans are absent from the letters that address these subjects.

The soldiers' experiences contrast sharply with the messages from the propaganda machine with which the Nazis battered the home front. Incessant in radio broadcasts and newspaper articles was the cant about the glorious army storming eastward, hurrying from one success to another. But the tone of most letters underscores the distance that existed between the Nazi imagination of the war and the real struggle in the vast expanses of Russia. The letters also contain many expressions of nostalgia for the years of peace experienced before the war. Five days after the invasion of Poland, on September 5, 1939, one soldier captures a frequently uttered sentiment: "Good-bye, my home, good-bye my youth, and good-bye my dear, dear [beloved]."

Their letters reveal a number of telltale clues about a soldier's devotion to the Nazi cause as well. While the fanatics talk about victory or triumph (based on their belief in racial superiority), the patriots speak of wanting to undo the Treaty of Versailles, while still others just dream of peace and life back home. Writing to his wife on November 11, 1941, Helmut F. even went so far as to propose a new Europe based on the American model:

> We were born during war. In WW I our fathers had to risk their lives. Now, more than twenty years have passed, and once again weapons speak. We, the people, the neighbors on our borders, no, we did not want war. And we have to try our very best to make peace with our archenemy, the French, so that we may become peaceful neighbors. The peoples all around us must have the good will to preserve peace. And Europe must be united. What am I saying here? It will remain a utopian dream. We should imitate America. The USA is really a good model. We have this fantasy, and it is really worth fighting for.

Helmut F. died in Russia. At the other end of the spectrum, a Gerhardt T. penned a striking example of Nazi fanaticism as late as March 3, 1945, two months before Germany's capitulation:

Even if Berlin falls, we never have to be afraid of a terrible end. After the wild celebrations of the others, we will carry victory, which now seems to have become almost impossible, back to our country. First of all, what counts now is to hold back the flood. And the counterforce has already been set in motion. Just as I believe in you, I believe in our victory, in our future, and in our happiness. Just as the others now plan to inundate us, they will have to realize one day that it is they who will have been overrun. Do you believe, Irene, I would be so full of confidence, if I did not know—and not I alone—that in the hands of our highest authorities rests a weapon that will be used at the decisive moment?

Quite another perspective can be found in a letter written as early as March 19, 1942, by Anton N. on his way to the eastern front:

Looking at the Polish population, the begging boys in rags, you think about the fate of these people. They all beg for bread . . . Who is not starving today? Then you really sense what war is. The trains filled with the wounded. A train stopped opposite us. Some apathetic-looking soldiers sat in front of the doors squinting at the sun. An endless number of trains roll through here with endless amounts of materiel and an endless number of soldiers, and one of these trains is ours. Just as we are ignorant about our goal, so are we ignorant about the war as a whole. But perhaps we are able to tolerate the war only because we do not know its course or its outcome. Perhaps in the end, it will swallow us up in its vortex—well, each one of us clings to his own hope.

The Nazi fanatics had an easier time accepting hardships because they believed in the *Endsieg,* the final victory of Nazi

Germany. Most of them had joined the SS voluntarily. On October 25, 1941, the *Obersteirische Rundschau,* a provincial Austrian daily newspaper, printed a letter written by a Sergeant Hiasl of the *Waffen-SS* to his friend Alois as an example of the SS fighting spirit. After recounting heroic battles and triumphs, the sergeant ends by invoking his Nazi faith: "Small was our unit after the battle, but great our success. In this spirit we push into battle for final victory. Only one can be victorious, and that is us." Whenever regular German soldiers mention the SS in their letters, it is either with a certain envy for their superior equipment and weaponry or with a cautious distance. One letter, written by a German soldier from Stalingrad on February 17, 1943, is more explicit: "The *Schwarze Korps* [Black Corps, the official newspaper of the SS] has landed here. I read one article. The writer must have been sick in the head or hyperventilating. I, for my part, want to save my skin as much as possible and bring it home safely. . . . More I cannot write. Oh well, all this will pass too and May will come." The writer, however, did not return; this was the last letter he ever sent.

As the war on the eastern front dragged on, in some letters the continued battles against partisans and their executions came to seem more and more routine, and the focus shifted to the suffering of the German soldiers. Kurt Weidemann articulates this in a diary entry of November 7, 1942:

> The "Ride of the Valkyries" moves past. You think you are in the Thirty Years' War. Stretched out in long lines, they [the troops] straggle past in no particular order or military formation. The weak and the bent bring up the rear, numbly straggling on. They come from the vortex. They had been part of the attack, but they made no progress and their ranks were severely decimated. You

can see it in their faces, their posture, their clothing. They were spared no hardship and they still are heavily burdened down by that experience, really unable to comprehend it. Their clothes were of many colors, coats torn, the wet snowy mud of the roads soaked into their shoes.[6]

In many letters, there is a subtle shift toward sympathy for the Russian people, who are the major victims of the war on their own territory. On May 15, 1942, Hans L. writes: "The misery on the roads is terrible. For a slice of bread, a boy carries your bags for kilometers. Hunger everywhere. These poor people! The Russian faces with exhaustion and suffering etched into their features. Is that the war, or was the Russian 'peace' always like that?" Another soldier, Karl U., captures the plight of the Ukrainians he has seen when he writes home on November 11, 1943:

Individually, or in groups with tiny babies and old grandmothers with heavy bags and their last cattle, they trek through rainy and stormy nights lit up by innumerable fires. Torn up and hastily abandoned, abodes still stand there with small, starving farm animals. What horrible misery. The human beings have nothing anymore, not only no home, but literally nothing at all. When evening comes, they bunk down next to a hay barn and huddle next to a small fire, and at the sound of every shot, they twitch with fear.

Fritz S. writes home on May 9, 1943:

I feel sorry for our Madka [a Russian widow in whose house Fritz S. is bivouacked]. Her husband died in Stalingrad, and now she is alone with her three children. Yesterday, her four-year-old son came by and looked at me so entreatingly that I took a slice of bread, put butter on it, and gave it to Madka for her children. It is the nicest reward for me when I catch a grateful glance. I cannot act in any other way.

Soldiers far from their families were eager to register any gesture of kindness—a smile, the gift of a bowl of cherries or a piece of clothing to keep out the cold. Whenever an army unit was stationed for a longer period of time in a particular village, away from the front and from partisan activity, contacts between families and soldiers became more personal. On November 6, 1941, Alfred B. writes:

> Babuschka [an old Russian woman] sat on her oracular chair yesterday. She took a flour sifter, stuck a pair of scissors into it, and examined the shapes that emerged. Then she performed her incantations and told me the results, namely, that I had to stay two more months in her house; then I would not remain in Russia but would go home to Germania. Well, I am not a believer in oracles and their predictions, and so I laughed out loud. She, on the other hand, remained dead serious and held on to her blessed belief that the oracle had never betrayed her. May she and the oracle be right! . . . So prepare the eggnog immediately, that upon my return by New Year's Eve it will ooze heavily out of the bottle— amen, amen!

Most German reactions to the strangers on the other side of the battle were brief but telling, particularly when it was their first encounter with an enemy soldier. "While combing through a forest—it was dark in spite of the snow . . . one fellow in my platoon was so frightened when a Russian suddenly came toward him that he forgot to throw his hand grenade and lost his left hand." Nonetheless, the impersonal aspect of war— "we killed another 187 partisans today"—far outweighs personal human emotions in the letters, and when soldiers try to connect the two, they reveal their own inner conflicts. In a letter of August 29, 1941, Hans L. draws a distinction between his own regular army unit and the SS or military police whom he observes methodically executing partisans:

> We are on the road. I am sitting in a hay barn. A strong wind blows in through the cracks. You can see a small dam and a very primitive windmill. And behind that, there are fir trees that probably still conceal partisans. Their end, if they are caught, is of such brevity and seeming irrelevance that we, the laymen, can only be puzzled. The Russian is led to a ditch, he looks into it, and at a moment's notice, someone shoots a bullet through his neck that goes right through his head. He falls forward, and while falling, gets a kick in the back. And straightway he lies on top of the others, who have already been sent to the unknown beyond. Another Russian jumps to the scene, pours some chlorine chalk over him, and it's the next one's turn.

In a letter that follows two days later, the same soldier writes that he cannot stop thinking about the "horrible end, swift as a wink of the eye," of those executed.

Most soldiers, lacking Hans L.'s narrative skills, write their observations in simpler language. Karl N., a farmboy turned soldier, states on August 29, 1944: "I can only write you that in Russia there are many industrious and decent people," and then, in several variations, states plainly: "I wish I were back home." Many such letters comment only about a day in battle or a day at rest, about the cold of winter or the heat of summer.

Having read a good sampling of the German soldiers' letters in the *Feldpostsammlung*, I have come to the conclusion that the German *Ostfrontsoldat* (eastern front soldier) did not exist. Quite aside from the uniqueness of each individual soldier, the specific circumstances in which they found themselves shaped their values and perceptions. This is evident if experiences of the *Ost-*

frontsoldat are compared with those of German soldiers in other European theaters of war, particularly those in Italy or France, where cultural affinities were acknowledged that did not exist in Russia. Herbert B., serving in Russia, wrote: "Something strangely non-European . . . emanates from these wretched huts, and you don't know what sustains these people, who know nothing about the world at large."

PERSONAL PORTRAITS

The excerpts and fragments quoted so far reveal a variety of experiences, attitudes, and values among German soldiers in World War II, ranging from Nazi fanatics with no sympathy for their enemies to courageous critics of the regime, including those who empathized with the plight of the people they were ordered to conquer. The longer letters that follow were written by soldiers from specific theaters of war who manage, even after sixty years, to leave us with a strong impression of their personalities and individuality, beyond their uniforms and steel helmets. By giving some of them an opportunity to speak to us, we may gain insights into a period in history when the individual counted for nothing and the grand design created in 1933 was everything. In each case the specific location or theater of war in which they found themselves determined to a great degree what they thought and felt and even how they were shaped as individuals and fighting men.

One such soldier, Lukas, writes home to his sister from the Russian front. He is a musician by profession, and he clearly prefers a musical instrument to a machine gun. Two letters tell his story. The first was written on August 13, 1943:

Yesterday I received a letter from Gretel. It included a few lines from you. My little woman has now settled in with you in Memmingen, and, as I can tell from the letters, you are quite well. I am really so pleased about that for you, because who knows what is in store for us. I haven't received a letter from you in a long time. I know you have to work very hard. How I would love to be with you now and climb up on the Nebelhorn [an alpine mountain] with you. I wonder whether something like that will ever be granted us again. I don't have much hope anymore. This life is for the dogs.

There is much to report from here. You may have heard about Kribyschervo [sic]. Well, that's exactly where our division is stationed. This is where the Russians have thrown two spearhead divisions into the fray and have achieved a breakthrough along a 20-kilometer front.[7] It began at 2:30 in the night. I just happened to be assigned to the front line in a village that soon fell into Russian hands. We retook the village a few days later. [General] Mannstein managed the affair. The *Stukas* [German dive-bombers] had a devastating effect. Everything was used: tanks, light and heavy artillery. And the Russians suffered terrible loss of life and materiel. For the time being, everything is quiet again. Our variety show[8] has been dissolved, but rumor has it that it will be established again soon. I don't know whether I have already written you about that. From our division (of 18,000) men, 11 musicians have been selected to perform under my musical direction. We have top artists, established professionals. Unfortunately, our magician died in battle. He had performed in the *Wintergarten* in Berlin [a variety show] and was tops. Everybody was represented: actors, musicians, even some who had played in the *Gewandhaus* orchestra [the renowned orchestra of Leipzig]. We put on a show of two and a half hours in length that would have rivaled the finest cabarets in Germany. It's too bad that this battle interfered, because we might have made it back to the *Reich* [for a performance]. Now, my little sister, that's enough for today. Next time, more. Greetings and kisses to you and Alice.
Your Lukas

On December 22, 1943, Lukas writes from Stalingrad:

You may have heard that our variety show has been dissolved once again. It's simply no longer feasible in Russia. The Russians are trying to encircle us. Their offensive has been going on for five and a half months and is expanding all the time. We should be renamed and called a variety show for the front lines. That would be more appropriate. But we [illegible word] have always been the unlucky ones and will likely remain so. Besides, we are all much too healthy. A healthy person is not allowed to leave. And on top of it, our general has received the oak leaf cluster [a high military distinction]. That makes it even more unlikely that we can extricate ourselves from here. At this time, foot soldiers are once again in high demand, and replacements will no longer be available. . . . From the start of the war, we've had to fight all over Russia, and in the end they assign us to the infantry once again, as a reward. Tomorrow, the decision will be made about who will be allowed to withdraw. It has not yet been determined who will leave. I may be among them. And besides, with human beings alone we cannot achieve anything. The Russian weaponry is much too powerful. . . . The variety show performances we had planned for Germany most likely will not take place. I never quite believed that it would happen, anyway. The situation is too serious, and our general brooks no [illegible word]. We had been promised, but promises are not kept around here. It's always been like that. I still fervently hope that I will be allowed to go on furlough in January. That would mean not being assigned to the infantry, because if I were, there would be no furlough. If that happens, I will put a bullet through my head. To be in the infantry means to die, or if you are lucky, to be wounded and shipped home. . . . We will all be glad when this nonsense is over. And as for the rest, I almost forgot to send Christmas greetings to you. . . . And now, my little sister, you have been informed about a few things from me. There is nothing else to report. You are informed about the overall situation. Winter has not yet arrived completely. Some snow has fallen, but since yesterday it has been melting. Well, until next time, my heartfelt greetings and kisses and wishes for a better New Year. Your brother

Lukas was killed in Russia.

•   •   •

One of the fiercest battles of World War II was fought over the famous Benedictine monastery perched on top of Monte Cassino in Italy. Over the course of several days at the end of January 1944, Erich S. wrote a letter to his wife that gives us a valuable view of the war in Italy as seen from the German side. Even the portion translated here shows that he had an eye for detail. A few lines of this letter are illegible; I leave out others that do not contribute to the overall portrait the soldier draws of himself and of the fighting in which he was involved.

Between Christmas and January 15 I received nothing from you. So I really don't know whether you received all my letters written during the time I was transferred. Take another look at the list to find out whether you received the two packages of coffee and my beautiful weighty books from Switzerland. . . . Outside, I hear captured Americans shouting, "Comrades, German soldiers" [in English]. They have great iron rations,[9] and I am chewing Wrigley's chewing gum and smoking their heavy cigarettes. . . . I know nothing about the general situation of the war. We are sitting here as if we were on the moon. . . . When I wrote you the last letter, we had five hours of a local armistice so that both sides were able to retrieve their wounded. After the Americans crossed the river, our Do[rnier] bombers really did their job. One hundred died. The other day we saw Americans peacefully taking a walk along the river in an upright position. Waving Red Cross flags, they crossed in rubber dinghies [to pick up their wounded]. You really can't imagine what has been happening here since last night. Our bunker rises and falls like a little boat in level-ten sea waves. All joints creak. . . .

January 25. It was impossible the other day to continue writing. It was just too wild. We expected a direct hit at any moment. No chance of writing when this is happening. At the drop of a hat the air pressure from the blasts cuts off our electricity. It's been going on like this for days. Now it's quiet, and you can stick your head out of the bunker. Since by day I was doing the most important thing that needed to be done, namely, catching lice, I will now continue writing as the successful hunter I have become. . . . Take good care of my books and the three rolls of film. They won't reach me here anymore. I have the cloverleaf, raisins, and photos with me. They are my most important possessions. Outside, reconnaissance planes are in the air all day long. There is going to be a magic show again tonight! . . . The 500 meters to get your food is always like running the gauntlet, a competitive game against death. The food is always cold and full of mud from throwing yourself down. Don't worry about me, if you don't get any mail from me. Things will get bad around here. We know that, but I have my guardian angel who sees to it that nothing will happen to me. I don't want to give you any proof of that, so you won't start to worry. . . . Now things will come to the boiling point here. Today there is a strange, uncanny silence. Usually, there isn't a single hour that passes without crackling explosions. . . . Just as an aside: to be in the infantry is the most horrible and hardest life you could imagine. As a civilian, I could not have imagined what it would be like, but now I know. It's the most stubborn, stupid bunch of people from top to bottom. I cannot understand how one is capable of fighting a war with them and maybe even of winning it. . . . By the way, since December 27 I have not shaved, and now I have a BEARD. But it is not well shaped, nothing for a cultured crowd. Well, that's it for today. With every letter I write, I have the feeling that it might be the last one. . . .

Erich S. was wrong about his guardian angel; about his premonitions of an imminent death he was right. It was his last letter before he was killed.

· · ·

When soldiers identified a geographical location in their letters, it was usually an obscure one, known only to military historians. But some places on the eastern front were well known. One was Stalingrad, where the Sixth German Army was destroyed, and another was Warsaw and its ghetto, where the starvation and mass murder of Jews took place. In a letter written at Nowy Dwor, a small Polish town approximately nine miles northeast of Warsaw, on February 28, 1942, a young army lieutenant, newly transferred from Germany, gives his first detailed impressions of what he saw and experienced on his journey.

> Dear Hilde, dear children! First of all, let me tell you that I arrived here this afternoon. . . . Last night at 21:16, I left Leslau together with my comrade, Private A., who has been assigned to me. His help in carrying my bags was most welcome. Sergeant H. brought us to the train. An unpleasant dampness hung in the air. The train was unheated during the first stage to [illegible], where we arrived at 23:30. From there we had an immediate connection to Warsaw. We were lucky to have a well-heated compartment all to ourselves. Toward 4 o'clock in the morning we arrived in Warsaw. However, we did not continue from there until 15:00. The clock showed 17:00 when the train arrived at the Modlin railroad station. To our pleasant surprise, a horse-drawn sled was awaiting me. It drove us through the wonderful winter landscape across the Narev bridge . . . to my future domicile. It consists of a small room at the far end of the barracks. It has two windows and two doors, one leading out into the open and the other to the interior of the barracks.

The lieutenant reviews many details of his trip before continuing:

After we had drunk a few glasses of beer for our farewell, I really became very cold. There is still no schnapps available. Therefore, I was very glad that my comrades and I had not consumed the schnapps, sent to me so lovingly, during the few days since I received it. I had poured the remainder into a small flask and put it into my pants' pocket for the trip. In the totally blacked-out train, I took a little sip from time to time. I hardly noticed the fellow travelers in the train because of the darkness. I only heard the lulling rattle of the train's wheels. Since I had not slept the entire night before, sleep would definitely have overtaken me if something out of the ordinary had not happened, as you will presently find out. Since the train stopped at every small station, and strangers, mostly Poles, entered and left, there was no way to go to sleep, because, after all, we are in the enemy's country, and even if it is pacified you always have to be prepared for trickery. . . . The entire region has already been integrated into Germany. We were now at the border town with its passport and customs' check of the travelers. The train that was to take us on to Warsaw . . . stood on the adjacent track ready for departure. . . . [some time passes before he writes the remainder of this letter] . . . As soon as the train wheels stopped rumbling at the first station, a huge crowd of people weighed down with packages and bundles descended. I stared as if hypnotized at the pushing and shoving and strange yelling, when all of a sudden my assistant, who up to this moment had been sitting there dead to the world, jumped up to the door opposite our compartment, uttering something inarticulate. When I looked, I noticed how men and women fought to get inside. But the first ones who actually gained entry into the [opposite] compartment were attacked and simply thrown out. Hours passed, and we found ourselves apparently at one of the suburban railroad stations of Warsaw. I looked out of the window, disturbed; a cold shiver ran through me as the ice-cold air touched me. Finally, the train stopped again. A thick, white, hissing fog from the steam of the engine penetrated our compartment. Whole hosts of shouting people left the train and the platform.

It was explained to him that "these people [were] just smugglers and hoarders, and that they left the train earlier in order not to be caught in the next station by security checks and relieved of the smuggled goods they had so laboriously obtained in order to resell them to sustain their lives, which were so full of worry and misery." This information roused his interest to reconnoiter further.

At the main railroad station [of Warsaw] we left our luggage at the baggage storage area for one mark. Then, after a cup of coffee, we took a streetcar that would take us to the Jewish ghetto. For hours, we rode all around the ghetto. Right in the middle of the city, a high wall surrounds it. We were not able to enter or go through it. We could gather only the smallest of impressions. They are not worth my writing about them. Four hundred thousand to 500,000 Jews are said to be cooped up inside, and if every day at least four to five hundred die, that will not be enough, or fast enough, as someone said, to empty the ghetto over time. Most likely, people arriving every day from all over the country augment the number of people already there. No one can explain what goes on in there, what these hundreds of thousands possess, how they feed and clothe themselves, and where they live. It is said that no one is allowed to leave the ghetto. But they must do so. They must have secret pathways and byways for smuggling, with the help of others, who assist them in selling jewelry and other dead objects for precious, life-preserving foodstuffs. The city looks dreary. You run into the traces of the horrible work our bombers have done (ruins and remainders of buildings) everywhere you look.... Behind the desolate, blown-out windows dwell horror and the seeds of death.... May a merciful spring spread its soothing cloak over us.... I wish you all the best, and I greet you and kiss you, with my thoughts deeply disturbed. Hans! Father!

This lieutenant, who was stationed near Warsaw for a long time, never returned home. What was his fate and final end? We can only guess whether or not he retained his sensitivity, evident in his first impressions, over time. Or did his devotion to duty turn him into a willing executioner of the Jewish ghetto dwellers?

. . .

While serving on the western front, Wolfgang K. wrote letters to his parents in the straight, legible handwriting he had learned in school. When the Allies landed on the Normandy coast, he was stationed close by. He wrote one letter before and two after the invasion. Each letter tells a different story, but this simple, young German remained the same.

June 3, 1944. Dear Parents, I want to send you some news from me once again. I am fine. Every night we have three hours of sentry duty. Starting Monday, it will be every other day. Today, I ate a whole cooking pot full of strawberries. About 2 kilos, for the price of 2 marks and 80 pfennig. Is little Irmy with you? How did you spend the Pentecost holidays? How is the weather? Is the fresh fruit already ripe, like it is here? What does little Irmy look like? What does she talk about? What's Ernst's address? Why has Gerda been sent away? Have you had an air raid alarm again? These are questions. Please answer all of them. By the way, how is Siegfried R.? In a few days, red currants and gooseberries will be ripe, too. I won't buy them, because you can find enough of them all over. I received the package of envelopes. I hope that the package embargo will be lifted soon, so that I will get a beautiful cake and cookies from home. How are you otherwise? What's Dad doing? I have not been to the movies for 3–4 weeks. The weather is not very good. Have you heard anything at home about how long furloughs for the western front will remain canceled? That's enough for today, because I have no more time. My most heartfelt greetings, Your Wolfgang. P.S. Have you received my package with the rubber bands?

Following the Allied invasion, Wolfgang K. pens a longer letter, because he has much more to write about.

June 23, 1944. Quickly, a few lines. For 14 days, we have been on the move, and we are now in Normandy, the richest region of France. We are on our way to Cherbourg. In three days, we will be there. The cities and villages are all empty of people. In one single house we found 50 lb. of butter, 10 lb. of lard, and 50 eggs, flour, sardines, apple cider, red wine, and schnapps. Today, we are going to make omelets. . . . We are living as snug as a bug in a rug. But for how much longer? Don't worry about me, because nothing is going to happen to me. I hope everything is in fine shape at home. No letter since May 28. All day we hear the sound of airplane engines. Unfortunately, they are English and Americans who are looking for troops at rest or in motion. German planes are nowhere to be seen. The artillery guns roar all day long. Today, Americans flew over our heads just 10 meters above the ground. It's a miracle that they did not discover us. The French who are still here—about 10% of them—are scared shitless. When the British planes arrive, they stand in the village square with a piece of white cloth so that the planes won't shoot.

Wolfgang wrote his last letter on July 3, 1944.

Dear Parents! I received three letters with much joy and many thanks. I am still well and I hope that the same can be said of you. I am still stationed at the same place. In my last letter I forgot to include the map. I don't know exactly where I am stationed, but I tried to mark our position as accurately as I could. We ate a rabbit today. There were two of us. My friend is from Stettin and he knows how to cook well. I am sitting by the fire guarding our chicken that is frying happily in the pan. We still want to eat it today. Unfortunately, it will be 10 p.m. or later. Today I bought 6 lb. of butter for 210 francs (11 marks). The chicken is swimming in it. Yesterday I ate four deep-dish plates filled with fried potatoes. I was stuffed. If nothing happens to me during this campaign, it will all have been somewhat of an advantage to me. I am going to weigh myself. I am really curious about that. No one is able to live like that in Germany. You can have all the butter you want here. I could now gobble up the entire three kilos, and I guarantee you that tomorrow I would be able to buy exactly the same amount again. For the rabbit and the chicken we used more than a kilo [of butter]. Now I want to answer your letters, that is, the letters from May 5, June 3 and 9. So our street also got bombed. You surely were lucky. Right at this moment there is a growl over our heads and bombs are falling. But the hits are still 3 to 4 kilometers away from here. Now, just at this moment I am going to duck . . . the bombing is getting closer and closer. Just one kilometer away. Nothing will bother us. I have received four packages, and I thank you for them. It is not as bad here as you imagine it. After all, we are still 20 kilometers behind the front lines. I would not want to be in the anti-aircraft unit, because you should have seen how "Tommy" [a relatively positive German nickname for the British] attacks, flying as low as 20 meters high or less. Thanks for the fruit. Time is short; I cannot write to everyone. Just received your letter from June 6 and I want to answer it right away. . . . Little Irmy seems to be right at home with us. Perhaps she will be a little bored. She is so much in love with music. If I were home, things would be different, because she writes very often and she is always sweet and happy. Has Gerda returned to Munich from Switzerland? You said she got herself a dog. I thought she did not like animals. I would love to see that little dog, because in our company we have a dog, too. That's enough for today, because I have to write more letters, and I still want to read the newspapers. With all my heartfelt greetings, Your Wolfgang

Four days after he wrote this letter, Wolfgang K. was killed. His mother asked the army to return his private belongings to her, and she received this reply:

Re: Belongings of soldier Wolfgang K., died on July 7, 1944. . . . In his army pack only materiel and equipment owned by the army was found. The valuables that you mention in your letter, your son most definitely had in his possession on July 7, '44. During battle they must have been lost. The men who were in charge of the burials of dead soldiers at that time have themselves died or were missing from that day on. Family valuables that were in the possession of members of his company could only be partly salvaged during those days. Nothing was brought in that belonged to your son. [the signature is illegible]

• • •

I will conclude this chapter with more detailed and differentiated portraits of four German soldiers. Each one left an extensive correspondence behind, safeguarded by his family. In the first case, an officer who became an ardent believer in Hitler in 1933 nevertheless reveals in many letters a great deal of individual insight and sensitivity about the world around him. Manfred von K. wrote a letter to his wife every other day for four years whenever circumstances allowed. He participated in the German invasion of France during the spring and summer of 1940. Later on he was appointed to the divisional staff as a junior officer during the German invasion of the Soviet Union that began on June 21, 1941. As part of the Sixth German Army, he was captured in early 1943 when the Soviet army liberated Stalingrad.

He was to spend thirteen years as a prisoner of war in the Soviet Union.

An almost equal number of letters is available in the correspondence of two close friends, one an artist and painter, the other a student of theology. Eugen and Hans were soldiers in the German army that invaded France in 1940, but they served mainly on the eastern front after Germany attacked the Soviet Union. With the sensitivity of the art historian and with a philosophical bent of mind, these highly educated individuals kept each other informed of what was happening around and to them, hoping one day to be reunited after the war.

Finally, there was nineteen-year-old Franz W., who, his letters make clear, was very close to his mother. He kept her informed of his personal feelings and his desire to experience an adventurous life as a member of the *Luftwaffe*. His boyhood dream turned into brutal reality, and he died as a turret gunner. More than the others, he represents an Everyman in the German army.

A BELIEVER

In October 1933, Manfred von K. writes to his future wife about the good times he enjoys as a student in Geneva, Switzerland. "We now have a very nice clique of international students that has a lot of fun and goes out frequently. Recently we roamed through the streets one night and ended up with 16 people at our place—with the result that we spent the next day writing letters of apology to the other residents for having disturbed their peace!!" In the same letter he comments about the election to be held on November 12 and his hopes that Hitler will be elected by a near 100 percent majority: "I am also sending you Hitler's famous last speech, which opened the election campaign. It is the most beautiful that the man has uttered. With it he has given us his soul. You must read it very slowly and imagine his voice; only then will it move you." He concludes the letter, "This evening I attended a concert of the famous Russian pianist, Horowitz."

Manfred von K. maintains his optimism about the new Germany throughout the decade that follows, even when the fortunes of war turn against the *Reich*. On September 1, 1939, the day Hitler attacked Poland, he writes home: "There is no doubt that England and France will be mobilized. We have to wait and see what form of opposition will materialize. And in that I am an optimist. I believe that England will go against us pro forma in order to save face." Yet two weeks later, now inside Poland, he adds: "I fear that overhasty optimism is inappropriate. If the affair turns out to be of long duration, I will be drafted into officers' training (September 16)." In the same letter he voices his grudging respect for British persistence: "If England really gets going, a change of government would hardly be expected from such a stubborn people; a change of mind on their part would be necessary to create the conditions for peace."

A few months later he led a reconnaissance mission of twenty soldiers behind the French lines. With a conquered machine gun in tow, his squadron returned unharmed. This success resulted in a medal of valor and officer status. His wish for an early peace dominates his thinking, however, and he reports a rumor associated with Hitler: "The *Führer* is supposed to have said to a group of soldiers in a bunker at Christmastime that he knew very well that they were only interested in how soon they could return

home; he said that they would definitely be home before the following Christmas. Such words make the rounds quickly."

In spite of his trust in Hitler, Manfred von K. remains skeptical about what the soldiers are told; on January 9, 1940, he writes:
"These speculations are all idle as long as we don't know more.
In this state that is controlled in an authoritarian manner, we
will never know enough about higher politics to form our own
opinions."

At the end of February 1940, Manfred von K. is granted a
special furlough because he has become a father. As time goes
on, however, he identifies more and more with his life in the
army and his job on the divisional staff, which involves organizational matters. German internal politics and even family
life fade into the background in his letters. Only international
politics and their effect on potential military conflicts seem to
interest him.

During the spring of 1940 the pace of the war slows down,
with no major military actions being waged, and Manfred von K.
has time to enjoy his officer status and assignment to the staff of
his division. He only regrets that his new status prevents him
from spending time with his soldier buddies as before. In an
aside he mentions that he is being trained as an officer for the
battlefront. He has enough leisure time to relate amusing anecdotes, and the fighting seems far away.

This period constitutes a peace before the storm. On May 10,
1940, the German army outflanked the Maginot Line and
invaded France via Belgium and the Netherlands. Later on,
Manfred von K. was to compare this war of six weeks with
the long battles against the Soviet Union. By contrast, the 1940
French campaign was a *Blitzkrieg,* and he adds: "When history

really gets rolling, losses are small." As the conquest of France ends he takes stock on June 25, 1940, of what he experienced. "In the last days we have seen unbelievable scenes, the dismantling of a defeated army. In Nancy alone more than 200,000 prisoners were taken. The big battle of Masuria [in East Prussia during World War I] produced about 100,000. And back then it was said, Those are just Russians."

The end of the successful war in France encourages Manfred von K. to dream of Germany as the superpower of a continental Europe, in which France would still, however, have a stake. "France has suffered a hard blow of fate, and a white France will soon emerge again; the power of its culture will still be able to play a significant and fruitful role in the European concert." As for England, he sees "the removal of a plutocratic clique that in its constant exaggerated influence stands in the way of the two Germanic peoples." Here he expresses for the first time a white supremacist belief, an attitude quite common in midcentury Europe and the United States.

Hitler employed the trump card of nationalism to rally the vast majority of the German population behind him, between the defeat of France and the second severe Russian winter of 1942. In his letters, the young divisional staff officer Manfred von K. reflects this reality, coming back several times to the symbolism of Verdun, as in a letter to his parents of July 22, 1940: "Because our division played a major role in the storming of Verdun, the honorable task of explaining the course of the battles to prominent personalities from Fort Douaumont fell to my general, who received the Knight's Cross *(Ritterkreuz)* for this achievement." For Manfred von K., as for so many Germans, the swift defeat of France erased what most Germans considered the shame of German defeat in World War I and the Treaty of Versailles with its harsh reparations.

Despite a negative view of the war itself, referring to it as "the grotesque war" *(der groteske Krieg)* and "the damn war" *(der verdammte Krieg)*, Manfred von K. has a keen eye for military limits and possibilities, as well as an unquestioned faith in the military hierarchy. As the fortunes of war begin to shift, any doubts he may have had are obscured by references to the upbeat assessments of higher-ups. He is, moreover, capable of poking fun at himself and his role as a junior officer in the staff of the division: "Since I am probably the youngest in years and also have the least experience as an officer in this illustrious assembly, which is to say mess hall officer, I make it my habit every morning to prance through the house and garden and show off as much as possible." He sent this letter, dated July 22, 1940, to his parents, not his wife.

A few times he gets carried away and imagines Germany as the leader of a new fascist Europe. "An empire, a unified Europe under German leadership," he observes on September 29, 1940, "is not handed to us as a gift." But even in this, his letters are not consistent, particularly when he allows himself to reflect on his personal life and wistfully admits, "One is a soldier as long as there is war." He continues with such thoughts the next day: "One doesn't remember that one is married. I really have bad luck: first the long years in South America . . . and then I finally find a nice woman, whom I get to see at best every few months during the war." His utopia involving a new German empire has room for a personal dream or two as well, as in this comment from mid-April 1941: "Perhaps in a peaceful future we will be able to maintain contact with a circle of friends who are not only famous, but also particularly worthwhile and pleasant."

By spring 1941 Manfred von K. is back in Germany. Radical changes are in the air and he senses them. What he doesn't know, however, is that his future assignment will make the campaign in France pale by comparison. Still in Germany, he writes on March 19, 1941: "Everything here is breaking up and therefore quite unpleasant. I myself will most likely experience a change of air on the 27th."

His trek eastward through German-occupied Poland takes him at first through places he had been two years earlier. On April 18, 1941, he writes: "We slept once again in the soldiers' barracks in the unattractive Jewish part of town, where we lodged for several days. Then we continued through a typical Galician landscape. Many a soldier's grave from the Polish campaign lined our way." Later in the same letter he notes, "We arrived in a village more Ukrainian than Galician in appearance. In any case, there are already Orthodox churches with their famous onion spires; the faces of the rural population also look different. Friendlier, brighter. They often greet the wagons spontaneously as they roll by. Villages are incredibly primitive." Then he adds an observation that he is to repeat in many of his letters from Eastern Europe: "Typical for the East: extreme poverty and extreme aristocratic grand style. A middle class is totally lacking." Four days later he notes, "The road conditions are unbelievable. And so is the Jewish quarter where I am lodged"—and where he remains for some time, commenting: "The pretty frame with the two photos [from home] always gives me great joy when I return to my Jewish quarters. But I'm really for not continuing this damn old war ad infinitum."

In a letter of April 28, 1941, he describes his sense of alienation: "The people are very friendly. Nevertheless, I always feel as if I were very very far away from you. Inside me it's the feeling that I'm exactly as far away as when I was in Brazil." Mention of his transfer in a letter of May 1 implies that at that time Jews still lived in their homes: "While half of the ghetto looked on, I moved out of the Jewish quarter this morning in order to spend the last night with Lieutenant Herfurth in the new summer quarters."

Finally, Manfred von K. arrives at the border of the Soviet Union, an event he describes on May 4, 1941:

> Very beautiful areas of forest and a mediocre stand of pines. In between, a landscape that was feeling the first sunshine of spring. It was a great pleasure to which I gave myself wholeheartedly. We were at the border and looked over into the empire [of the Soviets] where far and wide not a soul was to be seen. For Pfd [an army friend, apparently] and me a strange feeling. A year and a half ago we stood at the French border and looked across under similar circumstances. Only that in the West there were borders made of stone, whereas here only barbed wire runs along the frontier.

On May 16, 1941, five weeks before Hitler attacks the Soviet Union and seven months before the Japanese bomb Pearl Harbor, Manfred von K. detects clues in a speech by Hitler he has just heard, which he says "was definitely a preparation for a longer war. There is no longer any doubt about America's entrance into the war." He describes mounting tensions: "Again we face very tense weeks; again we stand prepared and wait for our orders, but this time we know even less where the orders will lead us. . . . The days are already quite warm, although nights still grow cool. Nevertheless, I sit at the open window to listen to the frogs' concert, which I have not experienced in such intensity since Brazil."

Hell breaks lose on June 21, 1941, when the German army begins its massive assault on the Soviet Union. Manfred von K.'s commitment to Hitler is total; a fanaticism creeps into his first letter following the attack that drowns out the reflective tendency found in earlier letters. This letter of June 21 begins with a warning to his wife: "As a true follower, you needn't always be surprised by the *Führer*'s methods. That the censor opened my letter of the 11th doesn't surprise me at all. For that reason, I asked you in my last letter to take into consideration the customs of our authoritarian state leadership."

The war against the Soviet Union brings into sharp relief for him, as for other German soldiers ordered to fight there, the radical differences in culture and mentality, which contrast with his experiences on the western front. The war propaganda and army training clearly had not prepared them for this. Writing again on June 21, he notes:

> Western European thinking must first adjust itself internally to this Asiatic manner of making war. If I were to describe the details to you, you would only see the gruesome sides of them without comprehending the inexorable internal laws of this war, the pitiless face of Asiatic-Tartar instincts . . . political commissars . . . female captains with red stars. Here you don't ask for pardon, and none is given. Two worlds stand facing each other. . . . Images of dull, Asiatic fatalism coupled with deceitful battle rage—between [them and us] there can be no compromise.

Based on this experience, he reaches a conclusion, which also contains a rare allusion to earlier atrocities in Poland: "Never again will I allow even a word about the SS and their methods

in Poland to be uttered in my presence." Although he provides
few details about the battle in which he personally was involved,
one nevertheless is very graphic: "I was among the first to enter
the central office of the GPU [State Secret Police of the Soviet
Union], where 9 people including two women shot themselves
as we entered. They knew full well that the people would betray
them. What faces! Jews and Tartars."

As his army unit conquers the eastern part of Poland, which
had been occupied by the Soviet Union since the Stalin-Hitler
Pact of 1939, Manfred von K. draws a vivid picture of the Poles
and the city of Lvov as he experienced them during the Polish campaign. He refers to the attack by the local population
on Jews who were rumored to have helped the Soviets, and also
to the murder of thousands of Polish officers by the Soviets in
the forest of Katyn. He is surprised that the Polish and later on
the Ukrainian population seem to be friendly, knowing that the
German army had not treated the Poles well two years earlier.

During this early part of the attack on the Soviet Union, he
is deeply impressed by the poverty of the general population
and the apparent wealth of the elite. He speculates about this
disparity in a letter of July 10, 1941: "In Russia there never was a
middle class and an upper class of workers, as there are with us.
Rather, a small stratum ruled in crass contrast to the working
masses that lived in primitive conditions. Sometimes one asks
oneself whether, from the standpoint of the Russian proletariats,
the Soviet system didn't constitute progress in certain things."
But in this same letter he shifts from discerning rational analysis
to straightforward racist views: "In any case, as carriers of civilization we will not be able to plant any industrious German seed
into foreign races and soils for many years."

238 / *German Soldiers Write Home*

All the violence and destruction that Manfred von K. now witnesses in the East is disproportionately greater than what he experienced on the western front, as he concludes on July 2, 1941: "When you have seen Lemberg, then you wish for a quick peace and you hope that the intense suffering of the people stops. But we are still far from it." This longing for peace is genuine, but in no instance does he suggest that Germany under Hitler is the main cause of all the suffering. Even this intelligent man with his cosmopolitan background, clearly capable of independent thought, falls victim to a selective awareness that prevents him from questioning beliefs he has held since 1933. Whenever doubts arise in himself or others, his recourse, like an act of faith, remains the figure of Hitler. He has internalized his *Führer's* pronouncements to such a degree that at times he passes them on as his own.

His unflinching loyalty to the *Führer* does not extend to Hitler's lieutenants, however. Also in the early summer of 1941 he writes, "The manner of the special Sunday broadcasts [official pronouncements about the war, usually introduced by a flourish of Franz Liszt's music] was sheer ballyhoo and therefore not worthy of the severity of the battles, which had something of the nature of a crusade about them." Then he becomes more specific in his criticism: "Mr. G. [i.e., Propaganda Minister Goebbels] obviously knows how to make propaganda. Up till now, his success proves him right. However, it seems to me that in this instance one can see that he was never a soldier. And I can't imagine that the homeland is already to the point that it needs a carnival Sunday with march music."

The initial success of the German army in Russia is proof enough for Manfred von K. that the Nazi cause is just. On July 18,

1941, he writes: "It is amazing how everything works. Sometimes one doesn't dare believe in the mathematically precise work of our leadership, but the law of providence has always been with us." But as time and the war churn on, his ideology about "Tartars, Jews and Asian peoples" is gradually replaced by a grudging respect for the Soviet army. "In this campaign superlatives were truly achieved," he observes, "because the enemy fights back quite differently in its toughness and obstinacy than the French and English in the West."

Manfred von K. also exhibits a keen awareness of the civilian population caught in the line of fire. Occasionally he wishes the common folk could be removed from the battle zones so that soldiers might fight among themselves as of old. On August 12, 1941, he writes:

> In general, the presence of the civilian population running around in the battle zone presents a strange picture. Most of the time the unfortunate people are stuck in their potato cellars, which, because of the winter temperatures in the East, are deep under ground. Whenever there is a break in the shooting you see our troops with steel helmets on their heads, and between them somewhat fearful, scantily clad farm girls picking up their skirts and running to the closest fountain. Because water in this country is the question that could almost unite friend and foe. If we had Frenchmen and not Bolshevists here, we would reach an accommodation over the water situation.

By early 1942, the fortunes of war had begun to shift. German military advances in the vast wintry plains of Russia were halted and the United States had joined the Allied forces. Manfred von K. was now transferred back to France, where his letters show the military strategist and the convinced Nazi ideologue to be in conflict. While he recognizes German military setbacks and the emerging shift in the balance of power, he still settles the score in favor of the propaganda he holds to be true, simply because Hitler has articulated it. Informed military knowledge and insight yield to reliance on the "natural superiority" propounded by the Nazi hierarchy. In referring to a speech by a "high authority" sent from Berlin, Manfred von K. makes a revealing statement on January 22, 1942, one that set the tone for him until the end of the war:

> From a high vantage point he [Baron von Lersner, from Berlin] portrayed the divergent developments of the two peoples [Germans and British] and presented a creative image of the German people over against the typical little English shopkeepers of today. He completed his remarks . . . with the point—which we must continually prove—that our inner assurance of victory is absolutely irrevocable, and that we must understand how to defend this assurance against all evidence to the contrary.

At this time, Nazi propaganda has begun to present real military setbacks as deliberate strategic retrenchments ordered by the *Führer* and his generals. Manfred von K.'s letter of January 22 reflects this position: "After the intense defensive battles in the East again demonstrated the clear superiority of German soldiers, so that any serious threat can no longer arise. . . ." Since Germany is now on the defensive, he draws his optimism in the same letter from Japanese advances in the Far East: "Today's reports about Burma are very encouraging and if successful mean that China will be cut off from the road to Burma, and India cut off from rice imports from Rangoon, because that source from Bangkok has already dried up."

Manfred's wife, Ingrid, seems to have answered all of his letters, and he makes marginal references to them in his own letters to her. After this lengthy analysis of the war in Europe and Asia, he admits: "You write about children and I write about politics."

Almost two weeks later, in a letter of February 5, 1942, he momentarily breaks through the veil of ideology to express an insight of his own: "I sometimes feel rather stupid when I simply answer all arguments with a reference to trust. Perhaps it is easier to believe than to try to deal with all possible doubts." But he immediately retreats to the usual, comforting reference to higher authorities, to whom he attributes greater wisdom: "Therefore one feels thankful to see one's own position confirmed by a man who has a completely different overview of things." Some of his letters reveal that other officers did not share his continued optimism about the war; one he refers to by name in a letter of February 26, 1942, saying that he would like to straighten him out with "superior" arguments.

On April 16, 1942, Manfred von K. is on his way back to Russia. Inside the Soviet Union he traverses territory in eastern Poland that had previously been annexed by the Soviet Union and the Ukraine. It is familiar to him from the year before. His letter of April 19, 1942, contains a rare reference to the presence of Jews: "On the way to an outlying freight railroad station, Cavalry Captain von B. and I rode in an open horse wagon through the walled-in ghetto, which, if possible, should be traversed in a trot." He doesn't describe anything he saw on this swift trip through the ghetto, however. Once he reaches the Ukraine he observes, on April 23, 1942, that "the populace is exceedingly friendly, much friendlier and more forthcoming than in France."

As time passes, with no end to the war in sight, Manfred von K. concentrates more on his officer's duties in his correspondence with his wife. On May 3, 1942, he writes: "In the end it is of minor importance in what capacity and where one performs one's duty, since for me the execution of war will hopefully remain a temporary commitment." While stationed in Kiev, he enjoys the cultural life of the city, attending operas and ballets, and on May 6, 1942, compares the city to São Paulo, with their "juxtaposition of large government buildings in the American style . . . and ramshackle huts. Moreover, the people are friendly to us. Therefore, we don't have to suffer under partisans, since it is the Ukrainians themselves who urgently wish Soviet agents etc. to be caught."

On May 21, 1942, finally back at the front headquarters as a member of the divisional staff, he writes: "I had a lot to do. I couldn't get away from the telephone. I got two hours of sleep at night. But that is nothing compared to what a warrior must endure. . . . It is a peculiar war in this huge, bare landscape with its endless horizon . . . shimmering, hot, dusty days and cold clear nights."

Manfred von K. no longer tries to integrate his experiences and beliefs into a coherent whole. Claims of German military prowess and of the invincibility of the German army, often dressed in well-established propagandistic cant; comments about the suffering of the local population; hopes for an early end of the war; continued faith in Hitler; and ever-more-frequent reference to the immensity of the Russian plains—all these elements alternate. In the letter of May 21, he also seems existentially adrift:

When at night you drive in a vehicle with lights off through this completely open terrain and see the infinite starry heaven above you in wonderful clarity, you can feel quite lost. And it always impresses you just as much in the daylight how lost a person is in this landscape. . . . Recently I saw an attractive young woman in a bright dress with exposed arms and legs planting potatoes. Not 20 steps from her lay a dead Russian whose arms stretched ghostlike into the air, a strange experience of the Russian spring.

At the end of May, Manfred von K.'s division arrives at Charkov, southwest of Moscow, on its way to the Volga River and Stalingrad. On May 30, 1942, he indulges in reveries of peace: "The wonderful chestnuts stood conciliatory and watchful on both sides of the long rows of graves. In this barren steppe a large tree is a consolation for our German eyes." His optimism about innate German superiority follows quickly, though mixed with concern about where Germans will draw their defensive lines before the arrival of the next Russian winter. "Here in the East . . . we have shown that the initiative again is in our favor. That is decisive. . . . Where we draw the border here in Russia in the fall is by comparison less important." After years of writing home almost every other day, by midsummer (July 13, 1942) he complains that he "really can't find time to write," sometimes making light of the increasingly difficult battles so that his wife won't worry about him.

Autumn comes early in Russia. On August 28, 1942, he writes: "How incredibly fast these summer months passed with the difficult campaign. What experiences we have had. Today German tanks reached the Volga. I hope the battle for Stalingrad won't last long, so that we can soon make the necessary preparations

244 / *German Soldiers Write Home*

for the winter." He rarely discusses details of military engagements, but he hints in this letter at the violence of the campaign that will precede the second Russian winter. "The impressions of this brutally executed war in the steppes are such that one doesn't want to burden the homeland with them." He grudgingly admits that "in defending itself, this primitive, natural people performs astonishingly well. . . . It would completely miss the mark to draw comparisons to France in June 1940." Yet knowing that the German army is bogged down, he shifts in his thinking from attack to defense. "We must get ready for a second hard winter, in which we have the advantage, in that we will prepare better and that Russia is gradually losing resources. How it will nourish its two largest centers, Moscow and Leningrad, throughout the winter is undoubtedly a problem. . . . Of course, I don't have an overview."

He underestimates the sheer will of the Russian people to survive, no matter how extreme the conditions, and he does not know that as the German army prepares itself for ice and snow, the Soviets are amassing a huge army for their winter offensive to the east. In autumn 1942, Manfred von K.'s division arrives in Stalingrad. Although he is cautiously upbeat in his assessment of the strategic situation, he is also aware that the Germans' flanks were unprotected during their advance and that several units cut off by the Soviets might be reunited with the rest of the army only after heavy fighting. Yet he rises for the last time to the challenge as he sees it. "Even if we don't have much going for us anymore, we'll still be able to go the last yard." He concludes one of his final letters, on September 21, 1942, with an impression of Stalingrad in ruins: "Strange images in the city, where here and there civilians crawl out of cellars. . . . There will be great suffering to come among the people in the poor villages. The city will probably be evacuated, one hopes; then it will be a purely male matter—the city of rubble and ruins, cellars and barricades—until winter snows lay down a veil of forgetting." His expected winter calm will not come to pass, however. The Russians are ready to throw their armies against the Germans to retake Stalingrad.

The intervals between Manfred von K.'s letters grow longer. His Sixth German Army is encircled by the Soviets and slowly cut off. On November 2, 1942, he writes about "battles of great ferocity. Russia saw its great chance after an initial success and continued to attack with extreme force." He tries to interpret an impending German defeat as a prelude to the eventual reversal of fortunes in favor of the German side. "Leadership and troops have passed this test convincingly; now we are in the process of turning the tables on the exhausted and fragmented Russians and sending them packing—so that we will finally have our peace for the winter." But this respite was not to come, as Manfred von K. seems to sense when, in his second-to-last letter, typed on December 21, 1942, he reflects on the hundreds and hundreds of letters he has written to his wife over the years: "I believe that you have received so many long letters from me," he writes, "that I don't need to send you a 'tragic farewell letter,' if it should come to that in the end, since one already knows its content in advance. I am fully confident that you will raise the boys in a sensible way."

Before the final showdown, an extended lull in battle gives brief respite, and Manfred von K. seizes the occasion to express his innate optimism one last time. The Soviet encirclement was not tight, and much German traffic of men and materials still made its way in and out of Stalingrad. Around Christmastime he writes about trivial family matters, even discusses detailed plans for a furlough, and generally makes light of the German situation in and around Stalingrad. "Perhaps we will even be encircled—who can know! But you shouldn't worry unnecessarily and think that that is necessarily dangerous. The broad steppes are like a desert. Whoever breaks through the line can wander around freely in the region." Following this letter, Manfred von K. falls silent for a very long time.

The period that follows in Manfred von K.'s story is known in history books as the battle for Stalingrad. It ended on January 31, 1943, when the Sixth German Army, under the command of General Friedrich von Paulus, surrendered to the Soviet army. The battle for Stalingrad became the turning point of World War II on the European continent in favor of the Allies.

Several years pass. Finally, nearly three years after Stalingrad, Manfred von K.'s wife receives a brief message from her husband, who is alive and a POW in the Soviet Union. "I am healthy and well," he writes. "I am hopefully and confidently looking forward to an early reunion." The message expedited by the Red Cross carries the date December 25, 1945. A half year later, on June 11, 1946, Manfred von K. has not yet heard from home and is worried. Over a year after that, in July 1947, he finally hears from his wife and is elated to learn that she and their two boys survived the war. On September 7, 1947, he writes to her: "I have recovered well, fresh, am confident, hopeful that this will be the last winter." His wish was not realized, though, and the brief messages written on cards continue intermittently—on March 27, 1948; November 1, 1951; May 19 and July 22, 1952. On April 4, 1954, he writes: "Dear Ingrid! Twelve years ago I held you and the children in my arms for the last time. Still we must hope and trust in the magnanimous promise of the Soviet government of last year." A similar card is sent on October 7, 1954. On March 7, 1955, he once again expresses his hope for release: "After 13 years may grace descend on us."

As per agreement between the Federal Republic of Germany and the Soviet Union, the last contingent of German POWs was released and sent home in that year. Manfred von K. was among them.

TWO CLOSE FRIENDS

Eugen L. and Hans L., who shared a world of art, literature, and theology, were drafted at the beginning of World War II, in 1939, and spent the years that followed apart. They continued to cultivate their own intellectual and artistic universe, however, in the many letters they wrote to each other, while at the same time putting into words what they saw and experienced of war and violence. At the beginning of the war, Eugen writes to his friend Hans on October 1, 1939: "Have you also been blessed with the handsome armband: 'German Army'?" They have the same feelings about their military service, with criticism of soldiering running though their correspondence until the end. Hans writes to Eugen on July 10, 1940, from France: "When my duties are done, then I'm done. I automatically change into my suit and go to the baptistry—I believe I won't have to pay an entrance fee anymore pretty soon—where I can't ever get enough of the frescoes. . . . Then I return to the barracks where you wash, eat dry bread, clean boots, climb into bed, and look forward to more nonsense. How dull is the day and how uncertain the future."

Eugen echoes some of the same sentiments when he writes to Hans on October 1, 1941: "I believe that soldiering doesn't come any easier for me than for you. . . . Or is it not the uniform but rather, much more, the long, indeterminate, inescapable duration of it all! At any rate, it takes so much effort to remain 'alert' to everything that is close to my heart."

Eugen's and Hans's fates as soldiers were closely tied to their assigned stations in the geography of the war. On April 16, 1940, shortly before Hitler's attack on France, Eugen writes: "Now my fate is approaching. I'm going to the front again; I already have the confirmation, it can happen any day now. The exact date, however, is still uncertain, so I vacillate between the East and the West." A week later, on April 23, he is exhilarated to report unexpected good news: "To make it brief, my new station is Vienna. This time they really gave us the runaround. We thought we were going to the front." Now Eugen's letters report on the operas he hears and the museums he visits. But on May 16, six days after Germany invades France, he writes an emotional letter to Hans, who is stationed on the western front: "I can't tell you how much I long for a sign of life from you. The commonly used phrase 'sign of life' has taken on very heavy overtones. I imagine that you have been a part of it [the attack on France]! My thoughts were with you all these days. One can only judge the impact of what has begun when one thinks of one's friends."

For both of them, France is not an enemy to be defeated but a country they love and admire for its culture. In order to understand its literature and philosophy better, Eugen translates key French texts that are close to him; the poetry of Baudelaire, Cézanne's reflections on art, and Pascal's *Pensées* are woven into

many of his letters. His friend Hans likewise practices translating to get a better feel for the French language. As the war
progresses, the tone of their letters becomes darker. As early as
May 10, 1940, Hans writes to Eugen: "Where are you, actually?
In Vienna, or facing the enemy perhaps? It doesn't matter. When
this reaches you I will have been with you again a thousand
times. In every picture, whether painted or in the great out-of-
doors, my vivid thoughts are immediately in your presence. I
always know you would feel the same way, both in awe of the
abundance of beauty and in revulsion over the terrible suffering
that our soldiers, but especially the French, endure."

It is during an early stage of the war that Eugen, in a letter
of July 5, 1940, refers to works by Goya, which in turn become a
kind of leitmotif throughout their correspondence:

> I own a beautiful edition of the *Désastres de la guerre* by Goya. At
> the end of the series of often horrifying scenes, the last page: the
> Truth: how this disheveled old man, a hoe in his right hand, holds
> his wife with his left as if dazzled by her bare breasts ... to the right
> the baby in the crib, a sheep, sheaves in the field, and a tree laden
> with fruit! Thus end *les désastres,* the horrors of war; they dissolve in
> the face of maternal fertility. In this way, following the upheavals,
> we all long for peace, which "fulfills"; after storms and fears, the
> clarity of midday.

A sense of foreboding begins to creep into their letters.
Eugen writes on July 10, 1940: "You are at the ocean. Loads of my
wishes accompany you into the future. Who knows? The question and the expectation of what's to come lie on each one of us;
in forebodings of terrible things: because fate has no power to
stop what has been set in motion so easily: the apocalyptic rider
of war."

Between Germany's occupation of France in May 1940 and its attack on the Soviet Union in June of the following year, the European continent experienced relative calm. There were even rumors that a compromise peace might be achieved. During this period the two friends took stock of their experiences and tried to find an emotional and moral compass for the mayhem that might lie ahead. They could not, of course, foresee the brutal horrors that the war in the Soviet Union would unleash, yet premonitions weighed on them already in late 1940. On November 19, for example, Eugen reports on a visit he made to a Viennese museum:

> The most powerful and truly most unsettling picture couldn't even be exhibited—we were allowed to view it behind a curtain. "1914–1918" is seen, as in old woodcuts, on a small roll on the ground. Two fighters in horribly shrunken format, stiffened at the moment of death on top of the mountain of corpses on the battlefield. One with his head pointed down and with his mouth open, as if from this lowest point of the picture the breath of death is exhaled. The color is really no color at all, but a corpselike, leathery brown. Here there's no trace of transfiguration . . . no mercy. Has art reached its limits here, a *non plus ultra*—or has it gone beyond them in this?

On June 22, 1941, Eugen expresses a thought that must have been in the minds of many Germans the day after Hitler's attack on the Soviet Union: "It is no longer predictable what boundaries of time and space we will have to stake out for this war."

Hans was soon transferred to the Russian front, and at the outset life was relatively peaceful. He writes to Eugen on July 8, 1941: "It's a very peculiar and calm war for us . . . and the things there are to see! Jews, wooden houses, and impoverished-looking Poles; the only sign of higher culture are the churches—even in this tiny burg where people speak a Hebrew type of German, there's a wonderful church as well as a Russian one with icons."

Within a few months' time, the relative peace had changed dramatically for Hans. On October 28, 1941, he writes to Eugen:

> A pause to catch my breath and to glance into the void across desolate, dark, burned-out fire sites. On top of this, the fatal uncertainty of our position—especially our very personal one. How I survived two shots that struck within meters of me I'd rather tell you in person. I am truly horrified whenever I think of it. . . . The view of bestially mutilated corpses who wear the same clothes as we do cuts deep into the world of imagination that surrounds us here. But also the rigid faces of those hung as well as those shot and tumbling into ditches—images darker than the darkest of Goya—oh, Eugen, you never forget these things even if you want to. . . . Here no beauty is possible, no stillness, no mercy; there's only fear and finally horror.

Aside from the widespread horrors, Hans retains a keen eye for the individual Russians with whom he comes in contact during extended stays away from the front line. On All Soul's Day, November 2, 1941, he describes an encounter with a Russian in a sauna:

> An elderly man in a dilapidated suit full of holes sat [in the room] where we were getting dressed after the sauna. Meaning no harm, I said to my adjutant, "Look, he has a suit made of Swiss cheese." When the Russian answered in a clear German, "My clothes are shabby and worn," I was so moved that I dropped the pants that I had just pulled up. After a few exchanges he told us about the [art] galleries in Moscow and Petersburg as if he were an expert. . . . I couldn't get over my astonishment and I asked him what his profession was. He was a forester; he taught himself German and French and previously had been a teacher. But the Reds had no use for him. For some time he had been learning Latin, and he recited passages

from Caesar, Ovid, Cicero, and—what a miracle!—from Virgil.
Virgil in the sauna! from the lips of a man who, out of poverty and
shame that others would ridicule the rags he wore, sits in the corner to get dressed.

By spring Eugen, too, was on the way to the Russian front.
On March 18, 1942, he wrote to Hans: "We are now one day and
two nights into our journey east. Never before have I traveled
so incredibly fast straight across Germany with the travel and
transport society 'Army & Sons.' Yes, it's going too fast. . . . But
since we're going east no matter what, it doesn't matter to me.
After us, the deluge."

The many letters Eugen had received from the East had
informed him in a general way of the happenings there, but what
he saw with his own eyes went beyond anything he could have
imagined. On March 24, while traveling through the Ukraine,
Eugen writes:

Another greeting from our journey. We're getting close to Dnje-
popetrowsk. With this news you will know approximately where
we are and approximately where we are going or are being moved
to. Outside, the wonderfully blue, transparent, winter sky over the
snowy Ukraine. Yesterday I finished translating the biography of
Cézanne that I dragged along all the way from France. . . . There
are things here that make you ashamed of being a German. What
one finds out about what we have done to the "chosen people"! That
has nothing to do with anti-Semitism; that is inhumanity that one
would have thought impossible in the enlightened modern age of
the twentieth century. How will it ever be atoned! When you hear
such stories (and here you hear them from eyewitnesses), you must
sink into despair over the meaning of our battle. But what can you
do? Shut up and continue to serve.

At about the same time (March 21), Hans writes to Eugen: "We still haven't been relieved; we are positioned in the main line of battle right across from the Reds. . . . The corpses that we tossed onto the heap are now sorted out as well as possible, and the more than half a thousand Jews that were shot have been covered with lime. The details of what happened here—to write about that is not the right place. . . . My 'state of mind' is desperate. But it will probably recuperate."

Hans never recovers from what he has seen and heard. His revulsion determines the tone of the subsequent correspondence between the two friends. The letters become less frequent, probably because the intensity of frontline battles prevented him from writing or perhaps because the delivery of army mail from one part of the Soviet Union to the other became increasingly difficult. But a letter written on August 15, 1942, captures Hans's state of mind:

Dear Eugen! I wish for peace in order to take a piece of it to give to you. Everything that I see and hear is so dreadful, so unbearable . . . that, although everything around us feels like peace, I often find myself thoroughly shaken and tired inside. I find that it would be unholy and a sin to communicate this darkness to you. . . . Our surroundings [a veiled reference to Germany] exalt and at the same time destroy community. Alone in our hours of despair, the best of us give our best, which we inherited from our mothers' wombs. But no angel blesses us when we are surrounded by the transgressions of others. All of this makes me very sad. How brutally cruel is man, and often how cool and horribly matter-of-fact.

Eugen and Hans were caught up in the maelstrom of the war in the East, ordered there as soldiers. Neither of them had ever joined the Nazi Party, and they had nothing positive to say about the regime. They were not admirers of the military hierarchy nor did they believe in Nazi claims of Aryan racial superiority. Early in the war, by chance, Eugen came to sit in a café near the leading Nazi ideologue of race, Alfred Rosenberg, who in 1934 wrote the infamous *Der Mythus des zwanzigsten Jahrhunderts* (The myth of the twentieth century). With the expert eye of an artist, Eugen assessed him. On April 16, 1940, he wrote to his friend: "We weren't allowed inside the city hall because Rosenberg was to speak there. In the afternoon when we sat in the casino in Jeppert and drank a cup of coffee, Rosenberg sat with regional Nazi Party leader *[Gauleiter]* Forster next to us at the table. I, of course, took a close, hard look at my subject." Although Eugen doesn't elucidate his impressions, his intimate friend, Hans, would have understood the disdain implied in this "close, hard look."

Eugen and Hans's world encompassed French art and literature, Cervantes, Tolstoy, Virgil, the medieval mystic Meister Eckhart, even Thomas Mann—who had been declared persona non grata by the Nazis—and Hermann Hesse. Their musical tastes ranged from classical music to French chansons. Eugen preferred Mozart to Richard Wagner, who had been cast into a Germanic icon by Hitler. After seeing *Don Giovanni* in Vienna, Eugen wrote to Hans on May 1, 1940, that Mozart's music would stand by itself even without the visual effects of opera, whereas "Wagner always comes off poorly because no one can stand that tooting without the glamorous sheen of the stage." Their preferred society is neither fatherland nor *Volk*, but rather a circle of like-minded friends cultivated while at university. At times they profess their distance from the bourgeoisie and its values, as when Eugen writes to Hans on January 24, 1941, "I increasingly take a dim view of certain bourgeois traits—a narrowness of perception, a rigid planning and striving for security and a comfortable life! How I must praise my home. The generosity of my mother."

Eventually, Hans, on the Russian front, begins to lose hope; on March 1, 1942, he writes:

> Dear Eugen! . . . since the 29th of January our otherwise so peaceful city [here unnamed] has been engaged in a continual battle with the Reds, who for as many days have surrounded us with a wall of people and canons. . . . I remain watchful and pray, since prayer has become as dear to me as the handful of bread that we receive. I also allow myself to write that I have become familiar with the thought that I won't come home—however, there is hardly anyone in our group who doesn't have some hope left for a happy ending.

Whenever the duties of soldiering did not eat up their time, the two friends continued to write long letters to each other. They sketched the sights around them or followed their deeply Christian faith by discussing biblical passages, a long discourse on Paul's letters to the Galatians being one such example. In spite of the violence and mayhem around them, they tried to stay true to their cultural values to the very end. Eugen relies more and more on his skill as a painter and drawer of sketches to keep on an even keel. He writes to Hans on March 28, 1942: "And these sights on the way! Emaciated horses, horse cadavers along the street, then left or right graves of soldiers, refugees, columns of women who shovel the snow from the streets. A gripping image is unforgettable for me—how a man and woman pull a sled through the snow with a stick; the tiny faces of two children peer out from the covered sled, and from behind a grandmother, black and bent, pushes. The villages lining the streets drown in the water from the melting snow."

As winter passes, spring and summer offer new vistas to the eye of the artist—idyllic moments in a brutal war. On June 4, 1942, Eugen writes to Hans: "To once spend a week in the village below and to sketch to one's heart's content! That would yield profits! How colorful these villages wake up from winter, how changed the people, bright girls who flirt like they do in big cities—in guiltless, naïve ways; barefoot and with a bright head scarf, the women at the fountain or in the fields; the old people in the meadow or in their front doors—untold visual impressions, which could all become studies for big new paintings."

But in the summer of 1942 the war on the Russian front intensifies once again and Eugen is increasingly affected by the fighting, as he explains in a letter of July 14: "Now you have this sober, businesslike report. Does it tell you anything, these facts and outer realities of the war? I wanted to speak about the various impressions one has in relation to the events—how one's 'soul reacts.' But that is a difficult undertaking—everything is simply there. The news does not rattle me, fatigue makes me indifferent." Four days later he continues: "No matter how hard the war is, and no matter how tough it has made us—so that we are prepared for anything—what thoughts fill me for every dead person who exhales his last breath, struck by a piece of iron, for everyone whose whole life is reduced to a cripple's existence by a piece of raw material hurtled against it. The meaning of suffering—I think about these things remembering my past readings in the Book of Job."

Finally, Eugen's time is almost up. Writing on August 1: "No one to see, I'm alone. I move forward. I only had my pistol. Then a hit! The pistol is shot out of my right hand. I am thrown to the ground, I feel the moisture—blood! Now I could only retreat, alone in the world." After a stay in a military hospital, Eugen is back at the front as the Russian winter arrives once more. Eugen's letters become less frequent and he relies more and more on his art as a survival strategy. In November he still indulges in a long discussion about the paintings of Franz Marc, wondering why this artist makes animals the subject of his art. By the end of the year, Eugen's own art and artistic eye are all that remain. On December 16, 1942, he writes: "Then I sketched the ruins in the half-destroyed houses in our base in Kolchos. With their black roof rafters sticking up against the sky, the standing chimneys, and empty window hollows, they evoked pictures of a deadly chastisement; they betray more about war than the pictures of actual war events. . . . The war has already become too much of a fate, too much a natural force, rushing forward and smashing things, indifferent to our thoughts and wishes. Can one demand of an avalanche the direction it should roll?"

In Eugen's last surviving letter, from December 31, 1942, Goya's *Désastres de la guerre*—as reproduced in the volume that accompanied Eugen throughout his war years as a point of artistic and existential reference—comes to describe his own fate:

So I still brought together [i.e., managed to sketch] a few pages based on themes—a kneeling figure of a girl with a wreath in her hair. . . . Then "a ghost on the plains" who saunters up behind a wanderer—you know, a sort of skeleton that looks like the bones and cadavers that lie here in Russia on the military routes, upright and as if in pursuit. Then a "demon of the steppes," a monster I invented, almost with the body of a shark but with dragon feet waltzing above the ground. Finally, yesterday, a Russian dance-of-death scene—a soldier in the act of painting with death hovering over his shoulders.

The last document we have pertaining to Eugen is the official report of his status as missing in action:

> I . . . inform you on behalf of the authorities of the following: on January 29, 1943, during a skirmish near Gussewka (west of Woronesch) Lieutenant L. was wounded and was treated at a temporary field hospital; his wound consisted of an upper arm fracture from gunfire. According to the military doctor, his general condition was poor. On January 31, 1943, he was transported to a major field hospital in Nist-Sewitz, from which location all the sick and wounded soldiers were transported away from the front by airplane. Since that date we have received no further information; neither have we received any report of his admittance into a military hospital. . . . Heil Hitler! W. Ernst, Petty Officer

Eugen was never heard from again. Hans died a year later, on the Russian front.[10]

.   .   .

Manfred von K. and the two friends Eugen L. and Hans L., despite differing political views, belonged to a sophisticated, educated class of Germans who reflected on their experiences, often with great sensitivity. The majority of German troops who fought in World War II, however, were soldiers from modest circumstances with little or no higher education.

EVERYMAN

Franz W., eighteen years old, belongs to the long list of simple German soldiers whose letters are stored at the *Feldpostsamm-*

lung. Franz was close to his mother and tried to write home every week. He bares his heart to her—about his life in the military, his ambitions as a soldier, and his professional plans once the war is over. He also confides about his secret love for a girl, whose picture is pinned in his locker. His letters are written between 1942 and the spring of 1944. In the earliest letters his handwriting is meticulous, as if he wants to prove his superior penmanship to his mother, whom he idolizes. As time passes, he takes less care with his handwriting, and his thoughts become more fragmented as he jumps from subject to subject—mother in her flower shop or kitchen, the blonde girl he loves, dreams about life after the war, and plans to become a carpenter. All are suffused with nostalgia for home and hopes for the future, and he puts them in the style of a person who led a simple life until he was drafted. On April 4, 1943, for example, he writes: "How is it at home? The cherry trees are probably blooming in the garden, there's already a lot of green; especially now I think a lot about home. How it will look when I come home again, something has already changed, the store; I won't serve anyone anymore, I'll be on the lookout for something blond, but that will happen in any case, even without buying flowers."

In many of the letters he tries to please his mother, as when he takes stock of himself in an early letter: "You must actually be satisfied with me; I'm not a good-for-nothing, I don't smoke and drink; of course, I have faults, but certainly only small ones, like insolence, which I can't get rid of here. But, you know, Mother, we have always gotten along well with each other even if this or that didn't always go the way it should have. Oh well, I'm a Hamburg Pighead."

He is also bent on convincing his mother that he does better and is smarter than the other recruits around him. On June 12, 1943, for example, he writes: "Yesterday I wrote a letter for you, I described for you the situation here. Up to now nothing has changed. Always the same questions. . . . Just now someone came from the office, a very clever guy. He knows for sure that we'll be joining a company of cadets at Bug. Poor fool, he believes everything he hears. Some of the others are already going nuts, every day we're told something else. So as soon as it's certain, I'll write. My duties are done for the day, fini."

Franz has one passion that seems to preoccupy him: food. He goes into great detail about his efforts to augment the rations he is served in the mess hall, such as wolfing down his first portion to gain the time to line up for seconds. Once, as he tells his mother, he almost succeeded in making it through the chow line a third time, but the food ran out with only three other soldiers in front of him. He is particularly fond of vegetable soup. "It's served three times a week on top of our regular rations, we call it 'straight through France,' because it contains just about everything; but no matter; the soup is so thick that the spoons stand straight up in it."

Franz's letters contain hardly a trace of nationalism, let alone Nazism. But he has a strong sense of local patriotism for northern Germany and Hamburg, and he loves his *Heimat* to the extent that he believes his personal characteristics were shaped by that city near the North Sea. He is not fond of people from the south of Germany, particularly Bavarians.

Above all, Franz is concerned about his future. He is proud of his drawing and woodworking skills and wants to become a cabinetmaker, outlining for his mother his plans for achieving this goal. Imagining his return home to start a new life, on August 15, 1943, he writes:

> Above all, keep my [carpentry] apprentice certificate in a safe place, because if I am to become somebody along the lines that we all expect, then the well-being of our family will depend on it for a long time. . . . Then I will spend many an evening over a drawing and figure things out. I'll build models again and come home in the evenings with a briefcase under my arm. . . . When we have a peaceful period behind us, then one day I'll stand in front of you with a suitcase knowing what I want and where I'm going; I'll be able to do what I want, seek out my own path and won't be dictated to; then I'll recoup the time that has been taken from me.

Franz also had a childhood dream of flying, and he now works hard to be become a cadet in the air force. Accepted on November 3, 1943, he proudly writes his mother that he had his first flight when a crew was one man short and he volunteered to take his place—even though he was, as he confessed to the pilot, only a simple gunner. Eventually, full of pride, he can report to his mother that he has become a regular turret gunner. He is not permitted to write in detail about his combat missions, however, and the mood of his letters begins to change. "Flying is really great, I would like to continue with it if only the word military didn't come before it," he writes in unpolished German.

Though still loyal in his mind to the blonde girl back home, Franz confesses that he is going out with other girls as well. He begs his mother not to tell anyone, especially not his girl, because it might break her heart. He adds, dramatically, that if she knew she might drown herself in the Elbe River.

In 1944 the air war over Germany became more and more intense, and one day Franz vanishes. His mother kept his letters and in recent years gave them to the *Feldpostsammlung* archives in Berlin. Franz apparently died in battle, but where and when is unknown.

·   ·   ·

The rise of Nazism in Germany and World War Two, with the horrendous destruction it caused, leave me with a profound sense of sadness that this cautionary tale against modern totalitarianism does not erase. The attempt to rescue the importance of individual lives in both my books, *An Uncommon Friendship: From Opposite Sides of the Holocaust* and now *German Voices: Memories of Life during Hitler's Third Reich,* provides some consolation. But, as I recently wrote a Jewish friend, the wounds our generation carries from the past will never completely heal.

NOTES

INTRODUCTION

Epigraphs: Sebastian Haffner, *Geschichte eines Deutschen: Die Erinnerungen 1914–1933* (Munich: Deutscher Taschenbuch Verlag, 2002), 198; translation mine. Eberhard Weinbrenner (translation mine) was one of the Germans I interviewed; see chapter 4 for his story. The final epigraph is from a letter written by Emil B. located in the *Feldpostsammlung* of the Museum für Kommunikation, Berlin. This letter as well as the letters and excerpts in chapter 5 are housed in this archive; all translations of these letters are mine.

1. The museum is located at Leipziger Straße 16, Berlin; Internet URLs for the *Feldpostsammlung* are www.feldpost-archiv.de and www.feldpostsammlung.de.

2. The institute is located at Leonrodstraße 46; Internet access at www.ifz-muenchen.de.

3. Hans Mommsen, "Der Reichstagsbrand und seine politischen Folgen," *Vierteljahrshefte für Zeitgeschichte* 12 (1964): 411. Translation of this and other quotations from German texts are mine.

4. Jochen Lang, *Die Gestapo* (Hamburg: Rasch Verlag, 1990), 84.

5. Hubert Gelhaus, *365 ganz normale Tage. Betrachtungen des national-sozialistischen Alltags in Kloppenburg und Umgebung* (Oldenburg: Holzberg, 1988), 109.

6. "Der Reichstagsbrand. Ursachen Wirkungen Zusammenhänge" (Paris: Defense Verlag, n.d.), 29; anonymous pamphlet in the archives of the Institut für Zeitgeschichte, Munich.

7. Thomas Berger, *Lebenssituationen unter der Herrschaft des National-sozialismus* (Hannover: Niedersächsische Landeszentrale für politische Bildung, 1981), 34.

8. Ibid., 37–38.

9. From a typewritten letter of May 24, 1933, to the Nazi ministry of the interior in Berlin from the local Nazi officials of Merseburg, Archiv für Zeitgeschichte, Munich, microfiche, p. 48—one of many such documents deposited in German archives. It is now difficult to reconstruct in a few paragraphs the scope, speed, and thoroughness with which the Nazis launched mass arrests of their political enemies throughout Germany.

10. Birgit Retzlaff, *Arbeiterjugend gegen Hitler. Der Widerstand ehemaliger Angehöriger der sozialistischen Arbeiterjugendbewegung gegen das Dritte Reich* (Werther i. W.: Paegelit Verlag, 1993), 65.

11. Hans-Dieter Schmid, ed., *Zwei Städte unter dem Hakenkreuz. Widerstand und Verweigerung in Hannover und Leipzig, 1933–1945* (Leipzig: Leipziger Universitätsverlag, 1994), 104.

12. Joseph Wulf, *Presse und Funk im Dritten Reich. Eine Dokumentation* (Frankfurt: Ullstein, 1989), 100.

13. Ibid.

1. JOBS AND THE OLYMPIC GAMES

1. Berlin had been scheduled to host the Olympics in 1916, but the games were canceled because of the war; Germany was subsequently barred from the games of 1920 and 1924. This made hosting the 1936 games an even greater matter of pride and legitimacy for the Nazis.

2. Adolf Hitler, quoted in Hubert Gelhaus, *365 ganz normale Tage. Betrachtungen des nationalsozialistischen Alltags in Kloppenburg und Umgebung* (Oldenburg: Holzberg, 1988), 93.

3. True to the principle that the economy is servant to the nation because dependent on the larger political goals of the state, the Nazi leadership made sure that the traditional captains of industry were no longer the only ones to make key economic decisions, especially those that involved the production and distribution of raw materials, particularly iron and steel. Steel was to be the crucial element in putting the economy on a war footing. This aspect of the economic recovery was set apart from the overall Four-Year Plan. See Gerd Ruhle, *Das Dritte Reich. Dokumentarische Darstellung des Aufbaues der Nation, mit Unterstützung des deutschen Reichsarchivs; das fünfte Jahr, 1937* (Berlin: Hummelverlag, 1940), 193.

Early in the Third Reich, Germany experienced job creation and astonishing economic growth, but without any official reference to military buildup. That came later when, for example, during the war the overweight Hermann Göring demanded that Germans fight harder and eat less. Most Germans were well aware of the discrepancy between his exhortations about frugality and his own extravagant lifestyle.

4. Lore Walb, *Ich, die Alte; ich, die Junge. Konfrontation mit meinen Tagebüchern, 1933–1945* (Berlin: Aufbau-Taschenbücher, 1998), 74.

5. Beatrix Hochstein, *Die Ideologie des Überlebens. Zur Geschichte politischer Apatie in Deutschland* (Frankfurt: Campus, 1984), 207.

6. Ibid., 210.

7. Helmut Heiber and Beatrice Heiber, eds., *Die Rückseite des Hakenkreuzes. Absonderliches aus den Akten des Dritten Reiches* (Munich: Deutscher Taschenbuch Verlag, 1993), 193.

8. For more details, see Anatol von Hübbenet, "Die NS-Gemeinschaft 'Kraft durch Freude.' Aufbau und Arbeit," in *Schriften der Hochschule für Politik,* ed. Paul Meier-Benneckenstein (Berlin: Junker und Dünnhaupt, 1939), 35.

9. The first "grand happening"—celebrating the Nazis' decisive victory in the March 5 election—was in audio form and broadcast all over the country from Königsberg. The accompanying fanfare that took place in Göttingen on this occasion was repeated in many cities all over Germany.

10. Helmut Schmidt and Wolf Siedler, eds., *Kindheit und Jugend unter Hitler* (Berlin: Siedler Verlag, 1992), 27.

11. Joseph Goebbels, "Ansprache an die Vertreter der ausländischen Presse," July 7, 1936; recorded from a radio broadcast; my translation.

12. Wulf, *Presse und Funk im Dritten Reich,* 54.

13. Ibid., 77.

14. Arnd Klüger and Theodor Lewald, *Sportführer im Dritten Reich* (Frankfurt: Bartels, 1975), 46.

15. Gerhard Kiersch, *Berliner Alltag im Dritten Reich. Fotographierte Zeitgeschichte* (Düsseldorf: Droste, 1981), 43.

16. Quoted in Jochen Köhler, *Klettern in der Großstadt. Volkstümliche Geschichten vom Überleben in Berlin 1933–1945* (Berlin: Das Arsenal, 1979), 127.

17. Kiersch, *Berliner Alltag im Dritten Reich,* 43.

18. Berger, *Lebenssituationen unter der Herrschaft des Nationalsozialismus,* 127.

19. Heinz Wetzel, *Politische Leibeserziehung. Beiträge zur Formung ihres Bildes* (Limpert: Frankfurt, 1936), 37.

20. Jörg Titel, "Die Vorbereitung der Olympischen Spiele in Berlin 1936," in *Berlin in Geschichte und Gegenwart,* ed. J. Wetzel (Berlin: Jahrbuch des Landesarchivs, 1993), 120.

21. Ibid., 121.

22. Arno Klönne, *Hitlerjugend. Die Jugend und ihre Organisation im Dritten Reich* (Hannover: Norddeutsche Verlagsanstalt, 1957), 19.

23. Wetzel, *Politische Leibeserziehung,* 24.

24. Ibid., 37.

25. Ibid., 43.

26. Siegfried Zoglmann (text) and Heinrich Hoffmann Jr. (photos), *Jugend erlebt Deutschland* (Berlin: Verlag für soziale Ethik und

Kunstpflege, 1936), 17. Quoted phrase was a song lyric and widespread slogan.

27. Wetzel, *Politische Leibeserziehung,* 58.

2. *JUNGVOLK* AND HITLER YOUTH

Epigraph: Gerhard Neizert, one of my German interviewees. His war experiences are recounted in chapter 4.

1. Franz Josef Heyen, *Nationalsozialismus im Alltag. Quellen zur Geschichte des Nationalsozialismus vornehmlich im Raum Mainz-Koblenz-Trier* (Boppard am Rhein: Harald Boldt Verlag, 1967), 120.

2. Hans-Ulrich Thamer, *Verführung und Gewalt. Deutschland 1933–1945* (Berlin: Siedler Verlag, 1986), 72.

3. Ibid.

4. Heiber and Heiber, *Die Rückseite des Hakenkreuzes,* 42.

5. Bradley Smith, ed., *Heinrich Himmler. Geheimreden 1933 bis 1945* (Frankfurt: Ullstein, 1974), 35.

6. A pastor by the name of Josef Müller was less lucky. He told a joke about a dying parachutist whose last wish was to be buried with a picture of Hitler and Göring on each side. That way he would die like Jesus on the cross. The invocation of the two thieves crucified with Christ did not escape the Gestapo. Müller was arrested and executed on September 11, 1944, in Berlin-Plötzensee, a prison where tens of thousands of Germans who opposed the Nazi regime were murdered between 1933 and 1945, sometimes for no more than a derogatory remark or joke.

7. After 1935, all German youths, both boys and girls, belonged to the Nazi youth organizations, by law, with the exception of the usual groups: Jews, Gypsies (Roma), and the mentally and physically handicapped.

8. Bernat Rosner and Frederic C. Tubach, with Sally Patterson Tubach, *An Uncommon Friendship: From Opposite Sides of the Holocaust* (Berkeley: University of California Press, 2001), 103.

9. Adolf Hitler, *Adolf Hitler an seine Jugend* (Berlin and Munich: Zentralverlag der NSDAP, 1937), 2.

10. Albrecht Günther, *Geist der Jungmannschaft* (Hamburg: Hanseatische Verlagsanstalt, 1934), 37.

11. E. Mischlich, *Führer im Geländesport für Hitlerjugend und Geländesportschulen,* ed. E. Hägele (Leipzig: Armanen Verlag, 1934), 55.

12. This movie can be viewed in its entirety at http://de.metapedia .org/wiki/Hitlerjunge_Quex; short segments can also be found on YouTube.

13. Adolf Hitler, in Walther Hofer, ed., *Der Nationalsozialismus. Dokumente 1933–1945* (Frankfurt: Fischer Bücherei, 1957), 88.

14. Gert Bennewitz, "Die geistige Wehrerziehung der deutschen Jugend," in *Schriften für Politik und Auslandskunde,* ed. F.A. Six (Berlin: Dünnhaupt Verlag, 1940), 16.

15. Fritz Brennecke, ed., *Vom deutschen Volk und seinem Lebensraum. Handbuch. Die Schulungsarbeit in der HJ [Hitlerjugend]* (Munich: Zentralverlag der NSDAP, 1937), 81.

16. Ernst Anrich, "Neue Schulgestaltung aus nationalsozialistischem Denken," in *Kulturpolitische Schriftenreihe,* Heft 4 (Stuttgart: W. Kohlhammer, 1933), 66–67.

17. Michael Buddrus, *Totale Erziehung für den totalen Krieg. Hitlerjugend und nationalsozialistische Jugendpolitik* (Munich: K.G. Saur, 2003), 66.

18. Adolf Hitler, quoted in Bernhard Haupert, *Jugend zwischen Kreuz und Hakenkreuz. Biographische Rekonstruktion als Alltagsgeschichte des Faschismus* (Frankfurt: Suhrkamp, 1991), 12.

19. Dr. Robert Ley, *Deutschland ist schöner geworden,* ed. Hans Dauer and Walter Kiehl (Berlin: Mehden Verlag, 1936), 3.

20. Ulrich Hermann and Ulrich Nassen, eds., *Formative Ästhetik im Nationalsozialismus. Intentionen, Medien und Praxisformen totalitärer ästhetischer Herrschaft und Beherrschung* (Weinheim and Basel: Beltz Verlag, 1993), 157.

3. WAR AND THE HOLOCAUST

1. Heyen, *Nationalsozialismus im Alltag,* 142–43.

2. Ibid., 143.

3. Martin Broszat and Hartmut Mehringer, eds., *Bayern in der NS Zeit* (Munich: R. Oldenbourg Verlag, 1983), 1:123.

4. Berger, *Lebenssituationen unter der Herrschaft des Nationalsozialismus*, 92.

5. Ibid.

6. Johann Stab, police officer in Kleinheubach; unpublished typewritten report of December 1945, no page numbers.

7. *Die Berichte des Oberkommandos der Wehrmacht*, vol. 1: *1. September 1939 bis 31. Dezember 1940* (Munich: Verlag für Wehrwissenschaften, 2004). This announcement was broadcast and disseminated in all German media.

8. Walb, *Ich, die Alte; ich, die Junge*, 129.

9. Adolf Hitler, quoted in Burt Naegele, *Jene zwölf Jahre: Erzählung eines Zeitzeugen* (self-published, 1993), 139; document archived in the Institut für Zeitgeschichte, Munich, F 7334.

10. Walb, *Ich, die Alte; ich, die Junge*, 133.

11. SS Brigadeführer Knoblauch, Letter to Heinrich Himmler and the chief of police of the ministry of the interior, SS Brigadeführer Petri, November 19, 1938, p. 1; Institut für Zeitgeschichte, Munich.

12. Broszat and Mehringer, *Bayern in der NS Zeit*, 1:138.

13. Ibid., 135.

14. Original Nazi complaint, quoted ibid., 137.

15. Ibid., 136.

16. Jutta Sywottek, "Mobilmachung für den totalen Krieg. Die propagandistische Vorbereitung der deutschen Bevölkerung auf den Zweiten Weltkrieg," in Sywottek, *Studien zur modernen Geschichte* (Opladen and Düsseldorf: Westdeutscher Verlag, 1976), 167.

17. Ibid., 169.

18. Adolf Hitler, quoted in Martin Broszat, "Hitler und die Genesis der 'Endlösung,'" *Vierteljahrshefte für Zeitgeschichte* 25 (1977): 757.

19. Ibid., 758.

20. Minister of Justice Thierack, notes of discussion with Heinrich Himmler, September 18, 1942, recorded by the Police d'Israel, 6th

Bureau, IMG vol. 26, pp. 200–203, archived in the Institut für Zeitgeschichte, Munich, Akz. 2903/62, Document 652-PS.

21. Gestapo office in Würzburg, from a report of November 28, 1944, concerning the removal of the last Jews on June 17, 1943, microfiche, p. 84; Institut für Zeitgeschichte, Munich.

22. Christian Mitschke, "Thema: Was ich so erlebte—Einige Episoden aus meinem Leben," in *Philosophische Blätter* (Bautzen: self-published, 1997), 13–14.

23. Berger, *Lebenssituationen unter der Herrschaft des Nationalsozialismus,* 92.

24. Max von der Grün, *Wie war das eigentlich? Kindheit und Jugend im Dritten Reich* (Frankfurt: Luchterhand, 1979), 16.

25. Berger, *Lebenssituationen unter der Herrschaft des Nationalsozialismus,* 60–61.

26. Quoted in Robert Gellately, *Die Gestapo und die deutsche Gesellschaft. Die Durchsetzung der Rassenpolitik 1933–1945,* translated from the English by Karl Nicolai and Heidi Nicolai (Munich: Ferdinand Schöningh, 2002), 73.

27. From a directive written for general distribution in the SS bureaucracy by the head of the SS, Heinrich Himmler, SS-Gericht Nr. Ch/12568, Munich, November 4, 1935; Institut für Zeitgeschichte, Munich.

28. Quoted in Heyen, *Nationalsozialismus im Alltag,* 313.

29. In the decades following World War II I have noted that many Jewish refugees from Nazi Germany have reconnected with their hometowns and with old German friends. They seem to hold a much more differentiated view of Germans than many of the second or third generation of Jewish refugees who maintain a negative, ideologically fixed view of Germans.

30. Heyen, *Nationalsozialismus im Alltag,* 71.

31. John S. Conway, "Augenzeugenberichte aus Auschwitz," *Vierteljahrschrift für Zeitgeschichte* 27 (1979): 268.

32. www.newworldencyclopedia.org/entry/Auschwitz

33. Heinrich Himmler, "General orders regarding executions," marked "secret," January 6, 1943; Institut für Zeitgeschichte, Munich.

34. Martin Broszat, ed., *Kommandant in Auschwitz. Autobiographische Aufzeichungen des Rudolf Höß* (Stuttgart: Deutsche Verlags-Anstalt, 1958), 190.

35. Much has been written about the Germans' pact with the devil. Following World War II, Thomas Mann devoted one of his masterpieces, *Dr. Faustus,* to this ancient myth. In spite of the insights available from such interpretations of German culture, there is a simple but important flaw in the analogy between Faust's pact with the devil and the contract between Hitler and the German people. In Goethe's epic of the legend, the pact that the devil makes with Faust is perfectly clear in its terms. In fact, Faust himself defines them from the start, before he consents to an oath signed in blood. He agrees that if he ever achieves a moment of perfect bliss, Mephistopheles may take his soul. The German people made no such pact with Hitler in 1933, since Hitler hid the key terms from them. Only particularly sensitive political and cultural analysts were able to read ominous signs between the lines from the very beginning. For Hitler, the most important aspect of the pact was to hide from the German people the full extent of his plans for genocide and hegemony in Europe. The year 1945 brought these aspects fully to light as Germany went down in flames and smoke, and after the great master of these sleights of hand committed suicide.

4. IN SEARCH OF INDIVIDUALS

Epigraph: Eva Leveton, in *Reconcile: Germans Jews and the Holocaust,* documentary film by Mariel McEwan and Sergio Palermo, 2004. Eva Leveton's Jewish father fled Berlin during the Nazi period. She and her non-Jewish German mother survived the Allied bombing of that city.

1. Sabin Bode, *Die vergessene Generation. Die Kriegskinder brechen ihr Schweigen* (Stuttgart: Klett-Cotta, 2004), 35–36.

2. Rosner and Tubach, *An Uncommon Friendship,* 3–4.

3. Dr. Camerer died in 2009. Several other interviewees have died since the time I interviewed them.

4. During the early years of Hitler's *Reich,* the young still had a choice whether or not to join the *HJ.*

5. Walter Kempowski, ed., *Das Echolot. Fuga furiosa: Ein kollektives Tagebuch, Winter 1945* (Munich: A. Knaus, 1999), 4:757.

6. Hans-Bernd von Buggenhagen, in Ruth-Erika, Fürstin zu Löwenstein-Wertheim-Freudenberg, *Es bleibt die Erinnerung. Berichte aus der verlorenen Heimat Buggenhagen* (self-published, n.d.), 49–50.

7. *Der Neue Tag,* Nr. 20, January 20, 1942, p. 3.

8. Dieter, Freiherr von Lersner, *Die evangelischen Jugendverbände Württembergs und die Hitler-Jugend, 1933/1934,* vol. 4 of *Arbeiten zur Geschichte des Kirchenkämpfes* (Göttingen: Vandenhoeck & Ruprecht, 1958), 72 pp.

5. GERMAN SOLDIERS WRITE HOME

1. Conversation with Marlis Prinzing, March 23, 2005.

2. Kurt Weidemann, *Kaum ich: Das Wort ICH kommt kaum vor. Die Feldtagebücher und die Gefangenschaft von Kurt Weidemann, 1940–1950* (Ostfildern: Cantzsche Druckerei, 2002), 45.

3. Heinz Schramm, *Das Hitlerbuch der deutschen Jugend,* 4th ed. (Hamburg: Hanseatische Verlagsanstalt, 1933), 47, 41. This was a widely distributed propaganda text for German youth.

4. Quotations in this chapter, including the mottos, are my translations of letters and excerpts from letters contained in the *Feldpostsammlung* archive. Many writers signed off only with first names or appellations such as "your son." Some letters included no names, dates, and/or places of origin; I have attributed these letters to fictitious first names and last initials.

Archival codes for the main letters and excerpts are: the lieutenant stationed in Warsaw: 3.2002.887; Manfred von K.: 3.2008.2195.0; Eugen L.: 3.2002.0210; Hans L.: 3.2002.0211; Franz W.: 3.2009.574.0.

5. Weidemann, *Kaum ich,* 29.

6. Ibid., 198.

7. If a censor had read this, it would have been deleted.

8. Lukas belonged to a unit that provided the troops with entertainment.

9. See http://www.dererstezug.com/IronRation.htm for an explanation of iron rations.

10. The location of Hans's grave in Russia was mentioned in a letter by a relative who visited the grave, though he did not specify its whereabouts.

Text:	10.75/15 Janson MT Pro
Display:	Janson MT Pro
Compositor:	Toppan Best-set Premedia Limited
Printer and binder:	Sheridan Books, Inc.